Making Enquiries into Alleged Child Abuse and Neglect:
Partnership with Families

Making Enquiries into Alleged Child Abuse and Neglect: Partnership with Families

Edited by Dendy Platt
and
David Shemmings

JOHN WILEY & SONS
Chichester • New York • Weinheim • Brisbane • Singapore • Toronto

First published in 1996 by Pavilion Publishing
This edition published in 1997 by John Wiley & Sons Ltd,
Baffins Lane, Chichester,
West Sussex PO19 1UD, England

National   01243 779777
International (+44) 1243 779777
e-mail (for orders and customer service enquiries):
cs-books@wiley.co.uk
Visit our Home Page on http://www.wiley.co.uk *or*
http://www.wiley.com

Other Wiley Editorial Offices

John Wiley & Sons, Inc., 605 Third Avenue,
New York, NY 10158-0012, USA

VCH Verlagsgesellschaft mbH, Pappelallee 3,
D-69469 Weinheim, Germany

Jacaranda Wiley Ltd, 33 Park Road, Milton,
Queensland 4064, Australia

John Wiley & Sons (Asia) Pte Ltd, 2 Clementi Loop #02-01,
Jin Xing Distripark, Singapore 129809

John Wiley & Sons (Canada) Ltd, 22 Worcester Road,
Rexdale, Ontario M9W 1L1, Canada

ISBN 0-471-97222-3

Typeset by Phoenix Photosetting, Chatham, Kent
Printed in Great Britain by Redwood Books, Trowbridge, Wiltshire
This book is printed on acid-free paper responsibly manufactured from
sustainable forestry, for which at least two trees are planted for each one
used for paper production.

Contents

PART 3 The enquiry in progress

CONCLUSION

Contributors

The editors

Dendy Platt is a senior lecturer in social work at New College Durham and course leader for the Diploma in Social Work course. His previous experience includes a number of social work posts, the most recent being project leader of a Barnardo's family centre. Before that he was a team leader with Newcastle Social Services and project director of a Save the Children community project. He has published a number of papers in the fields of child care, child protection, family assessment and community social work.

David Shemmings is a lecturer in social work at the University of East Anglia. He has been a senior research associate at the University of East Anglia, and has held management posts in local authority social services departments as well as having worked as a teacher of children with special needs. He wrote *Client Access to Records: Participation in Social Work; Family Participation in Child Protection Conferences: A Training Pack* (with June Thoburn and Ann Lewis); and *Paternalism or Partnership? Family Participation in Child Protection* (with June Thoburn and Ann Lewis). He has written various other contributions to books and articles on participation in social service provision and on management.

The contributors

Lyn Burns is area manager, Stroud and Dursley area office, Gloucester social services department and lead officer for operational child protection for the county.

Terry Burns is area manager in Cheltenham, and lead officer for child care in Gloucestershire social services department.

Jabeer Butt is a researcher/consultant with the Race Equality Unit .

Hedy Cleaver is a research fellow at the University of Leicester.

David Cooper is a senior lecturer in social work at the University of Plymouth.

Murray Davies is regional director for the NSPCC in Cymru/Wales and Midlands.

Contributors

Pam Freeman is a researcher at the Socio-Legal Centre for Family Studies at the University of Bristol.

Paul Gerber is currently leader of an NSPCC therapeutic project specialising in child sexual abuse and providing recovery services to children and to non-offending carers.

Melanie Phillips is a Black qualified social worker of Asian origin, currently working as a freelance trainer and consultant in child protection and race equality.

Philippa Russell, OBE is director of the Council for Disabled Children and associate director of the National Development Team for People with Learning Disabilities.

Yvonne Shemmings is a senior manager in Essex social services department.

Wendy Stainton Rogers is a senior lecturer in the School of Health, Welfare and Community Education at the Open University.

David Thorpe is a senior lecturer in applied social science at Lancaster University.

Corinne Wattam is NSPCC research fellow at Lancaster University.

Dr Jan Welbury is a consultant in community child health in Sunderland.

Jeannie Wells is project leader of a multi-agency child protection project for NSPCC Cymru/Wales and Midlands.

Tony Young is assistant area manager, Gloucester area social services office.

Acknowledgements

This book is the result of an exercise in partnership between different organisations, groups and individuals providing support to children and families who become involved in the child protection process. As editors we are particularly grateful to them for their encouragement and patience, but we have been especially pleased to receive their comments on the various drafts of each chapter.

We would like specifically to express our gratitude to Sue Amphlett (Parents Against INjustice), Barbara Hearn (National Children's Bureau), Philip Noyes (National Society for the Prevention of Cruelty to Children), Alison Richards (Family Rights Group) and Daphne Statham (National Institute for Social Work) for their constructive and perceptive comments; to New College, Durham for making available time and resources to support Dendy Platt's involvement; to colleagues at the Department of Health who, at a time of considerable change within the field of family support and child protection, helped us to see where and how our work fitted into the wider policies; and to the many family members who shared with us their thoughts and feelings about how the present way of making enquiries into allegations of child abuse and neglect can lead to much pain. Finally, we offer our thanks to Anne Sampford (of PAIN) who helped co-ordinate our efforts.

Crown copyright is reproduced with the permission of the Controller of HMSO.

Preface

We are currently witnessing a fundamental reassessment of the child protection system as it operates in the UK. The recently completed Department of Health Research together with criticisms from various professional bodies, interest groups, and policy makers are all suggesting that it is no longer adequate simply to try and fine-tune or modify the system. What is required is a fundamental rethink of basic principles and the policies and practices that represent them. This is no easy task when we remember that 25 years of investment and development have gone into what we have today.

For me the contemporary nature of child protection is best characterised by the policies and practices which attempt to identify 'high risk' to children. Notions of working together are set out in increasingly complex yet specific procedural guidelines and the work is framed by a narrow emphasis on legalism and the need for forensic evidence. However, increasingly it is being argued that the basic principles of the Children Act, particularly its emphasis on family support and partnership, are being undermined. It is felt that too many cases are being dragged into the child protection net and that as a consequence the few who might require such interventions are in danger of being missed. The impact for the children and families involved is severe.

Concerns about enquiries get to the heart of these current debates about our child protection system. It is in this context that this book is both very timely and much needed. While the focus is on making enquiries inevitably it raises issues and questions about child protection generally and how this can be reformed and rethought. It is clearly not appropriate to see enquiries in isolation, and a major strength of the book is the way they are located in much wider organisational, professional and social processes. It will be of real value to policy makers, managers, professionals and, not least, those on the receiving end – parents, children and families more generally. It brings together real strengths, both in analysis and in making recommendations for change to day-to-day policy and practice. The book makes a significant contribution to the major rethink of the nature and failure of child protection which we are now engaged in.

The process of developing and writing the book is itself important and instructive. The initiative for the project was originally taken by Parents

Against INjustice (PAIN) following the completion of some earlier research carried out on its behalf in relation to a case study of 30 families who claimed to have been falsely accused in relation to child abuse investigations. The research explicitly provided the families' perspectives and demonstrated there were major problems and concerns which required publicising and addressing (Prosser, 1992).

While this current book has been initiated by PAIN, it is a joint project between the National Institute of Social Work (NISW), the National Society for the Prevention of Cruelty to Children (NSPCC) and PAIN. Numerous other organisations and individuals also have been included on the Steering Group. This clearly demonstrates that there is now a wide range of interests — including those speaking on behalf of social workers, children and parents — who feel the current situation is in urgent need of attention. This book marks a significant development which we cannot afford to ignore. It is a major contribution to the literature but also acts as a significant policy and practice initiative in its own right.

Nigel Parton,
Professor in Child Care,
University of Huddersfield.

REFERENCE

Prosser, J. (1992) *Child Abuse Investigations: The Families' Perspective. A case study of 30 families who claim to have been falsely accused,* Stansted, Parents Against INjustice.

Introduction

David Shemmings

In his book *Flaubert's Parrot* Julian Barnes reflects upon the task of the biographer. He reminds us that what appears in the completed work is the *biographer's* view of a person's life; someone else might have interpreted things differently. Jane Gibbons and her colleagues drew a similar conclusion about child abuse: 'as a phenomenon child abuse is more like pornography than whooping-cough. It is a socially constructed phenomenon which reflects values and opinions of a particular culture at a particular time' (Gibbons *et al.*, 1995). It is at the point where concerns and suspicions are raised, and subsequently when enquiries into allegations are made – themselves the product of social processes – that these constructions begin to take on a more outward and visible form. Files are created, meetings are arranged, lives are affected permanently. Thus the way in which enquiries are undertaken is of considerable importance.

Returning to *Flaubert's Parrot*, Barnes invites us to consider something more complex: what of those aspects of the subject's life which the biographer overlooks or even chooses to ignore? He observes that,

> The trawling net fills, then the biographer hauls it in, sorts, throws back, stores, fillets and sells. Yet consider what he doesn't catch: there is always far more of that.

Unfortunately the waters of child protection are more murky and turbulent. There are concerns both about who gets trapped and about who swims free. The key questions seem to be, firstly, when social workers and others make enquiries what do they take account of, what do they leave out, and more importantly how do they decide which is which? Secondly, how many people get stuck inappropriately in the system in order to catch the right ones? The biographer needs to be concerned about 'the ones that get away'; so do professionals involved in the field of child protection but they also have to pay attention to those who get trapped by mistake. Fish and nets are used by Jane Gibbons and her colleagues at the University of East Anglia to describe the present system, which they believe consists of: 'a small meshed net in which a large number of minnows – which have later to be discarded – are caught as well as the marketable fish. Each fleet has its own mesh . . . and several net designs are being used' (Gibbons *et al.*, 1995).

Introduction

As a result of a major research programme comprising twenty studies commissioned by the Department of Health (DoH, 1995) it is possible, with a reasonable degree of reliability and accuracy, to quantify the number of fish caught inappropriately. The figures in the next two paragraphs are taken from the 1995 DoH summary report.

Of the 11 million or so children in England and Wales some 160,000 will become the focus of concerns connected with suspected child abuse. As a result of these concerns – 'referrals' would be the term best understood by social workers familiar with the system – about 40,000 reach a child protection conference of which approximately 24,500 are placed on the child protection register. Therefore about 120,000 out of the original 160,000 never enter the formal child protection system and only some 15 per cent of referrals reach the point at which members of a child protection conference decide that a child is not safe enough without their formal involvement.

Does this mean that 85 per cent of referrals are 'false'? Clearly not, but because only a tiny proportion (of the 160,000) enter the formal child care system – in 1992, for example, this figure was approximately 6,000 – the findings of the research suggest that, of the referrals which are *not* placed on a child protection register, some will have been unfounded; some will reflect situations where the concerns are justified (but not to the point where the child is felt to need compulsory intervention); and some will include situations in which the child is at risk – and should have been registered or even removed – but where, for whatever reason, there is not enough evidence to substantiate such a judgement (or where there were enough signs but they were misinterpreted). Unfortunately too, some of the names registered will include children who are not at risk at all and where mistakes have been made – the so called 'false positives'. What are the implications of these figures? Anyone acquainted with contemporary child protection services knows that there are families who are not part of the formal child protection system but who nevertheless need and would accept some help. They will also know that there are children on registers who are not receiving much support. The reasons for this vary. They concern not only the problem of working with scarce financial resources but also include a lack of technical and human resources – sometimes nobody knows precisely what to do to protect a child.

There are gaps in the research at present. For example, little is known about the feelings and experiences of children who were assumed incorrectly to have been abused. Such an experience will have lasting effects on the children and their families; life will never be the same. But what, if any, help do they get to learn to trust the adults around them again?

The legal basis surrounding the making of enquiries is complex. Whilst Dendy Platt covers this in more detail in Chapter 2, some of the key features likely to affect child protection and child welfare policy and practice in the future are worth examination. The present debate concerns the thresholds between three sections of the Children Act 1989: between services provided under Part III (section 17b) – which deals with children whose health or development is being or is likely to be 'significantly impaired' without those services i.e. children 'in need' – and the child protection procedures as defined by *Working Together* (DoH, 1991), section 47 of the Act, and the court system for making decisions about children suffering or likely to suffer 'significant harm' (section 31). The question, therefore, is whether a child can best be helped and protected under the 'in need' provisions of Part III of the Act or whether it is necessary to use the formal child protection system, or the court system (see Brandon *et al.*, forthcoming 1996). The major difference between, as Marian Brandon and her colleagues have put it, 'the "significant harm" . . . threshold and the "significant impairment of health and development" which triggers the provision of services under Part III of the Act is that the Part III definition is not linked to parental fault'. Whilst this book does not consider these thresholds in detail the most recent research by June Thoburn and her colleagues analyses how boundary decisions are made by practitioners and managers. It will contain important messages for all child welfare and child protection professionals. Here are two such examples:

Crucial in our study was whether social workers and team leaders perceived their work as primarily 'child protection' or 'in need' work . . . A majority said, with pride, that the bulk of their work was child protection . . . There was a marked difference between workers who prided themselves on all their work being classified as 'child protection' cases and others who prided themselves as having 'very few' child protection cases, and these differences appeared to be independent of the extent of deprivation in the areas of study. (Brandon *et al.*, forthcoming 1996).

. . . at worst, decisions about the allocation of resources, including social work support and therapeutic services, are based not on the extent to which a child's development is being or is likely to be significantly impaired, but on whether the parents are likely to be judged to be responsible for the impairment or harm, and if so, whether there is a risk that the agency as well as the parents might be found wanting. How else can we explain why a 15 year old known to be engaged in prostitution, or a pregnant homeless 16 year old, causes little concern and may not be given services as a child in need, but much energy is taken up by many professionals investigating and conferencing a 12 year old who receives soft tissue injuries as a result of a single incident of over-chastisement by a normally caring parent? (Brandon *et al.*, forthcoming 1996).

Introduction

Lastly from a legal point of view a 'cause for concern' may not be sufficient reason to make enquiries. Section 47(1)(b) of the Act states the basis upon which local authorities shall make enquiries: where there is 'reasonable cause to suspect that a child who lives or is found in their area is suffering, or is likely to suffer significant harm . . . '. Therefore in order to respond properly to referrals, professionals making enquiries as part of the Children Act 1989 should not do so without an adequate understanding of how to interpret 'reasonable cause' and 'significant harm'. Professionals involved in child welfare and protection are not moral crusaders. They are empowered in law to act in certain prescribed situations in certain prescribed ways; no more, no less.

The main conclusion from the research commissioned by the Department of Health is that the child protection system has separated *protection* from *support and help* to families. Attempting to redefine this balance is likely to usher in significant changes in social policy in the field of child welfare and protection. Those now involved in the child protection system will experience shock waves for some time to come but because the thrust of the changes marks a shift away from the twin activities of surveillance and social control toward a more welfare-oriented approach based upon family support, many working in this field will welcome them (including family members). But as with any policy and practice development, however positively these changes are viewed, they mask potential problems. There is a danger, for example, that more families could become enmeshed in a new, 'unofficial', system albeit with the good intention of providing help and support. The change of emphasis could result in some family members not being sure whether or not they are under suspicion. Similarly, social workers and directors of social services departments are likely to wonder whether they will be backed up when inevitably things go wrong: when the wrong family is 'supported', or the wrong child is 'protected'.

By now readers may have wondered why the word 'enquiry' has replaced the more familiar term 'investigation'. A detailed post-structural analysis of the power of language to construct and not merely to reflect thought is unnecessary in order to conclude that 'enquiry' sits better with an approach based upon support and help than does 'investigation', which is more redolent of formal or quasi-formal interrogative and judicial procedures. As Wendy Rose, Assistant Chief Inspector at the Department of Health, put it at a conference which explored the relationship between 'child protection' and 'family support': 'We have to ask ourselves whether in some cases children in need might be better served by a lighter approach. By this I mean a lesser emphasis on investigating for evidence regarding the alleged incident and a greater emphasis on enquiring and analysing whether family support services are needed' (DoH, 1994). Earlier she had wondered rhetorically: 'This may appear a pedantic or semantic point but investigation seems to convey to us a harder, evidence-based, police-led activity . . . Have we strayed too far from the notion of a social worker making enquiries and visiting a family at home to see if she or he can be helpful? Is this now a completely out-dated way of thinking?' (DoH, 1994).

Unless there was an obvious reason why the word 'investigation' had to be selected – for example, when quoting from another text or when an author is referring specifically to a more formal process – we have chosen to use the term *enquiry* throughout the book because, for much the same reason as articulated by Wendy Rose, it seemed to resonate better with the anticipated changes. And we have adopted the convention of using the term *Inquiry* to denote the formal process brought into operation when a child is thought to have died as a result of mistreatment.

Rather than become immersed in semantics at this point, however, it is more important to reflect upon these anticipated changes. In respect of making enquiries into alleged child abuse or neglect there appear to be three. Firstly, professionals must not assume automatically that mistreatment has occured. This may sound little more than common-sense and good practice but the extent of this problem came home to the contributors after the first drafts were circulated for comment. It soon became apparent that whenever terms such as 'suspicion of abuse' or 'allegation' were used, at some stage in their drafts virtually everyone – including the editors in the chapters written by themselves – went on to assume that abuse had happened. When this occurs in practice the enquiry will concentrate on 'what', 'when' and 'how' type questions rather than on 'whether' type questions. Such is the nature of preconception, bias and false assumption. Secondly, professionals may find that their language will need to draw less heavily upon metaphors from forensic science when they think about and describe what they are doing, especially with family members. Thirdly – but perhaps it is the one with the most potential to achieve the shift in emphasis – some professionals will need to overcome the habit of separating the need to *protect children* on the one hand from *supporting and helping families* on the other. That this tendency exists is not entirely their fault. It stems partly from an understandable concern that they will be blamed if they get the emphasis wrong but it derives also from a misconception in society, often fuelled by stories in the media, that children are likely to be removed from families if the enquiries conclude that they are in need of protection. In practice this happens rarely. Consequently, far from being separate and mutually exclusive, the twin aims of protecting children and of supporting and helping families are parallel processes which must be carried out simultaneously if children are to be protected successfully, from within their families.

At this stage in the development of policy there are many unanswered questions each of which needs more discussion and debate; it is not clear, for example, where the finance might come from to achieve the shift in emphasis. We welcome this debate; this book, we hope, will contribute to and stimulate it.

Whilst it is difficult to be precise about terminology at this stage, we are conscious of the need to adopt a working definition of *enquiries* in the chapters that follow. We appreciate that at different stages in the process *enquiries* will range from 'looking into' concerns at an informal level to formal 'investigations' of specific allegations of abuse or neglect. It was to this latter term that we returned in an attempt to formulate a working definition. Despite its procedural significance, however, we found that definitions of what constitutes an 'investigation' were varied and inconsistent. They tended to focus exclusively on objectives and not processes. To embrace the changes emerging from the research findings we believe that, in future, definitions of enquiries will need to take account of both. This book is concerned to examine processes which are broader than those understood generally by professionals more familiar with the term 'investigation'. For many social workers a child protection 'investigation' is seen sometimes as little more than the interviewing of a child and other family members after the reported allegation is first received. For children and families, on the other hand, it may start sooner and almost always ends much later, if it ever really ends at all.

Soon after this publication was first conceived two workshops involving over 100 professionals and family members familiar with the child protection system were asked to discuss a number of topics relating to enquiries and investigations. Some of the groups were invited to consider a definition of the enquiry process. The deliberations surrounding these workshops formed the basis of our working definition of enquiries used in this book:

Making enquiries into alleged child abuse or neglect is defined as the systematic process by which:

- facts and opinions are collected, recorded and analysed;
- by child care professionals from different agencies;
- from the child, parents or carers, other family members and others from the child's educational and social environment;

- up to and including an appropriate point of resolution such as a child protection conference, court hearing or internal decision to discontinue the process

What are the tasks of professionals making enquiries? Elaine Farmer (1993) crystallised those suggested by *Working Together* (DoH, 1991) under three specific headings. Modified slightly they shed light on the immediate broad aims of professionals who, she argues, should seek to establish information about the following:

Commission – whether abuse has occurred
Culpability – how and by whom it was caused
Risk – whether the child is safe enough.

In a similar vein, our working definition of the task of an enquiry is as follows:

The *task of an enquiry* into alleged child abuse or neglect is:

- to obtain as clear an account as possible of whether abuse or neglect has occurred, and then if appropriate,

- to assess how and by whom it was caused, and whether the child remains at risk.

The second thread, reflected in the book's title, is to consider ways of making the relationships formed during enquiries more like partnerships, or at least more participative. But how realistic is this? Is the intended metaphor of partnership (see Shemmings, 1991) that of a 'dance partner', a 'business partner', or is it perhaps a 'détente partnership' where each 'partner' tolerates the relationship out of fear of an abuse of power by the other person? A social worker appearing on the door-step with a uniformed police officer who announces, 'We are here to investigate an allegation of abuse to your child . . . no I'm sorry I can't tell you at this stage what that allegation is or who made it', heralds a predictable kind of relationship. To then add, 'but I want you to trust me because it's important that we work together in partnership', confuses everyone and leaves the professional on a hiding to nothing.

There is little doubt that virtually all families caught up in the current child protection system would prefer a supportive approach to one based upon surveillance. But the children who are abused at the hands of adult carers will say, 'Well they would wouldn't they – but what about me in all of this?' The research can help to resolve part of this dilemma. The Department of Health's summary report (DoH, 1995) contains findings which stress those aspects of

Introduction

the relationship between families and professionals more likely to be received positively. Although not listed in order of importance, of the five key features of effective practice identified, it is interesting to see that the first is 'close professional/client relationships'. Equally noticeable was the finding that, had the involvement of agencies been a little sooner and had an offer of help been made earlier, then re-abuse would have been lower. Whilst there are times when removing a child is the right thing to do, we need to remember that most families who abuse or mistreat children would prefer not to, and that in the early stages of an enquiry they are more likely to respond to an offer of help than they are to the threat of handcuffs.

So what does the worker need to do and say to reduce the suspicion of family members and to increase participation? Lesley Oppenheim wrote a practical and insightful article which addressed the first interview and she offers some useful tips to practitioners (Oppenheim, 1992). In addition, three of the twenty studies in the Department of Health's summary report provide professionals working in this field with some relevant and accessible principles for practice. The work of June Thoburn and her colleagues at the University of East Anglia (1995), that of Hedy Cleaver and Pam Freeman from the Dartington Social Research Unit (1995), and Elaine Farmer's and Morag Owen's research at the University of Bristol (1995), emphasise three key features concerning the development of trusting relationships. Firstly, unlike relationships which are chosen freely, in situations when there is suspicion as well as structural imbalance resulting from an uneven distribution of power between families and professionals, the promise of trust is not enough: it must be demonstrated. Professionals cannot expect families to have faith that trust exists; it must be affirmed repeatedly by their actions. Thus professionals must behave in ways which prove explicitly that they are reliable, honest, straightforward, scrupulously fair and, above all, are able to explain how they form assessments and use their judgement. Secondly, for trust and participation to grow, professionals need to appreciate just how violating suspicion of abuse can be to families. But, thirdly, being direct, honest and open is not enough. They are necessary conditions for the development of trust but they are by no means sufficient: a high level of sensitivity is called for too.

In the child protection system it is easy to overlook two key points. First, while their names are on the child protection register about 80 per cent of the children will live at home with their parent or carer and more often than not one or more of the adults they are living with is the alleged or the actual abuser (DoH, 1995). This is of course obvious: if it were not the case – if the child was not thought to be living with or was not having access to an abusing adult – then he or she would not have been considered in need of protection. The second point is even more obvious: because only around 15 per cent of the original 160,000 referrals end up on the child protection register then most of the remainder stay at home with one or more adult carers. As the likelihood of professionals removing children is remote and because first impressions are so important, whatever influence they might have can only come from patient and skilled work during the early stages when enquiries are made. Despite the search for both, to date there exists neither a quick-fix solution nor a magic check-list. Therefore professionals will have to be satisfied with perfecting their abilities to relate well to family members. As the chances are that both during and after enquiries have been made the adults and children will carry on living together, mostly outside the gaze of child protection professionals, arguments about whether the needs of children predominate over the rights of adults are misleading because, except in the most extreme circumstances, professionals always have to address both simultaneously. But to ensure that the purpose of any help and support given to families is not overlooked the original word 'protection' must not disappear from the professional's lexicon. The first task of an enquiry prompted by concerns about alleged mistreatment is to see if the child is safe; if the child is not, then the second aim is to work out what support is feasible to help keep the child safe in the future. An exploration of the factors likely to assist in this process is the subject of this book. It is not a 'how-to-do-it' book; neither does it seek to tackle the question of assessing the risk of significant harm to a child. The book is, quite deliberately, designed to encourage debate. It offers the reader an opportunity to paint afresh the subject of 'enquiry', partly by adding some new colours and partly by inviting the reader to look at what surrounds the subject rather than stare too long at the subject itself.

The book is divided into three parts. Part 1 includes three chapters which consider some of the background to the making of enquiries. It begins with an introductory chapter by Dendy Platt in which he sets the scene by discussing legal definitions of enquiries and investigations within the context of child welfare and child protection policies. Whilst anti-oppressive and anti-racist practice is referred to in most of the contributions in this volume, the next two chapters outline a background against which to appreciate how the power of the state, mediated by welfare professionals, remains essentially discriminatory and oppressive. Chapter 2, written by Melanie Phillips and Jabeer Butt, deals specifically with how racism exacerbates the way in which Black families in a White society can become marginalised and alienated by the process of child protection enquiries. They were hampered in their task by the lack of research concerning the effect of enquiries upon Black families. Philippa Russell in Chapter 3 undertakes a similarly critical analysis of the way our assumptions and prejudice about disability affect the way we react to allegations. In order to consider the impact upon the process of making enquiries of both race and culture, and of disability, it was recognised that Melanie and Jabeer, as well as Philippa, would need to consider the enquiry process within the wider system of child protection and welfare.

Part 2 considers specifically the question of partnership with family members during the process. Each chapter uses a critical lens to analyse the likelihood and limits of partnership in the fraught arena of making enquiries into allegations of child abuse and neglect. Yvonne Shemmings and David Shemmings start by reviewing critically the research findings on participative relationships and then apply them to the subject of enquiries. In Chapter 5, Hedy Cleaver and Pam Freeman use their research into the views of family members – primarily parents and adult carers – during the enquiry process to shed considerable light on the experience. Next, Murray Davies, Paul Gerber and Jeannie Wells provide the balance of the child's perspective and suggest ways of helping and encouraging them to become genuine participants.

Finally, Part 3 considers the enquiry process in more detail and the chapters are arranged in the order in which this process unfolds. It begins with David Cooper's chapter, in which some of the social and psycho-social contexts for referrals of alleged child abuse and neglect are given a refreshing analysis. Next, in Chapter 8, David Thorpe provides an analysis of how referrals are handled in social services departments and in particular draws on research which he undertook recently in Western Australia. He argues convincingly for approaches to enquiries which recognise the importance, firstly of understanding, and then of 'gate-keeping', the highly subjective impressions and judgements of the many different stakeholders involved in defining and producing state responses to allegations of abuse. He concludes by describing a powerful and practical way of monitoring the enquiry system at a local level which will be of interest to managers and practitioners alike. In Chapter 9 Lyn Burns and Tony Young provide a step-by-step approach to planning an enquiry with the focus on participation with families being uppermost from beginning to end. Similarly, Dendy Platt and Terry Burns in Chapter 10 demonstrate how recorded agreements can provide professionals with a method of making tangible the rhetoric of empowerment and partnership. Next, Wendy Stainton Rogers considers the legal and professional dilemmas which abound when children are interviewed. She manages skilfully to distil from the complexities and contradictions a number of pointers for practice which professionals, both those experienced and those less so, will find extremely helpful. Chapter 12 is written by Jan Welbury, a consultant paediatrician. It considers the vexed practice of medical examinations, but still from the point of view of openness and participation. It keeps as central the now well-known quote of Lord Justice Butler-Sloss in the Cleveland Inquiry Report: 'The child is a person, not an object of concern'. Based upon the recognition that judging and assessing the information gathered during the process of enquiries is highly subjective, in Chapter 13 Corinne Wattam helps deconstruct many of our pre-conceived ideas and attitudes concerning the nature of abuse. She provides an analysis of the types of structures used to make sense of information gathered. Interspersed throughout her chapter are the main implications for practice. In the concluding chapter, Dendy Platt tackles the particularly sensitive problem of how and when to end the enquiry, never forgetting that for many family members the process does not 'end'.

Three organisations – Parents Against INjustice (PAIN), the National Institute for Social Work (NISW) and the National Society for the Prevention of Cruelty to Children (NSPCC) – sponsored the book although the views expressed in this book are those of the authors and not necessarily of the sponsoring organisations. It is the result of a collaborative process involving key individuals and groups concerned with the provision of support to families, and with the welfare and protection of children. Early on, two workshops were organised and invitations were sent to family members, practitioners, managers and researchers. Participants were asked to consider specific topics concerning the way in which enquiries are conducted. These discussions were tape-recorded and subsequently were analysed by the editors. A Publication Steering Committee (*see* Appendix 1) was then formed to reflect different aspects of the enquiry process. Draft chapters were sent to all the members of the Steering Committee whose comments were passed on to individual authors – a mammoth task! Finally, the editors scrutinised the collection in order to achieve an appropriate degree of cohesion but without restricting the contributors.

The book is aimed at professionals and managers involved in the fields of child welfare and protection but as over half the chapters include up-to-date research findings the book also will be of interest to students and academics. It has been stated already that this book does not examine the thresholds between services aimed at children 'in need' and children 'in need of protection'. What the collection offers is an opportunity for readers to explore the debates and then to consider specifically the two main changes necessary if a more open and supportive approach is to be shown to family members. Firstly, when making enquiries social workers should stop acting as forensic scientists. This is not meant to infer that they are to blame for doing so now; it is merely a plea for them to resist doing so in the future . The message to social workers in this book is unequivocal: be social workers.

Secondly, the message to all professionals is to be even-handed and open-minded. So many of the problems encountered during the enquiry, for children and adult carers alike, can be reduced to one: the tendency to jump to conclusions, far too quickly. Unfortunately what then tends to happen is that, as the enquiry unfolds, only the information which confirms first impressions is taken notice of; any information which dis-confirms the original assumptions tends to be ignored. When making enquiries professionals are advised to consider the possibility that nothing abusive has happened. Such an approach is more likely to afford the right children the protection they need because professionals who are even-handed and open-minded are more capable of weighing-up, evaluating and assessing what they hear and see than those who make up their minds too soon. In the context of alleged child abuse and neglect, the consequences of professionals jumping to the wrong conclusion are devastating, both for the children who are being abused as well as for those who are not. As Michel Foucault and other post-structuralists have argued convincingly for some time, language has had a powerful part to play in the construction of socially-defined meanings (see for example Foucault, 1989). Reflect for a minute on the term 'disclosure interview': hardly a neutral term, for the word 'disclosure' assumes or suggests what is expected to happen during the interview. Similarly, the discourses which resulted a few years ago from the folklore message that children 'must be believed' – when presumably what should have been said was 'must be taken seriously' – no doubt led to a lack of even-handedness when the enquiries were made.

In conclusion, it is not only child abuse which as a phenomenon is socially constructed; the system designed to respond to enquiries itself also is socially constructed. Julian Barnes captures this with a characteristic display of lateral thinking:

> You can define a net in one of two ways, depending on your point of view. Normally, you would say that it is a meshed instrument designed to catch fish. But you could, with no great injury to logic, reverse the image and define a net as a jocular lexicographer once did: he called it a collection of holes held together with string.

Such a formulation conceives of nets not as fixed, permanent frames but as human constructions which are sewn, shaped and stretched for specific purposes. They can be redesigned, so that that less of the wrong fish are trapped and more of the right ones are caught.

REFERENCES

Brandon, M., Lewis, A. and Thoburn, J. (forthcoming, 1996) 'The Children Act's definition of "significant harm" – interpretations in practice,' *Health and Social Care in the Community*, Spring.

Cleaver, H. and Freeman, P. (1995) *Parental Perspectives in Suspected Child Abuse*, London: HMSO.

Department of Health (1991) *Working Together under the Children Act 1989: A guide to Arrangements for Inter-agency Co-operation for the Protection of Children from Abuse*, London: HMSO.

Department of Health (1994) 'An overview of the developments of services – the relationship between protection and family support and the intentions of the Children Act 1989', Department of Health paper given at the Sieff conference in September 1994 by Wendy Rose, Assistant Chief Inspector (Social Services Inspectorate).

Department of Health (1995) *Child Protection: Messages from Research*, London: HMSO.

Farmer, E. (1993) 'The impact of child protection investigations: the experiences of parents and children', in *Child Abuse and Child Abusers: Protection and Prevention*, Waterhouse, L. (ed.), University of Aberdeen Research Highlights in Social Work.

Farmer, E. and Owen, M. (1995) *Child Protection Practice: Private Risks and Public Remedies*, London: HMSO.

Foucault, M. (1989) *The Birth of the Clinic*, Routledge.

Gibbons, J., Conroy, S. and Bell, C. (1995) *Operation of Child Protection Registers*, London: HMSO.

Oppenheim, L. (1992) 'The first interview in child protection: social work method and process', *Children and Society*, 6, 2, pp. 132–150.

Shemmings, D. (1991) *Client Access to Records: Participation in Social Work*, Avebury: Gower.

Thoburn, J., Lewis, A. and Shemmings, D. (1995) *Paternalism or Partnership? Family Involvement in Child Protection*, London: HMSO.

Part 1

The background to the enquiry process

1

Enquiries and investigations: the policy context

Dendy Platt

The dominant feature of British 'child protection' policy is the enquiry[1] process (Hallett, 1993). The very centrality of this process has made for a system with particular characteristics and particular problems. It is a system in which making enquiries and (where appropriate) the initial protection of the child often take priority over support to child and family, therapeutic work, prevention, and indeed a partnership approach in general. This chapter will consider the enquiry process in its historical context first. It will then examine current issues for policy and practice as they relate to this process. A major argument which emerges will be the apparent growth of a legalistic approach to 'child protection' in recent years. The centrality of enquiries into allegations will be an important consideration. Finally, key themes will be proposed for the development of future practice.

The historical place of investigations and enquiries

The investigatory approach to alleged child abuse has a long history. The first Prevention of Cruelty to Children Act in England was passed in 1889 (Ferguson, 1990) although for at least a hundred years before that, child cruelty was condemned and punishable by the state (Pollock, 1983). A significant part was played in the investigation of alleged child abuse and neglect by inspectors of the National Society for the Prevention of Cruelty to Children. The principal methods (post-1889) were investigation of the allegations, removal of children to places of safety and punishment (often by imprisonment) of the offending parent(s). The justice requirements of the time were enacted using a punitive model which aimed to change behaviour by instilling a fear of the consequences. The welfare requirement was associated frequently with the rescuing of children by removal, although the general thrust of the approach was towards moral regeneration.

Practice and thinking has been developed and refined considerably, but it is clear that the twin elements of welfare and justice are as important today as they were 100 years ago. However, their interpretation and relative importance have fluctuated over the years. The individualised focus of concern about child abuse has continued from its base in the late nineteenth century, but the role of values and concern about morality has been re-emphasised. This focus has been supported and bolstered by a variety of factors including the role of the health professions, exemplified particularly by C. Henry Kempe and others, and of the various public inquiries into deaths of children from abuse (Parton, N., 1985). These developments served to emphasise the concentration on the individual rather than on the social conditions which may have lain behind a situation of abuse. The 1960s and 1970s witnessed the emergence of social work as a generic activity, and an increase in optimism concerning its potential. It was perhaps at this time that preventive and rehabilitative ideals took greatest hold.

Unfortunately they were to become short-lived in relation to child protection work. By the late 1980s:

> there was a general loss of faith in claims that wide-ranging prevention and professional intervention could control and reduce problems (Parton, N., 1990).

Although at least some of these claims were justifiable (e.g. Gibbons et al., 1990) the trend in official and popular thinking was, by then, well-established. Investigation rather than prevention has continued to be the fulcrum of British child protection policy. The key Inquiries into aspects of child abuse during the 1970s and 1980s have played a critical role which scarcely can be overemphasised (e.g. London Borough of Brent, 1985; Secretary of State for Social Services, 1988). They have led particularly to an increase in government guidance, with local procedure documents which address every aspect of the process. Over the past ten years or so, the size of such procedure guides has grown from slim A5 paperback booklets to A4-sized wedges of paper a centimetre thick or more, often ring-bound to allow updating, and appearing in several different volumes tailored to the purpose and readership.

They are obvious manifestations of the growth of legalism in child protection. The term 'legalism' refers not simply to a justice model or to the use of the law in child protection, but to a moral and ethical approach which values the adherence to rules and procedures of which the law is one example (Parton, N., 1991). Thus, even without invoking legal proceedings, a zealous

4

application of procedures designed to promote the welfare of a child would be described as legalistic.

The growth in legalism has now moved beyond the attention to deaths from child abuse in the mid-1980s. The various contradictory and contested pressures upon practitioners and policy-makers have become more marked. The Cleveland Inquiry for example, is well-known for having been the first major public inquiry to give prominence to the twin issues of families' rights and children's rights as well as to sexual abuse itself, which had then only just become established on the political and professional agenda. The Report's recommendations formed an important baseline in interviewing both child and parents/carers, which has influenced practice ever since (Secretary of State for Social Services, 1988). Detailed review of these principles is unnecessary here, since they underpin so much of what follows in later chapters; however, they have also reinforced the trend. The Cleveland report contributed to the greater legal clarification now contained in the Children Act 1989, and to an extensive rewriting of child protection procedures. The Report has been criticised for making fewer practical proposals for the child's voice to be heard than for the parents' (Parton, N., 1991). Families' organisations, however, would argue that even though the necessary requirements for consultation etc. have now been written in to most procedures, the correct processes often are not followed (Amphlett, 1991; Lindley, 1994).

The most recent development of policy and practice in the enquiry process is the change introduced by the Criminal Justice Act 1991, making video evidence from a child admissible in court. Whilst a step forward for many children, it is once again accompanied by the familiar mushrooming of procedures. The Government's own guidance, the *Memorandum of Good Practice* (Home Office and DoH, 1992), covers the principles of video interviewing of children, and is aimed at the legally acceptable recording of a child's evidence for criminal proceedings. Its application is currently rather variable, and will continue to be so while initial problems are being resolved. In some areas it is seen as becoming the 'industry standard' (Keech, 1993) for interviewing children when enquiries are made and a number of local authorities profess to require a video interview to be carried out in all cases of alleged child abuse or neglect (confidential source). Others allow considerably more room for discretion.

Clearly each historical attempt to improve procedures and to refine the law has been motivated, at least in part, by a desire for better practice. Whether things have been improved in reality, however, is open to debate. It is often suggested that the welfare of politicians and bureaucrats has been enhanced

5

by better protection of their backs. Some writers would go further. Milner (1993), for example, develops a feminist critique of child protection procedures and demonstrates how processes focus readily on the female parent, even when the male is the perpetrator. There is frequently a lack of success in involving men in the intervention or 'treatment' stages. She concludes that the bureaucratic systems reinforce this tendency. Policy-makers, often male, are protected from exposure to the reality of violence by fathers. Anecdotal evidence indicates that advocacy organisations frequently find that men experience a sense of exclusion from 'child protection' processes. To consider the issues raised by these recent developments, it is necessary to look more closely at the difficulties the system is throwing up, and at the experiences of the children and their families.

The legal context of enquiries

Enquiries into alleged child abuse and neglect are founded on a clear legal basis. Section 47, Children Act 1989 sets out comprehensive requirements for making enquiries by a local authority or (S.44) by an 'authorised person' (e.g. NSPCC). The principal element of these requirements is to make enquiries where the local authority has

> reasonable cause to suspect that a child who lives, or is found, in their area is suffering, or is likely to suffer, significant harm [S.47(1)(b)].

The critical point is that enquiries should be made when both 'reasonable cause to suspect' and the possibility of 'significant harm' are indicated. Government guidance explains these provisions (DoH, 1991a, 1995). Paragraph 5.14.2 of *Working Together* appears to indicate that all referrals should be dealt with under child protection procedures, but paragraph 5.11.5 does state that courses of action other than a formal investigation may be taken (DoH, 1991a). This approach is backed up and reinforced by *The Challenge of Partnership in Child Protection* (DoH, 1995, e.g. paragraph 5.9). The difficulty of deciding to initiate an enquiry is emphasised in *Working Together* (paragraph 5.11.3):

> The balance needs to be struck between taking action designed to protect the child from abuse whilst at the same time protecting him or her and the family from the harm caused by unnecessary intervention (ibid).

Comprehensive guidance on the conduct of an enquiry, as an entity on its own, is unavailable, although *The Challenge of Partnership* does expand on the guidance contained in *Working Together*. Both publications describe the enquiry as part of a wider process. Stages of work in individual cases are set out in paragraph 5.10 of *Working Together* (DoH 1991a):

    (i)   *referral and recognition;*
   (ii)   *immediate protection and planning the investigation;*
  (iii)   *investigation and initial assessment;*
  (iv)   *child protection conference and decision making about the need for registration;*
   (v)   *comprehensive assessment and planning;*
  (vi)   *implementation, review and where appropriate, deregistration.'* (DoH, 1991a).

The guidance goes on to affirm that the:

stages do not necessarily stand alone nor are they clearly divided in time. There is likely to be some overlap (ibid).

An attempt at definition

The first step in clarifying the meaning of the concept is to identify the purpose of making enquiries. Again, section 47, Children Act 1989 is of assistance. The enquiries, in particular, should aim to establish whether the local authority should make an application to the court (e.g. for Emergency Protection Order, Care Order etc.), or use any of its other powers under the Act [S.47(3)(a)]. *Working Together* expands the point.

The prime tasks are:
to establish the facts about the circumstances giving rise to the concern;
to decide if there are grounds for concern;
to identify sources and level of risk; and
to decide protective or other action in relation to the child and any others [DoH, 1991a, para 5.14.3].

This definition approaches the subject largely from the welfare perspective and tends to avoid the issue of criminal investigation. *Working Together* does indicate that cases may 'involve both child care and law enforcement issues'. But it does not describe enquiries in such a way as to clarify how these twin issues should be integrated.

Few earlier writers appear to have addressed the question of defining enquiries or investigations. Those who have present a picture not dissimilar to that of *Working Together*. For example, Noyes, in his analysis of inquiry reports on behalf of the Department of Health, states

> ... *the purpose of investigation is taken to be to obtain information to establish whether a child is in need of protection,* ... *to allow preliminary planning to be undertaken in relation to her needs and to allow additional information to be taken into account* (DoH, 1991b, p. 73).

Many commentators have addressed a similar dilemma: that of the overlap – or potential overlap, between the investigative and therapeutic functions. Hallett and Birchall (1992) identify that:

> *In many cases, perhaps the majority, the inquisitorial and therapeutic contents of a social worker's diagnosis and assessment are not easily divided into separate processes or time-sequences* (p. 185).

Similarly, Jones *et al.* (1993) identify the overall purpose of the investigation as discovering whether the child is at risk of harm, and, if appropriate, whether a crime has been committed. These themes are spelt out clearly by Brayne and Martin (1993).

> *The process of investigation will always involve tensions between outcomes that sometimes may appear to be incompatible.*

They list these outcomes as 'therapeutic intervention', 'statutory control' (meaning whether to apply for Emergency Protection Orders etc.) and 'prosecuting the perpetrator' (p. 167). Consideration of outcomes, however, takes us a little beyond the immediate tasks of the enquiry process.

For the purposes of this discussion the focus of an enquiry derives from two primary requirements. They are the need to protect the child (the welfare requirement) and the need to consider whether a crime has been committed (the justice requirement). The reality for many families experiencing enquiries and investigations will be that these considerations merge into a single experience (hence the need to distinguish the terms 'enquiry' and 'investigation' in the Introduction to this book). It is therefore preferable to set out a single definition of the enquiry. Elaine Farmer (1993, p. 49) identifies three dimensions for debate between social workers and parents concerning the finding of abuse or neglect. They can be adapted to help clarify the tasks of an enquiry. The three dimensions are, first, 'commission' (whether the abuse or neglect had in fact occurred), second, 'culpability' (who was to blame) and, third, 'risk' (the continuing or future risk to the child).

The families' perspective also draws our attention to a perceived lack of clarity concerning where an enquiry begins and where it ends,

... for families it's very much a perception of what that investigation is ... from the moment you are aware that a problem has been reported and investigations are being made about yourself and your family ... you are in an investigation (Parent, 1993).

A definition of an enquiry should therefore incorporate a clarification of the process as well as the objectives. The process indicated here is broader than the process which commonly is understood in professional circles. For many social workers, the 'investigation' is seen as little more than the interviewing of child and family members after the reported allegation is first received. In this book, which addresses *partnership with families*, it is essential to begin with a definition which encompasses both families' and professionals' perspectives.

An enquiry into alleged child abuse or neglect is, therefore, defined as the systematic process by which

- facts and opinions are collected, recorded and analysed;

- by multi-agency child care professionals and practitioners;

- from the child, parents/carers, family members and others within the child's educational and social environment;

- up to and including an appropriate point of resolution such as a child protection conference, court hearing or internal decision to discontinue the procedures.

The task of those making enquiries is to obtain as clear an account as possible of whether abuse or neglect has occurred, and then, if appropriate, to assess how and by whom it was caused and whether the child remains at risk. It is fundamental to the approach taken in this volume that the process should be undertaken in partnership with parents and children, and conducted in a non-discriminatory fashion. These themes are developed throughout the book. The 'point of resolution' is the moment or stage at which outcomes of the enquiry have been determined to the satisfaction of those involved. Viewed in this way it becomes clear that, in some circumstances, elements of an enquiry may be necessary up to and including a court appearance. Indeed there will be some situations where the enquiry is never resolved to the satisfaction of everyone. An enquiry may then be closed, but not concluded – and for some families it may never end completely. For the purposes of our definition, the various outcomes of an enquiry can be categorised by adapting Brayne and Martin's (1993) classification:

- no further action;

- provision of services of a supportive or therapeutic nature;

- statutory control (including placing a child's name on the at risk register, use of emergency protection order, or care proceedings);

- criminal prosecution.

An inherent drawback of our definition may be that it fails to differentiate the distinct and separate roles of social work and the police. It is important to emphasise that the social work responsibility is primarily for the welfare of the child. The police responsibility is to determine whether an offence has been committed, and then, if appropriate, to prosecute the offender. However, a single definition of an enquiry is preferred because increasingly it is coming to be seen as a single process, albeit with a combination of welfare and justice requirements. *Working Together* encourages a multi-agency approach (DoH, 1991a), and the *Memorandum of Good Practice* (Home Office with DoH, 1992) is founded on principles of joint investigation by police officers and social workers. A degree of care is needed in relation to this point. Anecdotal information from Parents' Against INjustice (PAIN) suggests that many families do not appreciate the differences between possible outcomes. The burden of proof, for example, differs between criminal proceedings and care proceedings. It may be difficult for someone to appreciate why care proceedings may be continuing, even though they may have been found not guilty in a criminal court. In this context, some separation of roles between police and social workers may be helpful.

A further problem for any definition of an enquiry is the overlap of the process of making enquiries with that of an assessment (see DoH, 1988). This overlap is inevitable given the need to establish the risk to the child. An *assessment* of factors contributing to risk to the child will need to take place alongside making of enquiries about the facts of the situation. However, the early stages of an enquiry realistically can only provide an *initial* assessment of risk. Detailed assessment will follow, where applicable, after the enquiries have been completed. Clearly, in most cases where allegations have been unfounded, further assessment will be inappropriate.

Some dilemmas of increasing legalism

The benefits of the legalistic approach may seem obvious and overwhelming. Tighter procedures lead to the better protection of children, and ultimately to the better prevention of abuse. In addition, if correct consultation processes are followed with parents/carers, and with alleged perpetrators, civil rights will be maintained. The benefits of the legal process itself are potentially extensive. Despite criticisms, the law can be seen to provide adequate powers to remove children when they may be in danger. In cases where a criminal prosecution is appropriate, it can be argued reasonably that a great many abused children will benefit from access to justice, and from the opportunity for their allegation – if warranted – to be upheld. Conversely, in cases of false allegation, access to the means of resolving the issue is vital for the accused person and for the child.

In reality, however, we must look more deeply in order to identify the difficulties and dilemmas of the current system. This critique can begin with the question of over-proceduralisation and the scale and volume of procedural guidance. With each 'mistake' (e.g. cases leading to public inquiries), and with each change in legislation, the attempt is made to re-write procedures in order to cover eventualities still further. The more that processes are tied up by procedure, the easier it is to blame the individual practitioner rather than the policy or the system if something goes wrong. The ultimate objective, however, is never attainable. It is not possible to cover every eventuality. Even if it were, it is no longer possible for every individual social worker to maintain a working familiarity with all the documentation. The writing up of improvements to practice will never even approach the goal of perfection in this, a human, endeavour.

The result of these developments is a system which places the procedures before the individual. Wattam (1992) draws attention to the criticism in the Cleveland Report (Secretary of State for Social Services, 1988) that the child had become 'an object of concern' rather than a person. She then identifies how the legal focus has moved on to make children 'the objects of evidence' (p. 25):

> What becomes problematic is that, if children are treated as people, with rights, feelings and wishes, and an entitlement to information about them, they can become tarnished as evidential objects (p. 29).

She describes how the highly-focused *Memorandum of Good Practice* establishes legalistic procedures for preserving children's evidence. These procedures, when applied at the level of questioning and communicating with a child may, by their very nature, militate against a supportive, welfare-orientated approach.

Costs and benefits of the enquiry process

The benefits of the investigatory system overall are also coming under question. Recent research has highlighted the 'drop-out' rate from child protection procedures. Giller *et al.* (1992), in a study of four Area Child Protection Committee areas, indicate that on average 78.2 per cent of all child protection referrals 'drop out' of the system at various interim stages prior to registration on the child protection register. Similarly, Gibbons (1993) found that only 15 per cent of referrals led to eventual registration. There are many explanations for these findings. One conclusion is that child abusers are extremely clever and therefore, in most cases, it will be difficult to provide adequate evidence. In this analysis many of the drop-outs are unsubstantiated cases where abuse has nevertheless taken place. Another might be that the residue of unregistered cases represents situations when abuse genuinely did not take place and when the child is not at risk. Clearly the reality will be somewhere in between these assertions. A proportion of the drop-outs will be cases of actual abuse or neglect where the necessary evidence has not been forthcoming. A proportion will be false allegations or other (correctly) unfounded cases, and some will be accounted for by inappropriate referrals, statistical errors etc. In addition, it is important to note that the decision to register is not an infallible process, and a group of children will still become registered inappropriately.

The findings of Giller *et al.* (1992), and of Gibbons (1993) are reasonably consistent with other researchers. Hallett and Birchall (1992) assert that 'there are about three enquiries for every child protection registration'. Anthony and Watkeys (1991) indicate that 52 per cent of all referrals of suspected sexual abuse were either unsubstantiated or insufficiently specific to merit investigation. Cleaver and Freeman (1995) found that 29 per cent of all reports led to registration, but suggest that this could be a considerable over-estimate due to the numbers of minor cases which go unrecorded. Clifford (1988) noted that child protection conferences only occurred following a quarter of the estimated number of referrals. Thoburn *et al.* (1995) suggest that 60 per cent of the conferences in their survey were necessary, the implication being that 40 per cent were unnecessary.

Recent evidence has suggested that reductions in children's homicide rates may be a significant indicator of the achievements of child protection processes (Pritchard, 1992, 1993). Unfortunately the picture is by no means clear, with other writers arguing convincingly that child protection systems have produced no such benefits (Creighton, 1993; Lindsey and Trocme, 1994). However, it may well be the case that greater attention to child abuse as a problem has brought more minor cases within the investigatory arena. This view is supported by Cleaver and Freeman (1995) whose study indicated that out of:

> . . . *over 600 families . . . we find that fewer than ten cases belong in this dangerous category* (p. 178).

They conclude

> ... *many families pay a high price. Disruption, lingering suspicion and resentment, the disintegration of adult and adolescent relationships can too easily become the side-effects of child protection work. Since the majority of cases investigated are minor, the cost in terms of human disturbance and misplaced resources may be considered unnecessarily high* (p. 199).

Similar debates have been taking place in the USA over a longer period. Douglas Besharov, noted for highlighting the problem of false allegations, is concerned currently to develop a more balanced approach to investigations of alleged abuse or neglect. He bases this on the view that:

> *as many as 65 per cent of all reports are closed after an initial investigation reveals no evidence of maltreatment* (Besharov, 1990).

His position is criticised by other well-known 'experts'. David Finkelhor (1990), for example, points out that, in comparison to the low clear-up rates of reported crime, the investigatory system in relation to suspected child abuse is 'surprisingly cost-beneficial'. Either way, if it is accepted that a proportion of families are traumatised unnecessarily by the process itself, our concern, at the very least, should be to improve the practice of making enquiries and to minimise this trauma.

The difficulty of identifying clearly whether child abuse has occurred in a given situation has been described and discussed at length in many other contexts. The very definition of abuse is problematic (Giovannoni and Becerra, 1979; Gelles, 1982; Parton N., 1985; Hallett and Birchall, 1992 etc.). Any professional will have great difficulty identifying a phenomenon she or he cannot define clearly. In the context of enquiries, there will be a whole variety of reasons why evidence may be difficult to obtain, specify and evaluate. Whilst evaluation of evidence is explored by Corinne Wattam in Chapter 13, it is important to identify some particular concerns here. Sexual abuse, for example, is characterised by a high level of secrecy and privacy. It is well known that medical evidence is rarely, if ever, unequivocal. In cases of physical abuse, physical evidence is more often a pre-requisite of the successful identification of its occurrence. Even here, evidence is often ambiguous. It must be accepted, therefore, that there will be a level of error when making enquiries into alleged child abuse which is determined by the nature of the phenomenon itself, *not* by inadequacies of the system. A key question is what proportion of the unsubstantiated cases arises because of these inherent difficulties, and what proportion derives from false allegations? Anthony and Watkeys (1991) suggested that 18 per cent of the investigations in their study revealed false allegations, but arriving at a precise figure is beset by problems of definition and interpretation.

Similar concerns are being raised about the operation of the *Memorandum of Good Practice* (Home Office with DoH, 1992). Whilst at the time of writing, detailed research findings have not been published, it is evident that video interviews of children are being held more frequently than was intended originally (Wattam, 1993). The chief constable of Gloucestershire has claimed that out of 15,000 video interviews recorded, only 44 were accepted by the courts as evidence (Cohen, 1993). This disastrously low 'productivity' associated with the *Memorandum* may be offset, at least in small measure, by an increase in guilty pleas but, as yet, there is no evidence that this is the case.

Does the process of making enquiries itself cause any harm?

Is harm actually being caused by the process of making enquiries? The results of research into children's experiences are not wholly consistent. Roberts and Taylor (1993) for example, identify a high level of satisfaction amongst sexually abused children who had experienced the child protection system. Nearly all of the 33 children in their sample who responded to the relevant question reported that they would encourage others in the same position to reveal the abuse. Other studies are less positive. Hallett and Birchall (1992, p. 200) are clear that the possibility of damage or distress to the child resulting from all the paraphernalia of a prosecution needs to be balanced against the benefits to be derived from such a course of action. They also quote Boyce and Anderson (1990) as reporting:

> Almost all the teenage girls we have worked with regretted disclosing the abuse and suffered great loss and personal turmoil as a result.

Farmer and Owen (1995) found that some older children felt responsible for family break-up. Those who were most worried were those who left home as a result of their disclosure and an important aspect appears to be the effect on the young people of subsequent actions rather than of the investigation itself. It may be interesting to contrast this research with that of Roberts and Taylor (1993) whose sample was drawn entirely from Scotland. Since the legal system is significantly different north of the border, the effects of this difference would be worthy of future study.

Butler and Williamson (1994) also present a worrying picture. Although not examining child protection processes specifically, their research has a clear message: that a significant majority of children and young people have little or no confidence in the ability of adults to take action to resolve serious problems without reacting inappropriately. Similarly, Davies and others argue in this volume that children's reservations centre on adults as being incapable of really understanding children's experiences and concerns. The ways in which adults approach confidentiality and consultation with children will appear as key themes.

Critically, in terms of our analysis of enquiries, Howitt (1992) concludes that previous research considered the impact on children:

> *in a way which prevents the effects of abuse from being separated from the effects of the interventions of the child protection system.*

Exploring this issue further is hindered by the absence of research into the effects of the enquiry upon children where the allegation or concern was false. Howitt's own conclusions do not take us much further forward than the above statement. Prosser (1992) describes particular features of 'system abuse', namely the use of explicit material to obtain information from children, and the problem of repeated medicals.

Little has been published until recently on the effects of enquiries on the wider family. Greater attention has been focused on specific or related areas such as parental participation in child protection conferences (Lewis, 1992). The general impression from the research is that investigations constitute an horrendous experience.

> *. . . most had found the investigative process, in the words of one 'a fairly devastating thing to go through' (Moran-Ellis et al., 1991).*

Parallel themes emerge to those identified by children. Some studies, for example Howitt (1992) and Prosser (1992), use samples drawn from the caseloads of advocacy organisations. They are therefore open to the charge that any conclusions will be unrepresentative of the average family experiencing child protection processes. Nevertheless, the trauma identified by Howitt (1992) and by Prosser (1992) is evident in other studies which have used more statistically representative samples. Farmer and Owen (1995), for example, report that:

> *. . . the majority of parents (70 per cent) felt angry and upset by the treatment that they had received during the investigation and conference.*

15

In addition, Farmer (1993) demonstrates how difficulties in subsequent working relationships between social workers and parents occur following disagreements on the three dimensions of commission, culpability and risk (see Introduction, p. xix). Cleaver and Freeman (1995) categorise in some detail the disagreements in perspectives which may occur. They nevertheless demonstrate the advantages, to both child (victim) and family, of parents being treated sensitively by professionals. Thoburn *et al.* (1995) analysed the development of 'partnership' relationships during enquiries:

> *In looking in more detail at those cases where working in partnership would not be easy to achieve, but was achieved, we conclude that the key factors are the attitudes, skill and efforts of the social workers backed by agency policies and procedures which encourage them to find creative ways to inform, involve, and eventually work in partnership with parents and children.*

Despite disagreement, then, it remains possible to foster successful working relationships in a great many cases.

Unfortunately one other area of possible harm arises from the current disquiet about enquiry processes. Anecdotal information from the UK suggests that a growing number of professionals are choosing not to refer cases of possible abuse because of anxiety about the way they will be handled subsequently (confidential source). Research from the United States paints a similar picture, of clear and intentional non-reporting of suspected child abuse, particularly amongst less serious cases (Sedlak, 1991). A situation where significant numbers of children may be denied services, at the same time as other families are traumatised unnecessarily, is of considerable concern.

Racism and the enquiry process

Many, if not all, families where abuse occurs are disadvantaged prior to any intervention and the intervention itself then causes further stigma and distress. Disentangling the effects of pre-existing disadvantage from those caused by the child protection system presents problems. Additional burdens are created by the effects of racism on Black people. Cleaver and Freeman(1995) consider the social class and economic status of Black families, and conclude that:

> *social and cultural factors lose their significance in the context of the enormous upheaval that follows a child abuse investigation.*

This conclusion highlights the trauma of the process itself, but is not necessarily consistent with some other views. Information regarding the experiences of Black families is lamentably rare in British research. Bell (1993) reports that five of the seven families of non-European ethnic origin from her study were among those who attracted the highest share of negative comments in case conferences attended by the parents. This proportion was higher than amongst White European families and was taken to reflect the particular pattern of difficulties, including racism, which the five families encountered. Information from the United States suggests that Black families are subject to a significantly higher proportion of interventions, despite an apparently lower rate of actual abuse amongst Black and Asian groups (Howitt, 1992). The conclusion may be drawn that the negative experience of (predominantly) White families will be compounded for Black families. Stubbs (1989) describes cases of alleged sexual abuse in Black families where the initial response involved precipitate removal of children, and police harassment of various family members including, in one case, storming a house in riot gear. He also suggests that Black children may not achieve the status of 'deserving victim' in the enquiry process, and consequently run a higher risk than White children of further system abuse. A sound basis for beginning to overcome some of these difficulties by promoting ethnically sensitive services is described by Baldwin et al. (1989/90). Other groups, such as parents and children with learning difficulties, may also be affected more deeply by the process – see, for example, Booth and Booth (1993) and Ward (1993).

The argument summarised

The growth of legalism in child protection has been represented most clearly by the predominance of the enquiry as a method of initial intervention. In turn, the enquiry itself has become more and more legalistic. At least for a proportion of families, the process is not tailored adequately to their needs. The area where practice is most lacking is in partnership with children and with adults.

The deficiencies in the child protection system may suggest the need for a radical re-think. However, some incremental change is achievable. For example, there is already considerable interest in the New Zealand system of family group conferences, introduced into the UK by Family Rights Group (1994) and others (Ryburn, 1992; Connolly, 1994; Tunnard, 1994). Family group conferences contribute a partial alternative to the traditional child protection conference. They provide a framework for the family itself, supported by extended family, to make the decisions about protecting the child. They may evolve as one way of enhancing the partnership aspects of the child protection system. Local authorities already have begun using family group conferences in at least ten areas (Tunnard, 1994).

The writer's position is that alleged child abuse is over-investigated. In no sense is this statement intended to minimise the huge trauma experienced by a large number of abuse victims. However, a system which appears to cause significant damage itself, in addition to the abuse which some of its subjects have suffered, must be subjected to more detailed scrutiny. An approach which generally is more supportive of child and of family, particularly those from oppressed minorities, is necessary. How can this be achieved?

Key themes in improving enquiries

There is now evidence that a debate about the need for change is emerging (see discussion in Introduction; also Rickford, 1993; Sone, 1994). This debate has been fuelled by the recent Audit Commission Report (1994) and, prompted by the current Department of Health Report of recent research studies in child protection (DoH, 1995), discussion undoubtedly will continue. The following identifies some key themes in the debate about how enquiries can be improved.

1. The child within the family

The primary focus of any enquiry into alleged child abuse or neglect is the child. The child's welfare is the paramount consideration (Children Act 1989). Experience and events over the past decade have tended to draw attention to the possibility that some social workers have given too much attention to the parents, and too little to the child. The balance has now swung the other way. The child has, in some instances, come to be seen exclusively as the social worker's client. This may leave social workers with the mistaken impression that they are fulfilling their duty to keep the child's welfare paramount. Neither extreme is sufficient or acceptable.

Integral to the Children Act 1989 is an approach which attempts to maintain the balance between the needs of the child when intervention may be necessary to protect her/him, and the rights of the parents and family to freedom, autonomy, privacy etc. Whenever possible, the child's needs are best met within their own family. The *child within the family* is favoured as a means of defining the focus of the enquiry, but there is still some way to go before the spirit of the Children Act 1989 achieves full expression in practice.

At the moment, maintaining this balance between the child and the wider family is very difficult. Professionals seem to fall into one 'camp' or another. Good supervision is often a pre-requisite of a balanced perspective, as are future models for good practice. The development of the family group conference offers a way of locating the needs of the child firmly within the family context. The involvement of the extended family is critical in sharing the burden of responsibility for meeting the child's needs. Unfortunately it is not yet clear to what extent the family group conference can play a role in determining or evaluating the results of an enquiry about alleged child abuse.

2. Widening and clarifying of accountability

Central to the principles of working in partnership – whether with children or with parents – is the need to demonstrate openness, to share information, to consult appropriately, to involve them in the process, and to offer an adequate structure for reparation and complaint. This does not imply that parents (some of whom may be perpetrators of abuse) should take charge of the process, but it should be open to their scrutiny and influence without prejudicing the safety of the child. Similar considerations would be opened up to the child. The growing evidence of children's dissatisfaction with adult interventions in the name of 'child protection' is leading to calls for a child's wishes to be respected much more widely. This practice should extend to developing a clear understanding of what children see as the primary cause of their trauma, a greater consideration of their need for confidentiality, and ensuring that they are given maximum possible choice and autonomy (Hopkins et al., 1994). The principles of partnership with children and with parents are so similar that ideally they should be seen to operate side by side.

In practice many social workers believe that partnership is not possible when enquiries are made concerning alleged abuse or neglect. This route will require new priorities, new training, and some new formal structures, including an appeal process against decisions about registration of a child, as well as effective reparation and complaints procedures.

3. The redefining of professional judgement

The main response to serious mistakes in child protection work over the past two decades has been to hold an Inquiry and then tighten up the procedures. Unfortunately, at the same time as identifying what should be good practice, this process has often resulted in practitioners focusing on the most interventive aspects and applying them as a straitjacket. In these instances, the 'following of procedures' has become a goal in itself. The danger in part is that procedures are pursued beyond the point at which they become unnecessary. Paradoxically, there is also a concern that procedures which are inconvenient (e.g. providing written material for children and families) may be ignored.

The suggestion is that the role of professional judgement should be enhanced throughout the child protection system. There are many points at which professional judgement can be exercised more explicitly. The obvious example is that of introducing effective gatekeeping and is described more fully by David Thorpe in Chapter 8. The term 'gatekeeping' is used to refer to those decision-making 'gates' which should be 'guarded' more carefully to ensure that appropriate decisions are made. Examples include initiating a child protection enquiry or a case conference. Many of these decisions can not be taken using a set of procedures alone; however they are construed they must rely on professional judgement. Our growing understanding of the way child abuse allegations unfold will be of assistance here. For example, a recent study found that children referred because of a suspicion of abuse, but who had not themselves disclosed the allegation, were unlikely to disclose abuse during formal investigation (Keary and Fitzpatrick, 1994). Whilst further research is needed, this information clearly would assist professionals making judgements about when to initiate a formal enquiry. Staff should be encouraged to use their judgement, suitably backed up by training and research, to be explicit about its use, and in return to have that judgement supported by management in the event of difficulties. Procedures should be relegated to a role of enabling and promoting good practice.

There is one key area concerning the use of appropriate judgement in making decisions which is considerably more difficult to incorporate within current decision-making approaches. Families and children suspected to have suffered abuse are often able to make judgements of the most critical kind, and yet professional caution errs on the side of taking this responsibility away from them. Nevertheless, the best decisions are often those where the people affected have the greatest 'say'. Once again the family group conference offers potential for those involved most closely to exercise their own judgement, and the safeguards to prevent further danger to a child are part of the model. Other approaches rely much more on the determination of family and worker to achieve best practice.

4. A re-focusing on the early stages of the enquiry process

Child protection processes absorb a considerable amount of professional time and resources, not to mention the effects upon children and families. There is also a significant number of cases where less formal involvement of services would be preferable, but where 'child protection' procedures nevertheless are being used. A recent Audit Commission Report (1994) claims that, 'It ought to be possible to tighten and clarify the guidelines and risk indicators that trigger a full child protection investigation' (para. 54). Whilst many question their idea of reliable risk indicators as significantly over-ambitious, agencies should consider, for example, what types of referrals may not warrant investigation at all. For referrals which do enter the 'system', emphasis should be placed on resolving any child protection issues at an early stage, without recourse to unnecessary formalities. 'Children in need' (S.17, Children Act 1989), identified during these processes, should be able to receive adequate support *without* having to be registered as 'at risk' (Gibbons, 1993; Cleaver and Freeman, 1995). In terms of practice, it is envisaged that a significant number of minor injuries, for example, to children where previous concerns are minimal, could be managed through family support services. This is not to suggest that the occurrence of abuse should be assumed in such cases and if a parent wants enquiries to be made in order to 'clear their name' this request should be met.

When an enquiry is judged to be necessary, various types of supportive activity could be enhanced. For example, the importance of directing support to the child through the parent who is not accused of abuse (Farmer and Owen, 1995) has been identified. Similarly, in cases of sexual abuse, Roberts and Taylor (1993) and Dempster (1993) highlight the improvement in outcomes for children when the mother 'believes' the child's allegation. The focusing of support and work on the child–non-alleged parent relationship becomes an important feature of practice, particularly for the child. The value of support from the non-alleged parent in reducing stress for child witnesses in court also has been demonstrated (Lipovsky, 1994).

5. A re-examination of the use of criminal law in cases of alleged child abuse

The increasing emphasis on the prosecution of alleged offenders is leading to a debate about whether child abuse and neglect should be removed substantially from the criminal arena. This debate has a number of strands.

Whilst a proportion will have a need for legal redress, children's most powerful concerns are a desire for the abuse to stop, alongside a fear of the family being broken up (BBC Childwatch). The heavy-handedness of current interventions often fails children on both these counts. The focus of English child protection practice is on collecting legally admissible evidence (Cooper,

1994). As such the process distracts attention from the needs of the child and family for support and services. NACRO (1992) has argued that the prospect of prosecution may well act as a deterrent to perpetrators who might otherwise admit their crime and, in doing so, help the children considerably. Given the low level of successful prosecutions compared with the volume of actual abuse, NACRO argues that the role played by the criminal justice system is minimal. When prosecutions are successful, the prison system, by and large, has been notable in its failure to enable offenders to address their behaviour, still less to prevent further abuse of children upon release (NACRO, 1992). Overall, it has been suggested that:

> only about 7 per cent of men who abuse children are picked up and dealt with by the legal or court process. This means that a staggering 93 per cent of abusers continue to live unhampered in the community (Borthwick, 1994).

If this is the justification for a child protection system which gives priority to collecting evidence, over support to children and families, the need for change becomes much more than rhetoric.

On the more positive side, confidence seems to be growing, despite low levels of resourcing, in intervention programmes with child sex offenders (Probation Inspectorate, 1991; NACRO, 1992; Procter, 1994). The acceptability of community-based work with families where physical abuse and neglect have occurred is already well-established. The practical conclusion is that a dramatic change in policy towards diversionary schemes, particularly in cases of alleged intra-familial abuse, should be considered. Where such schemes have been introduced, support and intervention can be offered to child and family at a much earlier stage. The most promising type of programme is that of diversion from legal proceedings (Skibinski, 1994). In such circumstances an offender would be expected to produce a signed admission of guilt, which would be lodged with the prosecuting authorities, and a contract for therapeutic intervention then drawn up. Only if the contract were broken by the offender would the matter be brought before a court. Schemes of this kind are in operation in a variety of countries, including the USA (Skibinski, 1994), Germany, Sweden, Italy, Belgium (NACRO, 1992), and, in the form of the confidential doctor service, in Holland (Marneffe, 1992).

An important objection to schemes like these is that they can be applied only when a perpetrator admits a crime. As such, they would discriminate against alleged perpetrators who have been accused falsely. It is to be hoped, however, that measures of this kind would assist in humanising the process. In this event, arguably it would be of benefit to all families involved in the system.

6. Preventive and community-orientated approaches

Both diversionary schemes and better gatekeeping should lead to a search for appropriate alternative supports to offer families who would be better assisted outside the enquiry system (Audit Commission, 1994). The value of community-based approaches has been strongly indicated, if not conclusively demonstrated. For example, the link between physical abuse and social isolation has been shown by many researchers (e.g. Starr, 1982). Our understanding of how isolation affects families is growing slowly, but the simple activity of linking up families with other social contacts in their area is unlikely to be sufficient. Very often, difficulties such as poor social skills and low self-esteem mean that such relationships are difficult to handle. However, the value of neighbourhood approaches to prevention has been indicated strongly by Gibbons *et al.* (1990), who also show that practical forms of support such as childcare (see Little and Gibbons, 1993) have a very important place. Unfortunately, there is less research information to back up community strategies related to child sexual abuse but positive, preventive responses may be possible in relation to individual circumstances. One of the greatest areas of relevant experience arises from feminist practice, particularly in community work and community education. Most of this experience has been built up from work with groups of either child or adult survivors of abuse (Parton, C., 1990).

Conclusion

This chapter has described the historical and policy context of enquiries into alleged child abuse. It represents one view of factors which have contributed to the practice developments examined in subsequent chapters. Predicting the future is never easy, but a humanising of the system is the shared aim of many. The six concluding themes are intended to bring the debate closer to this objective.

BIBLIOGRAPHY

Amphlett, S. (1991) *Working in Partnership: Coping with an Investigation of Alleged Abuse or Neglect*, Parents Against INjustice.

Anthony, G. and Watkeys, J. (1991) 'False allegations in child sexual abuse: the pattern of referral in an area where reporting is not mandatory', *Children and Society*, **5:2**, 111–122.

Audit Commission (1994) *Seen But No Heard; Co-ordinating Community Child Health and Social Services for Children in Need*, London: HMSO.

Part 1 Background to the enquiry process

Baldwin, N., Johansen, P. and Seale A., on behalf of the Black and White Alliance (1989/90) *Race in Child Protection: A Code of Practice*, Race Equality Unit.

BBC Childwatch. Quoted in NACRO (1992) *Criminal Justice and the Prevention of Child Sexual Abuse*.

Bell, M. (1993) 'See no evil, speak no evil, hear no evil', *Community Care Inside*, 28.10.93.

Besharov, D.J. (1990) *Recognising Child Abuse: A Guide for the Concerned*, The Free Press.

Booth, W. and Booth, T. (1993) 'Family undoing', *Mental Handicap*, **21**, Dec. 1993.

Borthwick, I. (1994) 'A manager's view', *Scottish Child*, February/March.

Boyce, L. and Anderson, S. (1990) A common bond. *Social Work Today* 21, 34, 38. Quoted in Hallett, C. and Birchall, E. (1992) *Co-ordination and Child Protection: A Review of the Literature*. London: HMSO.

Brayne, H. and Martin, G. (1993) *Law for Social Workers*, Blackstone Press.

Butler, I. and Williamson, H. (1994) *Children Speak: Children, Trauma and Social Work*, Harlow: Longman.

Cleaver, H. and Freeman, P. (1995) *Parental Perspectives in Cases of Suspected Child Abuse*, London: HMSO

Clifford, B. (1988) Child abuse in Gloucestershire: a statistical review of trends to March 1988. Referred to in Hallett and Birchall (1992) *Co-ordination and Child Protection: A Review of the Literature*, London: HMSO.

Cohen, P. (1993) 'In the frame: children's evidence', *Community Care*, 28 October, 1993.

Connolly, M. (1994) 'An act of empowerment: The Children, Young Persons and their Families Act (1989)', *British Journal of Social Work*, **24**, 87–100.

Cooper, A. (1994) 'In care or en famille? Child protection, the family and the state in France and England', *Social Work in Europe*, **1**, no 1.

Cornwell, N. (1989) 'Decision making and justice: do they register?' *Social Work Today*, **20** (47), 3.8.89.

Creighton, S.J. (1993) 'Children's homicide: an exchange', *British Journal of Social Work*, **23**, no 6, pp 643–644.

Dempster, H. (1993) 'The Aftermath of Child Sexual Abuse: Women's Perspectives', in Waterhouse, L. (ed.) *Child Abuse and Child Abusers: Protection and Prevention*, University of Aberdeen Research Highlights in Social Work.

Department of Health (1988) *Protecting Children: A Guide for Social Workers undertaking a Comprehensive Assessment*, London: HMSO.

Department of Health (1991a) with Home Office, Department of Education and Science, Welsh Office, *Working Together Under the Children Act 1989: A guide to arrangements for inter-agency co-operation for the protection of children from abuse*, London: HMSO.

Department of Health (1991b) *Child Abuse: A Study of Inquiry Reports*, London: HMSO.

Department of Health (1995) *The Challenge of Partnership in Child Protection: Practice Guide*, London: HMSO.

Department of Health (1995) *Child Protection: Messages from Research*, London: HMSO.

Family Rights Group (1994) *Family Group Conferences: A Report Commissioned by the Department of Health*, Family Rights Group Publications.

Farmer, E. (1993) 'The impact of child protection interventions: the experiences of parents and children', in Waterhouse, L. (ed.) *Child Abuse and Child Abusers: Protection and Prevention*, University of Aberdeen Research Highlights in Social Work.

Farmer, E. and Owen, M. (1995) *Child Protection Practice: Private Risks and Public Remedies*, London: HMSO.

Ferguson, H. (1990) 'Rethinking child protection practices: a case for history', in The Violence Against Children Study Group (1990) *Taking Child Abuse Seriously*, Unwin Hyman.

Finkelhor, D. (1990) 'Is child abuse overreported? The data rebut arguments for less intervention', *Public Welfare*, Winter 1990.

Gelles, R.J. (1982) 'Problems in defining and labeling child abuse', in Starr, R.H. *Child Abuse Prediction: Policy Implications*, Ballinger.

Gibbons, J. (1993) *Operation of Child Protection Registers: Summary Report of a Research Project Commissioned by the Department of Health*, Social Work Development Unit, University of East Anglia.

Gibbons, J. with Thorpe, S. and Wilkinson, P. (1990) *Family Support and Prevention: Studies in Local Areas*, National Institute for Social Work.

Giller, H., Gormley, C. and Williams, P. (1992) *The Effectiveness of Child Protection Procedures: An Evaluation of Child Protection Procedures in Four A.C.P.C. Areas*, Social Information Systems Ltd.

Giovannoni, J.A. and Becerra, R.M. (1979) *Defining Child Abuse*, Free Press.

Hallett, C. (1993) 'Child protection in Europe: convergence or divergence?' *Adoption and Fostering*, 17 4.

Hallett, C. and Birchall, E. (1992) *Coordination and Child Protection: A Review of the Literature*, London: HMSO.

Home Office with Department of Health (1992) *Memorandum of Good Practice on Video Recorded Interviews with Child Witnesses for Criminal Proceedings*, London: HMSO.

Hopkins, N. with Butler, I. and Williamson, H. (1994) '. . . and well?' in Butler and Williamson (1994) *op. cit.*

Howitt, D. (1992) *Child Abuse Errors: When Good Intentions go Wrong*, Harvester Wheatsheaf.

Jones, D.P.H., Hopkins, C., Godfrey, M. and Glaser, D. (1993) 'The investigative process, in Stainton Rogers, W. and Worrel, M. (eds) *Investigative Interviewing with Children: Resources Booklet*, Milton Keynes: Open University.

Keary, K. and Fitzpatrick, C. (1994) 'Children's disclosure of sexual abuse during formal investigation', *Child Abuse and Neglect*, 18, no. 7.

Keech, S. (1993) Personal communication.

Lewis, A. (1992) 'An overview of research into participation in child protection work', in Thoburn, J. (ed.) *Participation in Practice: A Reader*, University of East Anglia.

Lindley, B. (1994) *On the Receiving End: a study of families' experiences of the court process in care and supervision proceedings under the Children Act 1989*, Family Rights Group.

Lindsey, D. and Trocme, N. (1994) 'Have child protection efforts reduced child homicides? An examination of data from Britain and North America', *British Journal of Social Work*, 24, pp 715–732.

Lipovsky, J.A. (1994) 'The impact of court on children: research findings and practical recommendations', *Journal of Interpersonal Violence*, 9, no. 2.

Little, M. and Gibbons, J. (1993) 'Predicting the rate of children on the child protection register', *Research, Policy and Planning* (1993) 10, no. 2.

London Borough of Brent (1985) *A Child in Trust: Report of the Panel of Inquiry Investigating the Circumstances Surrounding the Death of Jasmine Beckford*, London: Borough of Brent.

Marneffe, C. (1992) 'The confidential doctor centre: a new approach to child protection work', *Adoption and Fostering*, 16, no. 4.

Part 1 Background to the enquiry process

Milner, J. (1993) 'A disappearing act: the differing career paths of fathers and mothers in child protection investigations', *Critical Social Policy*, 38, Autumn 1993, 48–63.

Moran-Ellis, J., Conroy, S., Fielding, N. and Tunstill, J. (1991) *Investigation of Child Sexual Abuse: An Executive Summary*, Department of Sociology, University of Surrey.

National Association for the Care and Re-settlement of Offenders (1992) *Criminal Justice and the Prevention of Child Sexual Abuse*, NACRO.

Parent (1993) Verbal contribution to PAIN 'Thinking Day', 21.6.93.

Parton, C. (1990) 'Women, gender oppression and child abuse', in The Violence Against Children Study Group, *Taking Child Abuse Seriously*, Unwin Hyman.

Parton, N. (1985) *The Politics of Child Abuse*, Macmillan Education.

Parton, N. (1990) 'Taking Child Abuse Seriously', in The Violence Against Children Study Group, *Taking Child Abuse Seriously*, Unwin Hyman.

Parton, N. (1991) *Governing the Family*, Macmillan Education.

Pollock, L. (1983) *Forgotten Children: Parent-child Relations from 1500–1900*, Cambridge University Press. Referred to in Ferguson (1990) *op. cit.*

Pritchard, C. (1992) 'Children's homicide as an indicator of effective child protection: A comparative study of Western European statistics', *British Journal of Social Work*, 22, no. 6, pp 663–684.

Pritchard, C. (1993) 'Re-analysing children's homicide and undetermined death rates as an indication of improved child protection: a reply to Creighton', *British Journal of Social Work*, 23 no. 6, pp 645–652.

Probation Inspectorate (1991) *The Work of the Probation Service with Sex Offenders: Report of a Thematic Inspection*, HM Inspectorate of Probation.

Procter, E. (1994) 'A four year evaluation of the Cherwell Group – a programme for convicted sexual offenders', *Social Services Research*, no. 2, University of Birmingham.

Prosser J. (1992) *Child Abuse Investigations: The Families' Perspective*. A case study of 30 families who claim to have been falsely accused, Parents Against Injustice.

Rickford, F. (1993) 'No room for doubt', *Community Care*, 21 October.

Roberts, J. and Taylor, C. (1993) 'Sexually abused children and young people speak out', in Waterhouse, L. (ed.) *Child Abuse and Child Abusers: Protection and Prevention*, University of Aberdeen Research Highlights in Social Work.

Ryburn, M. (1992) 'Family group conferences', in Thoburn, J. (ed.) *Participation in Practice: A Reader*, University of East Anglia.

Secretary of State for Social Services (1988) *Report of the Inquiry into Child Abuse in Cleveland*, Cmnd 412, London: HMSO.

Sedlak, A. (1991) *National Incidence and Prevalence of Child Abuse and Neglect: 1988*, Revised Report (Rockville, MD: Westat) quoted in Besharov, D.J. and Laumann, L.A. (1994) *Reporting Child Abuse and Neglect: Some Lessons from the USA*, Unpublished.

Skibinski, G.J. (1994) 'Intrafamilial child sexual abuse: intervention programs for first-time offenders and their families', *Child Abuse and Neglect*, 18(4), 367–375.

Sone, K. (1994) 'Balancing act', *Community Care*, 16–22 June.

Starr, R.H. (1982) 'A research-based approach to the prediction of child abuse', in Starr, R.H. *Child Abuse Prediction – Policy Implications*. Ballinger.

26

Stubbs, P. (1989) 'Developing anti-racist practice – problems and possibilities', in Wattam, C., Hughes, B. and Blagg, H., *Child Sexual Abuse: Listening, Hearing and Validating the Experiences of Children*, Harlow: Longman.

Thoburn, J., Lewis, A. and Shemmings, D. (1995) *Partnership of Paternalism? Family Involvement in Child Protection*, London: HMSO.

Tunnard, J. (ed.) (1994) *Family Group Conferences: A Report Commissioned by the Department of Health*, Family Rights Group.

Ward, L. (1993) 'Losing out on parenthood', *Community Care*, 29.4.93.

Wattam, C. (1992) *Making a Case in Child Protection*, Harlow: Longman.

Wattam, C. (1993) 'Kids on Film', *Community Care*, 7 October 1993.

NOTE

[1] The term 'enquiry' is used throughout this chapter as a general convention. 'Investigation' is used in quotations, and where there is an appropriate historical context, where reference is made to research which properly examined a process generally termed 'investigation', or where the type of enquiry referred to is particularly formal in nature.

2

Enquiries into allegations: a Black perspective

Melanie Phillips and Jabeer Butt

Introduction

There is little research at present which focuses on the experience that Black children and families have of enquiries into child abuse (we are using Black in this instance to define people of African, Caribbean and Asian descent, who have a shared experience of White racism). There is evidence however which supports the conclusion that, whilst all families experience child protection enquiries as intensely traumatic and emotionally devastating, the effects of racism exacerbate further the negativity of this process for Black families.

This chapter considers enquiries into allegations of child abuse from a Black perspective. We first set the context by discussing the perspective that we have brought to this issue as well as commenting on the dearth of relevant research for us to draw on in marshalling our arguments. We proceed to discuss the perspectives that have dominated the response to child abuse in England and the shift in child protection enquiries codified by recent guidance, the result of which has been a pre-eminence of the search for evidence of criminal activity in such enquiries. The implications of these developments for making enquiries and Black families is discussed next. We conclude with a discussion of good practice.

But first a note of caution. There is a danger in two Black people writing a chapter such as this. Often an invitation to write such a chapter is a way White people, or White organisations or White publishers, try to gain credibility for their work, or disguise a glaring omission, or attempt to increase their potential audience. You, the reader, will have to judge if any of this is true with the inclusion of our chapter in this book.

There is another danger too: that of being silent. In turning down this invitation it may have allowed those who have ignored the needs of our children and families to persist. It may also have left those who are interested in protecting Black children and families without an opportunity to consider what needs to change in their practice. It would be arrogant of us to suggest that this chapter will stop the former, but we hope that it will contribute to the work of the latter.

The context

In considering the experience of Black children and families of child protection enquiries we bring a Black perspective to bear. This Black perspective is drawn both from our experiences as Black people in Britain today and our analysis of how British society has responded to the presence of significant numbers of people who originate from Africa, the Caribbean and Asia. Adele Jones and Jabeer Butt have written:

> In defining ourselves as Black, we are referring to our collective experiences and struggles in challenging and resisting racism.
>
> A Black perspective is a perspective informed by that experience; thought and action based on the understanding of race, class and gender oppression as directly experienced and as it is reproduced in this society. . . . A Black perspective is part of a political process in which, in and beyond the act of resistance, Black people seek to define and express themselves. Informed by an understanding of oppression, a Black perspective also encompasses cultural identity and the rich, diverse traditions and backgrounds from which we come and is therefore more than just a response to oppression (Jones and Butt, forthcoming).

An implication worth highlighting is that we reject the notion of neutrality. We do not see ourselves as neutral in exploring the experience of Black children and families. Similarly, we would argue, all those involved in making enquiries into allegations of child abuse are not neutral: they all bring their own perspective to any allegation of child abuse, as does the legislative framework which attempts to govern their responses.

An essential element of our Black perspective is an understanding of racism. Racism is a complex phenomenon; it cannot be explained just in terms of attitudes, behaviour, or institutional policies. A definition of racism has to encompass the dynamic which operates between the historical legacy of slavery and colonisation, social policy, institutional and personal practice, as well as attitudes and behaviour. It is the interaction between these elements that is as important as each of the component parts.

The issue is not how 'natural' differences determine and justify group definitions and interactions, but how racial logic and racial frames of reference are articulated and deployed, and with what consequences. (Rattansi, 1992)

It is how racial logic and racial frames of reference relate to child protection enquiries, and the resulting outcomes for Black families, with which we will be concerned in this chapter.

Research

One place where racism operates is in the dearth of British child protection and Black families research. Importantly, not only does the majority of research fail to focus on the Black experience, nor even acknowledge that it may be different from the population under investigation; neither does it adopt a Black perspective. The experience of research into 'Black criminality' in the 1970s and the 1980s has demonstrated the need for more than the research just to focus on Black communities. A Black perspective is essential to ensure that we do not see the creation of a new orthodoxy, on this occasion replacing the acceptance of criminality by Black communities with some suggestion that Black communities accept child abuse.

Child protection

As a part of the child protection process, enquiries do not raise substantially different issues for Black families than from any other area of child protection work. The issues are detailed in depth elsewhere (Dutt and Phillips, 1990; Phillips, forthcoming; Gambe et al., 1992) but they are worth summarising here:

- the Eurocentric nature of British social work;

- stereotypical views of African, Caribbean and Asian families;

- stereotypical views of men and women in African, Caribbean and Asian families;

- a concentration on culture as defining the difference between Black and White families, rather than racism;

- White middle-class notions of good parenting and what constitutes a normal childhood are used as criteria against which Black families are assessed negatively;

- White middle-class notions of what constitutes child abuse and where and how the state should respond.

Enquiries are at the most acute end of the child protection spectrum, where rapid decisions have to be made about the protection of the child and the potential prosecution of an alleged abuser. If there is enough evidence to suggest that a child is not protected, and that an offence has been committed, police and social workers may take action through the criminal and family courts.

Both Black and White families experience enquiries as frightening and invasive, but for Black families the impact of racism on the assessments and decision-making of professionals means that they have cause to be particularly concerned about the outcome of the enquiries. In part, this is based on the history of social work intervention with Black children and families. Shama Ahmed (1991) has recounted that in Coventry the Black communities referred to welfare workers (social workers as they were then known) as 'farewell workers'. It was suggested in Black communities that when you approached a welfare worker you could say 'farewell' to your children.

This perception is supported by statistical evidence. A number of studies have shown the over-representation of Black children in public care. In the 1960s, one of the first studies conducted showed that children of 'mixed origin' were four and a half times more likely to come into care than 'White indigenous' or 'Afro-Caribbean and Asian' children (quoted by Barn, 1990). The Soul Kids Campaign (1977) and studies in the 1980s, such as the Adams study in 1981 and the Wilkinson study in 1982 have all shown that Black children make up over 50 per cent of the care population (Rowe et al., 1989; Barn, 1990). In a number of these research findings, there is a suggestion that the evidence is contradictory. This often hinges on the reluctance of those conducting the studies to consider children with one White parent as being part of Black communities. Bebbington and Miles (1989) in their examination of the backgrounds of 2,500 children in local authority care concluded that a child of mixed race is two and a half times as likely to enter care as is a White child.

Not all of these children will have been the subject of child protection enquiries, and so we cannot easily draw the conclusion that Black children are more likely to be removed from their families than are White children. Also we do not have statistics which tell us whether or not Black families are more likely to be the subject of child protection enquiries than their White counterparts. But what we can conclude is that Black children whose families come into contact with social welfare agencies are more likely to end up in state care than are their White counterparts.

31

There can only be two explanations for this. Either, in proportionate terms, more Black children are abused, abandoned or neglected than White children, or it is the perception of welfare agencies that Black children are less well cared for than White children. Studies have shown the latter to be the case. American research for example has shown that there is little variation between rates of abuse in Black and White communities:

> across the board studies have consistently failed to find any Black–White differences in rates of sexual abuse (Finkelhor, 1986).

In terms of physical and emotional abuse: 'Race stands out due to the similarities between Blacks and Whites' (Jones and McCurdy, 1992).

The only consistent variable in studies in relation to physical abuse or neglect appears to be one of economic circumstances, i.e. poverty. Although Black families are disadvantaged economically by the effects of racism, there is nothing to suggest that a disproportionate number of Black families, as compared to White families who are on the breadline, abuse their children. Indeed, the little British evidence that does exist appears to contradict this. Barn's investigation of Black children's admission patterns into local authority care found that:

> Black children were much more likely than White children to come from higher socio-economic groups. For example, 47 per cent of the Black children's mothers were in White collar and skilled manual occupations compared to 22 per cent of White children (Barn, 1993)

Barn also found that it was less likely that preventative work was done with Black families in comparison to White families. In addition, Black children were admitted into care at twice the speed of White children. Finally, Black children were more likely to be made subject to parental rights resolutions than were White children.

These findings are particularly significant because, although most of the Black children in her study entered care on a voluntary basis, they were as likely as White children to be made subjects of care orders. The implication is clear: that even when Black families approach welfare agencies for support and help, they are likely to experience control rather than care.

This is in keeping with the research on other aspects of provision of welfare services, such as in the field of mental health. Studies have shown that Black people are more likely to be subject to compulsory detention, and less likely to be in receipt of preventative services, than White people who are mentally ill. Bowl and Barnes (1990) show that, although Afro-Caribbeans are more often referred for assessment by approved social workers (ASWs), which do not normally lead to compulsory admission, the outcome is different:

> *The assessment by an ASW appears . . . to amplify the discriminatory effects of referral patterns, reinforcing the tendency for Afro-Caribbeans to be subject to compulsory detention* (Bowl and Barnes, 1990).

The historical basis for Black communities' fears of the outcome of contact with welfare agencies has been compounded, we believe, by recent changes in enquiries of alleged child abuse. Any analysis of the development of current joint investigation policy and procedures will show a move away from treatment and prevention, towards statutory and legal intervention, and it is the impact of this on Black children and families that we consider next.

Treatment or punishment?

The central tension that besets child protection policy and practice is maintaining a balance between treating parents and punishing them. A 'treatment' response originates from a social welfare model where the task of professional agencies is to help and support parents with the aim of achieving change. A 'punishment' response blames parents for their behaviour, and holds them accountable through criminal prosecution.

The 1960s brought the discovery of 'child abuse', spearheaded by Henry Kempe in America. He was the first to coin the term 'battered baby syndrome' in an attempt to describe the children that he was seeing who had bone fractures which appeared to be linked with the parents as the possible source of the injuries. Kempe suggested that the parents he saw were characteristically immature or inadequate. For him, protection was not just about the punishment of parents for cruelty, it also involved a programme of treatment for the parents in an attempt to change this behaviour.

Kempe's work laid the foundations for current social services policy. In the late 1960s and early 1970s family treatment was the main focus of any child protection work that was undertaken. The NSPCC and local authority departments carried the main responsibility for the work. Their emphasis was on keeping families together, and changing the behaviour of deviant parents.

Following the death of Maria Colwell in 1973, the resultant public and media outcry focused attention on social services' responses to situations of child abuse. The police were particularly dissatisfied with social services' approaches to the issue, and publicly stated at a Police Superintendents' Conference in 1976 that social services were failing to notify the police of cases of battered children, and were working with families at the expense of adequately protecting the child. As a result of this the DHSS issued a circular in 1976 which set out the importance of closer involvement of the police in child protection work and the need for better co-operation between police and social services (Parton, 1985).

But it was the fall-out from the Cleveland Inquiry which spurred local authorities to begin to develop joint investigation procedures. The political, media and public response to the criticisms of social services and the medical profession laid out in the Cleveland Report (Butler-Schloss, 1988) meant that no local authority could afford to ignore such advice. The police were no longer to be sidelined; they had to be involved as joint and equal partners. The focus of the work for social services was not just to be treatment; it also had to include punishment.

In 1991, the Criminal Justice Act took joint investigation a stage further by extending the use of video links in courts, and by introducing video-recorded interviews into courts to represent the evidence-in-chief of the child as the main witness. Department of Health guidance in the form of the *Memorandum of Good Practice* followed, which set out the principles and procedures to be followed in conducting video recorded interviews. It states that 'A major element in the *Working Together* approach is joint interviewing by police and social worker' (DoH, 1992).

As the primary purpose of the interviews is to obtain evidence from the child which can be used in the criminal court, this meant that for the first time social workers were to be involved directly in gathering evidence for criminal proceedings. The inevitable outcome has been the establishment of joint police and social work teams, with some being based in police stations.

The rationale for joint interviewing has frequently been stated as child centred, on the basis that it avoids duplication, enhances inter-agency co-operation and enhances the opportunity to link prosecution with protection. However, this process is causing increasing concerns on the part of a variety of professionals, not least many social workers. The emphasis on prosecution is an inappropriate way to deal with enquiries, particularly as so few result in criminal convictions. (Research yet to be published from Plotnikoff and Woolfson (1993) at the University of Birmingham has recently found that of almost 15,000 video interviews recorded only 44 were accepted by the courts.)

Parton summarises this shift in policy:

. . . the demise of the optimistic rehabilitative ideal, with its search for underlying causes, has been replaced by a pessimistic neo-classicist approach relying on multi-agency surveillance to identify the high risk in order to 'protect' the individual child from the abusive parent (Parton, 1990).

It could be argued that this shift is damaging for all families: Black or White. Furthermore, while statistics do not reveal what percentage of the cases being investigated involve Black families, any suggestion that this shift is more problematic for Black families will have to be tentative. However, evidence shows that the criminal courts are not fair and equal places for Black people. In an article in the *Independent* in 1989 Kirby stated that:

Black people are more likely than their White counterparts to be stopped by the police. If stopped they are more likely to be charged. If charged, more likely to be remanded in custody, and if convicted, more likely to receive a sentence of imprisonment (quoted by Skellington and Morris, 1992).

In another article in the *Independent*, in 1988 the director of NACRO, Vivien Stern, commented on a NACRO study which showed disproportionate sentencing in respect of Black people. She said:

. . . these figures do not show that Black people are more prone to crime than White people, but they do suggest that Black people who offend are more likely to go to prison (Skellington and Morris, 1992).

With the increased 'criminalisation' of child protection the chances are that Black people will suffer the consequences differentially. Even if conviction rates are low, the opportunities for racial discrimination are as apparent in relation to child protection enquiries as they are in any other area of criminal justice.

We would certainly not suggest that Black people should not be prosecuted as a result of enquiries. It is as important that Black perpetrators of crimes against children are convicted of their offences as it is for White perpetrators. What does give cause for concern, however, is the process by which convictions are achieved, and the impact that racism has on that process. If Black children are to protected, it is prosecution as well as protection which needs to be just and fair.

Enquiries

In considering the protection aspect of enquiries, there is evidence that racism also affects the judgements, assessments and decision-making of professionals in relation to the protection of children and this process can start from the first point of contact. Consider this example of a Black manager who was reviewing duty referrals:

> ... Well, it happened that a Black woman who once came in just to seek some help in terms of Section 1 money, she was talking about how difficult it is for her to manage her children and she was using her hands to express herself and put some emphasis into what she was trying to say. That was totally misinterpreted by the White worker, that she was aggressive and she was violent and that it was quite possible that the children may be at risk. Whereas when another assessment was done it was found that there was absolutely no danger at all and in fact she was a far more caring, loving person to her children and she looked after her children far better under the circumstances (Butt, 1994).

We have suggested already that Black families have a different experience of social work intervention as compared to White families. But in enquiries into allegations of abuse or neglect, there is a specific process by which professionals are required to assess the potential for protection which is present in the families being investigated. This process is governed by the Children Act 1989, illustrated in the Department of Health Guidance to local authorities, and translated at a local level by each authority into policies and procedures for making enquiries into allegations of abuse. Essentially the regulations and guidance in relation to conducting enquiries largely ignore racism. They prefer instead to focus on 'culture' and to promote 'cultural sensitivity' as the best approach to working with Black families. However, 'racism' and 'culture' are different. While there is a linkage between the two, 'culture' cannot be understood properly unless it is seen within the context of racism. Racism distorts White people's perception of Black cultures often through negative stereotyping of the lifestyles of Black families and sometimes through positive stereotypes like the ever-resilient Caribbean mother, or the enterprising Asian businessman.

'Cultural sensitivity' is the adaptation of multi-culturalism into a social work context. The Children Act 1989, *Working Together, Protecting Children* and the *Memorandum of Good Practice* all adopt a multi-cultural perspective in relation to Black families. Taking a lead from the Department of Health, most local authorities have incorporated this approach into their child protection procedures.

In *Working Together* the only reference which could be construed as referring to Black people is the following, under the heading 'Children and Parents with Communication Difficulties':

> *Children and parents whose first language is not English will also have special needs during the interviews. Efforts should be made to help them have a clear understanding of what is happening and what may happen in the future. Enlisting the services of an interpreter should be considered, but care taken in their choice.*

While important, the definition of difference encapsulated in this guidance inevitably focuses on effective communication with the Asian community, even though the majority of child abuse enquiries have probably been with the Caribbean community. Cultural sensitivity may suggest that you speak in the same language but it does nothing to ensure that the message is not discriminatory.

The effective protection of children is dependent on the ability of professionals to engage effectively with families, and to assess accurately the level of risk to a child. Both parts of the process require that child protection workers approach enquiries with an open mind, and that their judgements are not clouded with preconceived ideas.

In practice, assessments are not value-free, but are influenced by the worker's own views and values. Judgements of parents' and carers' abilities are affected by culturally racist views about Black family lifestyles and these in turn affect professionals' assessments about protection.

When these stereotypes are applied to assessments of families, it becomes clear that there are serious pitfalls in the culture-based model:

> *It is becoming increasingly apparent that the caring professions, particularly social work, are operating at two extremes in relation to Black children and their families. Either they seem to have a liberal or safe approach, anxious not to be labelled as racist, so keen that they tend to shy away from their duties of protecting the Black child from abuse, or they do not hesitate to remove Black children from their families, who according to them are not suitable parents or whose child care practices are perceived as sub-standard* (Ahmad, 1989).

Under-intervention, as a result of 'avoidance', will result in Black children being unsafe whilst over-intervention, as a result of a pathological view of Black families, will result in the inappropriate removal of Black children from families. Neither of these approaches will result in effective protection for the child.

Barn (1990) has demonstrated the significant disparity between Black and White families' experience of supportive children services, but more importantly the speed with which Black children come into care as compared to White children. It is difficult not to conclude that an element of the explanation for this is over-intervention. A sad feature of the past 20 years has also been the examples of under-intervention: Jasmine Beckford, Tyra Henry, Sukina Hammond.

To explain why social workers should respond to Black families in a way which produces such dramatically opposite outcomes involves a more detailed examination of the impact that stereotypes of particular groups have on practice. It also requires a consideration of the influence that gender has on the child protection process.

Both men and women abuse children, but it is also clear from the research that gender is a factor in rates of abuse. Some research suggests in child sexual abuse 90 per cent of abusers are men (Finkelhor, 1986). In physical abuse and neglect, the numbers of men and women who are responsible for the abuse is roughly equal, but as men spend a significantly smaller proportion of time with children than women do, and more seldom perform childcare tasks, research suggests that children may be at greater risk of physical and sexual violence from men than from women (Parton, 1990).

Concern about male violence, spearheaded by a feminist approach to child sexual abuse, has led to changes in child protection policy and practice in recent years. Under current procedures, the emphasis is on supporting the women in her role as a protector, and on the removal of the man where he is an abuser. Within this context, gender-based stereotypes can be as influential on practice as culture-based stereotypes. In assessments of Black families, gender and culture often combine to produce complex stereotypes which can have a dramatic outcome on practice. An examination of these stereotypes, and the consequent images which they provide of Black men and women, helps to explain the differential outcomes of social work practice with Black communities. Stereotypes of Caribbean families are particularly negative:

> *Afro-Caribbean life in contemporary Britain is seen as weak and unstable, with the lack of a sense of parental responsibility towards children* (Pryce, 1979), *a failure by the family to apply adequate social control over its youth* (Cashmore, 1979) *and a negative (personal) self image* (Fernando, 1988).

In the Beckford Inquiry (London Borough of Brent, 1985) social workers were criticised for their apparent inability to confront Morris Beckford, Jasmine's step-father, with their concerns about Jasmine's situation. In the report into the death of Sukina Hammond it is stated that several professionals had already formed a view of her father prior to meeting him, '. . . they . . . had an account of how they felt fearful of meeting Sukina's father' (BCCCS, 1991).

In both cases fear of these men seems to have resulted in professional avoidance, and in both of these cases the men referred to were of African Caribbean origin. Whilst we would not suggest that stereotypes were the sole reason for inaction, the picture that emerges for each of these men conforms to the typical stereotype of an aggressive and threatening African Caribbean man. Whatever the precise impact that this may have had on the White workers involved in these cases, it is likely that fear of Black men will have been one of the dynamics which contributed to the lack of professional action.

For Asian families the image of subjugated and passive women calls into question the protective abilities of Asian women. This may lead professionals to assume that Asian mothers are unable to believe and support their child in situations where the child alleges that they have been abused by their father. The assumption is that the mother is unable or unwilling to question her husband's authority. On a number of occasions these stereotypes have led to the inappropriate removal of children.

Conclusion

There is an inevitable desire that a chapter such as this should conclude with some suggestions of how to avoid the pitfalls identified earlier. Whilst we do attempt this below, it is also important to emphasise that an aim of this chapter is to suggest that making enquiries into allegations of child abuse or neglect with Black communities is a complex task. As with all complex tasks any attempt to put forward simple answers inevitably will be fruitless and possibly damaging. There are no simple formulae for conducting enquiries with Black families, any more than there are for White families. But the aim of any child protection enquiry should be to ensure that decisions which are made are informed by accurate assessments, which are as free as possible from the distorting effects of racism. This requires that attention be paid at all stages of the process of the investigation to the collation of information and to the interpretation of that information.

This process needs to begin at the point of referral. At this stage professionals have a duty to check out the accuracy of the information being presented to them. Where does this information come from? Is it fact or assumption? Is it influenced by stereotypes?

The investigation plan also needs to consider the accuracy of information in respect of a particular family. In deciding who should comprise the investigation team, consideration needs to be given to who are the most appropriate people available to conduct the investigation. This does not mean that it should always be Black workers who have the responsibility to investigate Black families, but it means that White workers must question and evaluate their own skills in assessing Black families.

In formulating a protection plan with the family, and in assessing the potential of the 'non-abusing carer' to protect, care should be taken to avoid gender-based stereotypes which might affect an accurate assessment of a parent's ability to protect. It is important at this stage that the worker remembers that families are experts on themselves. No amount of preconceived notions about Asian or Caribbean families will help a worker to identify how a particular family will respond to the situation, and what strengths or weaknesses may be present in this particular situation.

By asking non-alleged abusing carers how they think that they can protect their child, in the context of the options open to them, and referring to the child's particular need for protection, workers may be able to initiate a much more meaningful dialogue about protection than any preconceived professional plan could achieve. It would also have the advantage of being related to the particular cultural context in which that family lives. If the family is unable to offer a plan which would provide protection, even with practical assistance from professional agencies, then state care may be the only option, but at least workers will have attempted to negotiate with families in a way which respects culture, but rejects stereotypes. Just as White children, Black children deserve protection from abuse. However, for Black children this also means protection from the damaging effects of racism and its pervasive influence on the practice of child protection professionals.

REFERENCES

Ahmad, B. (1989) 'Protecting Black children from abuse', in *Social Work Today*, 8 June 1989, Reed.

Ahmed, S. (1991) 'Routing out racism', *Community Care*, **869**, 27 June, pp. 16–18.

Barn, R. (1990) 'Black children in local authority care: admission patterns', *New Community*, **16**, pp. 229–246

Barn, R. (1993) *Black Children in the Public Care System*, British Association of Adoption and Fostering.

Bebbington, A. and Miles, J. (1989) 'The background of children who enter local authority care', *British Journal of Social Work* **19**, pp. 349–368.

Bowl, R. and Barnes, M. (1990) 'Race, Racism and mental health social work: Implications for local auhtority policy and training', in *Research, Policy and Planning* **8**, no. 2 ,pp. 12–18, SSRG.

Bridge Child Care Consultancy Services (1991) *Sukina: An evaluation report of the circumstances leading to her death*, BCCCS.

Butler-Schloss (1988) *Report of the Inquiry into Child Abuse in Cleveland*, London: HMSO.

Butt, J. (1994) *Same Service or Equal Service?*, London: HMSO.

Cashmore, E. (1979) *Endless Pressure*, Harmondsworth: Penguin.

Dutt, R. and Phillips, M. (1990) *Towards a Black Perspective in Child Protection*, Race Equality Unit.

Fernando, S. (1988) *Race and Culture in Psychiatry*, London: Routledge.

Finkelhor, D. (1986) *A Sourcebook on Child Sexual Abuse*, Beverley Hills: Sage.

Gambe, D., Gomes, J., Kapur, V., Rangel, M. and Stubbs, P. (1992) *Improving Practice with Children and Families*, CCETSW.

Department of Health, Department of Education and Science (1991) *Working Together under the Children Act 1989*, London: HMSO.

Department of Health in conjunction with Home Office (1992) *Memorandum of Good Practice*, London: HMSO.

Jones, A. and Butt, J. (forthcoming) *Taking the initiative*, London: NSPCC.

Jones, E. and McCurdy, K. (1992) 'The links between types of maltreatment and demographic characteristics of children', *Child Abuse and Neglect*, **16**.

London Borough of Brent (1987) *A Child in Trust: The Report of the Panel of Enquiry into the Circumstances Surrounding the Death of Jasmine Beckford*, London Borough of Brent.

London Borough of Lambeth (1987) *Whose Child? A report of the Public Inquiry into the death of Tyra Henry*, London Borough of Lambeth.

Parton, N. (1985) *The Politics of Child Abuse*, Macmillan.

Parton, N. (1990) *Taking Child Abuse Seriously*, The Violence Against Children Study Group, London: Unwin and Hyman.

Phillips, M. (forthcoming) 'Issues of ethnicity and culture', in James, A. and Wilson, K. (eds) *The Child Protection Handbook*, Harcourt Bruce Jovanich.

Plotnikoff, J. and Woolfson, R. (1993) *Community Care 'News'*, 28.10.93.

Pryce, K. (1979) *'Rastaman'; The Rastafarian Movement in England*, Allen and Unwin.

Rattansi, A. (1992) '"Race", culture and difference', in Donald, P. and Rattansi, A. (eds) *Racism, Culture and Education*, Milton Keynes: Open University.

Rowe, J., Hundleby, M. and Garnett, L. (1989) *Child Care Now*, British Association of Adoption and Fostering.

Skellington, R. and Morris, P. (1992) *'Race' in Britain Today*, Milton Keynes: Open University Press.

Soul Kids Campaign (1977) *Report of the Steering Group of the Soul Kids Campaign*, Association of British Fostering and Adoption Agencies.

3

Children with disabilities and special needs: current issues and concerns for child protection procedures

Philippa Russell

Introduction

> *Children with disabilities are particularly vulnerable. They have the same rights as other children to be protected* (Children Act Guidance and Regulations, Volume 6, Children with Disabilities).

> *Yet still the myths persist that disabled children are not vulnerable – that while others may pity them they will not find them attractive or desirable, that if the children don't understand what is happening to their bodies, it can't be so harmful, that they don't feel things in the same way as others; that they cannot benefit from therapy; a series of further misconceptions that contribute to the 'let's sort out the normal children first' attitude which still, unfortunately, persists* (Margaret Kennedy, 1993).

There are about 360,000 children with disabilities (aged 16 years and under) in the United Kingdom (Office of Population and Census Surveys, 1989). These children form about 3 per cent of the child population in this country and many present major challenges to both their families and to statutory and voluntary services which provide support. The facts and figures set out below provide some background information for this chapter.

Disabled children – families in the UK

1. 360,000 children of 16 and under with significant disabilities;

2. 189,000 children have very severe disabilities;

3. 5,500 children live in residential care;

4. 16,000 children with disabilities and special needs attend residential schools;

5. Of the children living away from home,
   33% had major health or behaviour problems;
   33% had problems at home (e.g. parent unable to manage without additional support;
   15% had been sexually or physically abused;

6. 45% of parents had health problems; felt they had less time for other children and had additional costs because of caring for a child with disabilities.

The past decade has seen greater public (and professional) awareness of disability, with increasingly positive images about the capacity as well as incapacity of disabled people to make decisions about their own lives and to contribute to the planning and development of support services. But positive images are insufficient without a corresponding awareness of the increased vulnerability of disabled children, and their families, to abuse within a variety of settings; also of the need for improved training opportunities for all professionals working in child protection services to ensure that they are aware of disability issues and in particular know how and where to locate expert advice when required.

Disability and abuse: evidence from research

Evidence of the possible incidence of abuse and children with disabilities or special needs currently comes mainly from studies in the USA. Sullivan, Vernon and Scanlon (1987) found that out of 150 children with hearing impairments attending residential schools, 75 reported sexual abuse, 19 reported incest at home and 3 reported physical and sexual abuse. Margaret Kennedy (1990), in a UK study of deaf children, found 192 suspected and 86 confirmed instances of physical and emotional abuse, with 70 suspected cases of sexual abuse and 50 confirmed. She concluded that not only were disabled children more likely to be candidates for physical or sexual abuse but also they were likely to be abused for longer periods of time than their non-disabled peers. Kennedy noted that, although her study reflected a relatively small sample, it highlighted the need to include disabled children within local child protection procedures and to consider how children with communications problems might disclose any abuse and, equally, be heard and believed if abuse took place.

From 1977–1983, the Seattle (USA) Rape Relief and Sexual Assault Centre found over 700 reported cases of sexual abuse involving children and adults with learning disabilities from the Seattle area. This was considered to be significant under-reporting of the true incidence. Sexual abuse was defined in this study as 'rape, attempted rape or incest.' Of the reported victims 99 per cent were sexually abused by relatives or care-givers.

In another UK study of 65 adults with learning disabilities, all attending a work activity centre, Hard and Plumb (1987) cited in Westcott (1992) found that 83 per cent of the women and 32 per cent of the men had been sexually abused. Abuse in this context was described as sexual contact caused by force, coercion or manipulation, or otherwise entered into unwillingly or unknowingly. It included oral, anal or vaginal intercourse and touching breasts and genitalia.

As in the Seattle study, the researchers found that in 99 per cent of cases the abuse was carried out by someone known to the individual concerned. 64 per cent of the women said they told someone about the abuse – but 55 per cent were not believed and no action followed. 40 per cent of the men who told were believed.

Westcott (1992) has reviewed over twenty articles on the physical, emotional and sexual abuse of children with a range of disabilities. She notes that much of the current literature focuses upon *sexual* abuse (although children's vulnerability to sexual abuse may be greatly increased by emotional and physical abuse). She also notes that there has been little attention paid to the views and experiences of disabled people themselves – particularly with regard to *prevention* and *how* children and young adults might have been supported in disclosing abuse at an earlier stage. A study of the experiences of disabled survivors of abuse (Westcott, 1992) emphasises the importance of communication between carers and disabled children and the need to listen carefully to children's fears or complaints.

The existing literature on this subject demonstrates clearly the need for much greater vigilance in order to protect children and young people with disabilities and special needs and to ensure that these special needs are neither marginalised nor misunderstood within local child protection strategies. But it also provides some important messages about disability and child protection – and the myths which need to be dispelled in order to ensure that children with special needs do not experience a double jeopardy through misunderstandings and complacency about the quality of care and life experiences which are offered to them.

Parents of children with disabilities or other special needs are no more likely than other parents to abuse their children. But the additional responsibilities (and frequent lack of support) may make such families and children more at risk of abuse – and pressures of care may make families and professional carers hesitant to voice suspicions when there may be no obvious alternative source of help. A number of studies in the UK have shown the particular pressure placed upon families by the additional care needs of disabled children. A study by Glendinning (1983) found that out of 361 young children with disabilities, 50 children could not be left alone for even ten minutes in a day. A study by Wilkin (1989) of the lives of families of children with severe learning difficulties noted that they received little significant help from relatives, friends or neighbours in terms of day-to-day caring. Siblings (particularly sisters) frequently played an important role. Other studies of disability in adults have shown a growth of young carers, who may miss school or ordinary recreational activities in order to provide extra support at home. Carey (1982) cited in Glendinning (1983) similarly described the support network of another group of families with young disabled children as 'negligible in terms of the informal social network'. Looking at sleep disturbance in young children with disabilities, Quine and Paul (1989) also stressed the depression and anxiety caused by disruptive behaviours, and the particular vulnerability of single parents with no extended family and limited social contacts for mutual support.

A new group of vulnerable parents is that of parents who are themselves disabled. 'Elizabeth' (in a personal and anonymised communication) has described her experiences of being a physically disabled parent of a nine-month baby. 'No-one has confidence in me', she commented, 'I was expected to be careless, to take risks, to be an inadequate parent. I had to seek "permission" to carry my baby up and downstairs. Nappy rash, a scratched face, a stomach upset – I don't feel I can ask for help like any other parent. My childcare is always suspect, almost pre-judged a failure. We need disability equality training amongst all professionals working in the area of child protection. If you are disabled you are currently seen as super-woman or as totally inadequate, not an ordinary family living under pressure.'

Families from ethnic minority groups may also fall victim to misjudgments about the care of their children. 'Khalida' (personal communication) describes how she was suspected of alleged child abuse because she regularly either 'tethered' her very hyperactive brain damaged child with children's reins or locked him in his bedroom for short periods of time. 'Ahmed' had meningitis when he was three; it has left him with major behaviour problems: a hemiplegia which makes his walking very unsteady and constant screaming. Khalida speaks little English and is living in a short-term housing flat on the third floor, with unsafe windows and heating only through the use of electric fires. She has another child with spina bifida who has to be taken down to the school minibus each morning. The bus driver refuses to drive into the estate and leave his minibus because of vandalism. The escort is unable to carry Ahmed. His mother therefore has to carry him down and across a courtyard littered with tin cans, glass and barking dogs. Khalida cannot manage both children; her husband and brother have left for work much earlier. As she said at a parent workshop, 'They expect me to send Ahmed to school. How can he go, if I can't carry him to the school bus? My other son, he should go to school too. But they couldn't manage him, he is at home waiting for an assessment'.

A shortage of interpreters in the borough means that Khalida is unsure exactly what the 'assessment' will be. It is impossible for her to visit her other son's school, where there is a parents' group for Bangladeshi parents. A health visitor has reported 'possible neglect', having called and heard screams from the bedroom while Khalida carried Ahmed back from the bus. Khalida, depressed and tired, felt that she had only avoided a major problem because of the support of an Asian worker with a local disability organisation. She was able to demonstrate that, far from being neglectful or abusive, Khalida was actually the reverse. Her son was seriously at risk from his unsafe and unsuitable environment. As Shah (1995) has indicated in her study of Physical and Mental Handicap in the Asian Community, many families from an ethnic minority group with a disabled child are doubly disadvantaged. The disability may mask associated racism (which may make it difficult for a mother to attend a clinic or attend parents' group). It may be assumed, without asking, that the family will reject any help offered because of the extended family, or the family may be judged to be putting children at risk when in the context of poor housing, hostile communities and other difficulties, the parents in question are actually doing extremely well.

Pressures of care have to be put in the wider context of recent social and demographic change in UK society. Jonathan Bradshaw (1985) have found that poverty is increasing sharply in families with children in the United Kingdom. The OPCS studies on the lives of disabled people (1989) found that families with a disabled member were *significantly* worse off than other families without disability. Additional costs for heating, clothing, laundry and food were particular strains on low incomes, with many women unable to work because of the care needs. 50 per cent of parents interviewed in the OPCS studies said that they could rarely go out, because of a lack of sitters, and felt that their own health had suffered because of the extra anxieties and physical care.

Parents under stress can of course receive support from a range of sources. Respite care is one obvious and very popular service, although currently only around four per cent of parents receive it. But the use of services such as respite care, which remove a child from the family home, may in turn create problems and expose children to risk of abuse.

Many parents express great anxiety about their child's safety and care. In a study of respite care for young adults with multiple disabilities or challenging behaviour, Hubert (1991) found many parents who were desperately anxious about the quality of care available to their son or daughter. One mother described how her son always seemed to have been sedated heavily during his stay. Another anguished over her son's poor physical care, sitting in a wheelchair wet and dirty – 'so lacking in any dignity'. A third mother told how she prayed that her son Callum would not die while he was away. She knew he hated going. The care was not good enough. But her husband felt they must have a break and she felt respite care was the choice that would keep the marriage together. Parents frequently are well aware of the risk of abuse. Susan, a parent reading the Hubert study (personal communication) commented:

If you have a child with a disability, you often feel everything you do is wrong. My family are surprised and critical that I let my son use respite care. But they never offer to care for him, he is 'too difficult'. I think they are ashamed of having a family member receiving something from social services, as if he was on a child protection register or something. Actually, I wonder if he should be – he goes to a small residential home which is the only place which will accept a child with severe learning disabilities, limited mobility and continuous episodes of self-abuse (scratching his face). I have to let him go for his brothers' sake. They've got GCSEs this year – what can I do? But I think they dope him up there, he comes home like a zombie sometimes. He always gets nappy rash – sitting in a wet nappy is no fun when you're fourteen years old. He doesn't always have his own clothes. I do like him to look nice; he likes bright colours – last time back he came in a tatty old jersey, cuffs over his hands, food spilt on it. He smelt. . . I mean he really smelt. . . but what do we do? There's no-one else will take him; at least they smile when he comes . . . but honestly, would social services accept that standard of care if he did not have a disability? I often think we are all conniving, all playing a game – what is abuse for other children is not abuse if you've a child with a disability. But no-one would investigate, would they? What would happen if I decided I couldn't care. I'm a 'provider' in the brave new world of the 'market place' in health care. But no-one can afford to think of quality assurance. I'm just there. . .

Assessing risk will never be easy for children with such complex disabilities. But it can be done. Ruth Marchant (1992) in *Bridging the Gap* demonstrates the possibility of using the observations and skills of parents, staff and whatever communication aids the children use, to assess the occurrence of abuse, and to identify potentially abusive behaviour early and avoid it if possible. Parents themselves can be supported and encouraged to join local parents or support groups which in turn act as information-givers, counsellors and advocates in getting appropriate services.

Children with disabilities: assessment issues

Assessment of potential abuse of a child with a disability should be assisted by the various assessments and reviews which the majority of children already will have experienced. *Working Together* (DOH, 1991) identifies a number of different assessment procedures which children may go through. Although the definitions are not linked specifically to disability, many children with special needs will have experienced many of them. Indeed, many children will have become part of an 'assessment industry' which may (or may not) contribute significant knowledge to an enquiry relating to abuse. An awareness of the multiple assessment processes is particularly important in the context of working directly with children. Children with disabilities (like other children) have new powers under the Children Act 1989 to refuse examination if they are judged to have sufficient understanding. But many will give consent (and will be able to communicate) if supported by a trusted and familiar professional. Teachers and paediatricians in particular (together with some therapists) may have long-term and detailed knowledge of a child and be readily able to identify uncharacteristic behaviour. Such familiarity is important not only for diagnosing actual abuse but also for avoiding misdiagnosis when a child self-abuses for instance, or where the cause of the child's disability predisposes the child to broken bones or bruising. Equally, parents may be willing to talk to trusted professionals and an honest and open working relationship may be achieved before actual abuse takes place.

Working Together (DOH, 1991) lists the multiple assessment hurdles some children (with or without disabilities) may have to work through in order to get services. But when a child has a disability, the process may become much more complex. The Audit Commission (1993) has highlighted the poor co-ordination of assessment arrangements for children with disabilities. Around 50 per cent of parents felt that assessment was always poorly co-ordinated and that they did not understand the assessment process. Assessments were often felt to be negative (even when the outcomes were intended to lead to positive action) and many parents expressed the wish for a key-worker or 'named person' to help them interpret the maze of assessments, professional consultations and sometimes apparently conflicting advice. Services working with children with disabilities and their families in a child protection context need to be aware of the different assessment processes and also of potential sources of professional advice. Such assessment arrangements may involve some or all of the range of options set out below. Some children with disabilities will have child care plans (particularly if the child is using respite care or if he or she is 'looked after' by the local authority). There is also increasing interest in the integration of assessment arrangements (with particular reference to statutory assessment under the 1993 Education Act) but the majority of local and health authorities still operate a number of parallel assessment arrangements. Table 3.1 sets out some of the assessment arrangements which may be used and which may contribute relevant information in any enquiry into actual or potential child abuse.

Table 3.1 Assessment – an industry or a process for children with disabilities?

School-based assessment of children with SEN (special educational needs): the earlier school-based assessment arrangements for children with special educational needs introduced in the Code of Practice on the Identification and Assessment of Children with Special Educational Needs and the 1993 Education Act.

Statutory assessment (1993 Education Act): a compilation of reports from a range of professionals (including health and social services) and evidence from the school-based assessments mentioned above. The statutory assessment may result in a statement which must now be reviewed formally on an annual basis.

Health assessment: an examination usually carried out by a health visitor or community nurse to ascertain the child's health status (e.g. information on height and weight; immunisation; vision and hearing).

Medical assessment: A specific examination by a doctor usually for a definite purpose, e.g. a court request, as part of a child's health surveillance programme for a statutory (education) assessment. This may be more far-reaching than a physical examination of the child and may include information on development and behaviour.

Developmental assessment: An objective assessment of a child, often to an agreed protocol, carried out by a doctor, health visitor, child psychologist or others to determine the child's developmental level. Developmental assessments normally are part of a child health surveillance programme.

Initial assessment: an agreed multi-disciplinary composite report on the child's health and welfare in the context of his or her family which will enable participants in a case conference to plan the child's immediate future.

Comprehensive assessment: A structured, time-limited exercise to collect and evaluate information about the child and family as a basis for long-term decisions.

Family assessment: A report over a period of time to assess the functioning of a particular family in relation to the needs of the child. This is usually undertaken by a social worker but may be carried out by a psychologist, family centre worker or others.

Precisely because the experience of disability may be disempowering for children (and families), and because the need for special care may mask inappropriate behaviour, the Children Act procedures, which include children with disabilities within a common legal framework for *all* children, offer important new opportunities for also including such children within local child protection procedures.

The Children Act requires that every local authority 'shall have services designed:

(a) to minimise the effect on disabled children within their area of disability; and

(b) to give such children the opportunity to lead lives which are as normal as possible' (Schedule 2, para 6).

Volume 6 of the Guidance on children with disabilities (DoH, 1991) and the Children Act itself, stress the crucial importance of looking at the *whole lifestyles* of children with disabilities in order to provide appropriate help. Misunderstandings about the abilities (as well as disabilities) of children can lead to major risks being taken and opportunities for early preventive intervention being missed. The Children Act does not specify procedures for the assessment of children with disabilities (or indeed for children in need). But as noted in *Working Together* and in Volume 6 of the Guidance on children with disabilities, *existing* statutory assessment procedures – such as those relating to special educational needs under the 1993 Education Act and sections 5 and 6 of the 1986 Disabled Persons Act – can be used as a basis for assessment of special educational need and of other aspects of a child's needs. However, education and other assessments may not be sufficient in many cases. At present there is frequently a significant gap between the expertise of disability-specific services and the experience on child protection issues in local authority teams. This gap may lead both to under-reporting of actual or potential abuse, and also to inappropriate concerns about abuse, because the management of a child with a disability or a challenging behaviour simply may be misunderstood. There may also be a reluctance on both sides to acknowledge abuse when support services are scarce or when there are serious (albeit often inaccurate) assumptions about the inability of children with special needs to describe accurately their feelings and experiences.

The Children Act places considerable emphasis upon *listening to children*. But how can children with multiple disabilities or major communications problems be 'listened to'? The work of Margaret Kennedy and the 'Keep Deaf Children Safe' project has demonstrated how positive outcomes can be achieved when there are realistic approaches both to reducing the vulnerability of children through specific training and support and awareness of how to communicate when communication seems problematic or even impossible. Similarly, in her work at Chailey Heritage, Ruth Marchant (1993) explores strategies for listening to children with complex disabilities who can communicate only through Makaton or Bliss Symbol boards. Her work has demonstrated the importance of placing assessment for abuse firmly in the wider context of assessment of the whole child and listening to all relevant care-givers about the child's level of understanding, and how best to listen to his or her views. Although major anxieties still exist about the acceptance by Courts of evidence given by child witnesses through some of the alternative or augmented communication methods, growing expertise in this area suggests that all local authorities should at least be aware of where to get expert advice in this area, and that staff working in direct services for disabled children should have shared training arrangements with their colleagues in generic services to ensure mutual understandings and to raise awareness of the importance of collective approaches to combating disability.

Similarly, Area Child Protection Committees and teams need to ensure that they have relevant disability expertise; and parents need to be aware of the importance of discussion early on about any concerns which they have about their child's care and development. Assessment should be a shared and inter-active process, for all children; for disabled children, it is unlikely to be accurate or constructive without close involvement of representatives from all three statutory services as well as families and any other service providers.

Defining abuse in the context of disability

Children with disabilities are 'children first' and their experiences of abuse, neglect or disinterest will be similar to those experienced by all children. But disability may result in greatly increased risk, and certainly it may expose children to greater risk of inappropriate care because of the likelihood of multiple care-givers and the increased dependency resulting from a disability of special needs.

Firstly, it is important to acknowledge the discrimination and disadvantage which many people with disabilities experience as part of their daily lives. The language of disability in itself demonstrates the negative connotations of incapacity and inferiority which easily may be attached to a disabled person. The language applying to 'learning disability' (mental handicap) shows the struggle which people with such disabilities have experienced in being recognised as people first. The terms 'educational subnormality', 'idiocy', 'feeble mindedness', 'learning difficulties' have in their time all been attempts to create new and more positive images. But even contemporary media images – particularly those attached to charitable giving – perpetuate the notion of 'cripple' and 'helpless' and perhaps 'inadequate' person or personality. In the past decade the majority of local authorities have confronted the need for equal opportunity policies which acknowledge and promote the diverse cultural and racial origins of their local populations. But, historically, disability has not been part of generic social work practice – at least in children's services – and benign but dangerously inadequate ideas may abound about what disability means. There may be reluctance to believe that anyone *could* abuse a disabled child (as if the disability confers some special protection). Disabled children may be seen as so 'different' that ordinary child care practices cannot apply to them. They may be viewed as too unattractive to become victims of sexual abuse and too 'pitiful' to be physically or emotionally abused.

Equally, parents (on whose care society depends very heavily) may be viewed unrealistically as 'super-carers' without needs (or problems) of their own. One mother of a seven-year-old child with a rare genetic disorder commented (personal communication) that parents caring for disabled children form 'an invisible army, using statutory services only for emergencies because we are too difficult, too hard, to understand the rest of the time.'

Care and control – safeguarding children or abusing human rights?

'Penny' is our first child. When she was four – we live in a dreadful block of flats you see – she was playing around one day. I wasn't feeling well and I lay down for a minute on the sofa. Next minute it was all quiet. No Penny, nothing. Then the neighbours were banging on my door. Penny had got out and fallen straight down the stairs. Head injury – but we were lucky (well, sort of lucky). She recovered. Trouble is she is a different child now, so active and dangerous. She'll climb absolutely anything and she screams all the time. My other children can't stand it. When the holidays come and they are in and out, I lock her in her room sometimes. I don't leave her long. But if I have something to do, I lock her up or I 'tether' her by a scarf to the kitchen table leg. The school was horrified when I told them, told the social worker and all that. I said, 'you come and see my flat. If she fell and was killed, you would be after me then. Give me some respite care or something and I wouldn't need to lock her up.' But there isn't anything for kids like this, is there? They won't come looking too hard in case they have to do something.

(Said by a parent of a seven year old with very difficult behaviour and learning difficulties following an accident.)

Social services suspect that Penny is locked up for long periods of time. But the flat is totally unsuitable for such a disturbed child and no local services will accept her. The local authority has no residential provision, and no foster parent likely to accept a child with very challenging behaviour. Penny has been left with residual health problems after her accident and is often at home and out of school for long periods. Her mother believes that 'keeping her quiet' (i.e. physically restraining her) is actually good treatment.

Penny's mother is typical of many parents of disabled children, who present complex problems and who may well be excluded rapidly from local services. There are many unresolved issues relating to what constitutes 'reasonable care' for children whose behaviour puts them and others at risk. Penny may well be subjected to arrangements which would constitute abuse for other children. But there is nowhere for her to go. Any attempt to assess her risk and the quality of her family's care have to be put in the context of the clear need for family support services and the fact that most local authorities would find it difficult to offer positive alternatives. Treatment as abuse may be a particular theme in enquiries into allegations of abuse when a child has a medical condition or disability. The wide range of alternative therapies and the optimistic belief by some families that new treatments may produce miracle cures means that many children are being treated at the frontiers of science and current knowledge. Exclusion diets, rigorous therapy programmes, the use of medication and sometimes rigid behavioural approaches may have a rationale behind them and may (if properly monitored) have a place in the repertoire of interventions drawn upon for a child with special needs. But the lack of guidelines about how to assess quality of treatment and interventions, and whose rights are predominant, means that each case has to be evaluated carefully on its merits. Parents may easily find themselves caught up in allegations about potential abuse simply because there is a lack of clarity about the purpose of a particular treatment regime or because there may be insufficient understanding about the limited options that are available to a family in order to cope.

'Marcia' is another child with special needs. She has had three kidney transplants – two failed – and at thirteen has, in conjunction with her doctors and her parents, decided that she is just not going to go through another. She is aware that she will literally 'fade away' and that she may not see another Christmas. She has been to Disneyland and made her 'will', even choosing the music for her funeral service. So far she is happy with the decision. She says she is 'at peace'. The family is deeply religious and feel that they are implementing 'God's will'. But Marcia's school take a different view. They are pursuing the local authority to insist that Marcia does have another transplant or, at least, that she continues with dialysis. They insist that no child is able to give an objective judgement on their treatment (although they should be involved in discussing it). Marcia and her parents argue that they have consented to the current arrangements and that there is a 'right to die' for children with chronic or intractable illnesses. Although the Children Act 1989 is clear that children can consent to treatment (or its withdrawal), subject to sufficient understanding, both Marcia and her family will be vulnerable to allegations of abuse if their views are not considered fully (and respected) and if all those working with them are not helped to resolve their feelings about cessation of active treatment in a child.

'Daniel' is also a child whose treatment causes problems. Following meningitis, Daniel has developed major behaviour problems. His mother describes him:

> Daniel is held down or tied up most of the time. Sounds like a gangster film, doesn't it? But we are trying to get him into the real world. Sometimes we use special clothes to restrain his hand, or we tie him into the buggy major. I have a lovely big red woollen scarf to do it with. It looks OK too. Of course he doesn't need a buggy – but we couldn't face outings otherwise. We keep hoping he will improve. We have a social worker now. She says we can't tie Daniel up in his buggy. I think Daniel has a right to be restrained. He'll be locked up if he is not kept in order. What can parents do when all the professionals have failed?

Daniel's health is now causing problems. He needs minor surgery but no-one feels confident about performing it because of the convalescent period. Daniel's mother feels that child health services are doing the abusing, not her. She is thinking of suing the health authority for unreasonably refusing Daniel access to primary health care. But in practice children like Daniel may be seen as simply too difficult and in effect 'untreatable' because of the severity of their care needs. She feels that the hospital, 'is guilty of inverse abuse because they won't treat Daniel's *medical* problem because of fear of being accused of abuse themselves if they had to hold him down or restrain him in some way. That isn't protection, it's denial of basic rights.'

Risk factors for children with disabilities

Limited life experiences and social contacts mean that many children with disabilities have had no chance to acquire the 'street-wise' behaviours and judgements which their non-disabled peers use in assessing the behaviour and attitudes of other people. Some children with disabilities may have had almost no contact with non-disabled people and therefore are more at risk in terms of failing to understand inappropriate adult behaviour. Specifically, children with high dependency needs may have learned from an early age that it pays to be pleasing and compliant and may be reluctant to challenge carers (family or professionals). Lack of experience, together with a wider lack of control or choice over their own lives, will be compounded if children with disabilities lack appropriate sexual education – including personal and social education. Middleton (1992) found that lack of sexual, personal and social education creates problems which are compounded further if isolation and rejection increase the need for affection and attention, which makes such children (and some adults with learning disabilities) particularly vulnerable to adults' attention and favours.

Children (and many adults) with disabilities are likely to use a much wider range of services than their non-disabled peers and, furthermore, to use services which are distant from their family home. 'Lucy' is twelve years old and has cerebral palsy. She attends a special school eight miles from her country home. She travels by taxi, but with frequent changes of driver. There is no longer an escort, due to recent local authority retrenchment. She goes to a local club for young people and to a swimming club two nights a week, usually travelling with volunteer drivers. Although this involves a minicab driver and other children, her isolated home always means that part of the journey is spent alone with the driver. A neighbour sometimes takes her shopping in town and she spends one weekend in six in a residential respite care centre thirty miles away. She usually spends a further two or three weeks away in the summer on a holiday scheme. Her medical care is divided between a tertiary referral hospital (eighty miles away), her local paediatrician, the orthopaedic department and community health services which provide speech therapy and physiotherapy. Her parents are divorced and she spends time with both new families (and step-parents and step-children).

All the evidence about child abuse suggests that she is most likely to be abused by someone she knows well. But who do children like Lucy know? Almost every activity involves spending time with different adults. At her last review the social worker identified twenty different people helping her or her family. Frequently, she is dependent upon practical help for personal care. Transport is scarce and expensive and the background of her escorts has never been queried. Lucy herself would be unlikely to complain. She enjoys going out and would not do anything to threaten her social activities. She is also a passive and very compliant child who is anxious to please. She has few friends of her own age on which to base her knowledge of appropriate teenage behaviour. Her parents and step-parents have new lives after a period of considerable stress. Lucy's complex programme of services supports them all. They are all aware that there are waiting lists for many services and are reluctant to be critical. Lucy's situation is such that no-one is likely to complain or query any service for fear of losing it or alienating one of the many supporters who maintain the family lifestyle. The Children Act may require Lucy's social worker to consider her 'ascertainable wishes and feelings' within her Child Care Plan. But the fragility of a complex network of support will make all concerned reluctant to query any aspect of her care.

Impaired communication skills may make disabled people appear to be 'safe victims' because they are unlikely to complain and may indeed lack the language skills in order to avoid the abuse in the first place. Sometimes the absence of communication skills will be obvious, for example in a child who is profoundly deaf and can only communicate through sign language or when a child has a significant learning disability which restricts vocabulary and language. But they may also be lacking in children who theoretically *can* communicate but whose social skills and life experiences make it difficult for them to do so. A forthcoming study from the National Children's Bureau (Wertheimer and Bargh, in press) of young women with moderate learning difficulties found considerable evidence of bullying and emotional abuse (such as teasing) in families and the local community which was neither reported nor discussed. The young women in question needed considerable peer support in order to confront their difficulties and to think through strategies for dealing with them. Their own low self-image and their awareness of their 'differentness' severely limited their own survival skills. The project concluded that all young people with special needs require positive discrimination in terms of assertiveness training – using role plays if necessary – and that parents may need help to really listen to what their children are saying. The project parents were particularly surprised (and alarmed) by three key issues which emerged in the group discussions, namely that:

1. The young people admitted painfully that they were not able to handle bullying or teasing and that, even within their families, frequently they experienced exploitation and even derision for their perceived lack of ability.

2. The project also demonstrated that peer support for children and young people with disabilities has been developed insufficiently. The groups learned assertiveness through role-play and through mutual support in challenging abusive behaviour in their own lives.

3. The same project also indicated the importance of acknowledging race and gender issues in assessing the need for services for young people

with disabilities. In one case, the young woman's learning disability was being 'treated' with no real awareness of the racial harassment to which she and her mother were subjected in everyday life. Similarly, many of the young women saw themselves as 'inferior' and less valued and valuable than their male peers. An important part of the group work was to give them the confidence to be assertive (which in turn made them feel safer).

Treatment or care may in themselves be abusive. The 'Pindown' Report (Levy and Kahan, 1992) demonstrated the dangers of young, inexperienced and unsupported staff carrying out treatment regimes which they did not understand fully. The past decade has seen a major growth in programmes for children with disabilities, and in particular behaviour management programmes for challenging or difficult behaviour and a range of alternative treatments involving combinations of medication, diet and therapy for a variety of problems. Many programmes are effective, carefully planned, monitored and help to sustain children with very complex needs in their local communities. But others are not supervised, may be implemented out of context and can result in children experiencing loss of personal possessions; being confined to their room for long periods of time; suffering humiliation or ridicule or being denied a full diet or appropriate clothing. Guidance on the Children Act is quite clear that sanctions and treatment programmes should not interfere with basic human rights. But unless the care of children with disabilities is planned carefully and reviewed regularly – and children living away from home are visited and given the opportunity to communicate their feelings in private – inappropriate patterns of care are likely to continue.

The need for intimate care presents a major challenge. Many children with multiple disabilities require constant physical care and assistance with eating, dressing, toiletting and general mobility. Others require periodic intimate care (if, for example, they have to use a public toilet which has not been adapted for wheelchair use) but may manage very well in a suitable environment. Managing intimate care in a 'safe' and acceptable way means acknowledging a number of important preventive factors:

(i) *The home environment*. Bathrooms and toilets need to be conveniently located and designed to permit maximum independence and privacy. As more children are integrated into mainstream services, environmental factors may become more problematic.

(ii) *Staff training*. Practical help should be as unobtrusive as possible. Staff need clear messages about acceptable and unacceptable approaches to personal care. Children can be asked what they want, and their ideas and perceptions incorporated into training, which needs to be seen as providing opportunities for staff support. Anxiety about abuse can create emotional abuse if staff believe all personal contact must be monitored strictly. Insistence on open doors when intimate care is taking place and the rigid insistence on the absence of any physical contact with children or lack of attention to children's preferences for personal care, can actually create a regime where abuse may be un-monitored because there is no clear and comprehensive child care policy. Many disabled children (particularly those living away from home) need friendship and affection, but may be indiscriminate about how they seek or give it. Prevention of abuse is most likely to occur when there are warm and open relationships between staff and children. A rigid institutionalisation of care routines is unlikely to offer protection and may increase children's vulnerability.

(iii) *Social skills and independence training.* It can be easy to under-estimate a child's capacity to acquire self-care skills. Positive encouragement to self-management of incontinence and dressing etc. is crucial. Better partnerships between schools, parents and professional carers can offer greater protection.

(iv) *Listening to children.* 'Listening' may mean 'observation' for some severely disabled children. Listening may mean using a range of communications, and asking key questions about the needs of particular children using a service. If a child communicates through signing, or through cued speech, then he or she will need a regular member of staff who can communicate with him or her. Ruth Marchant (1993) has described how Chailey Heritage uses communication boards with children with multiple disabilities. Good record-keeping by staff (including the use of video) can also indicate when children are unhappy or having difficulty with a particular routine.

(v) *Listening to parents.* A number of studies have suggested that negative perceptions of disability (sometimes regarded as the Cinderella of equal opportunities policies) may apply to parents as well as children. Frequently parents feel that they themselves are not to be believed, or are regarded as trouble-makers if they complain about a service. As noted, many families are multiple service users. Such services may involve a child periodically staying away from home (for example for respite care). One mother described (personal communication) how she 'sat in the drive to the respite care home and cried every time she left her child'. Her father had been seriously ill and she had been obliged to agree to her teenage son using a local residential respite care home. Because of his difficult behaviour there had been no alternative, but she felt her son came home each time 'wearing someone else's clothes, dopey, too much medication, and desperate not to go back'. She did not think her child was actually abused, but his personal neglect and her anxiety combined to make her 'quite desperate'.

Crisis management – care and control

Children with learning disabilities and challenging behaviour probably are the group of children with disabilities which most local authorities find hardest to manage and over whom both the local authority and family, or carers, may have different perspectives concerning the acceptability or the abusive nature of different styles of intervention. The following comments from parents illustrate the dilemma about deciding when control or restraint should be seen as abusive behaviour.

'Nicholas' went to a residential school when he was 13. To be honest, we couldn't have coped a day longer. But he comes home for holidays. He had started scratching his face all the time. He looked terrible and the cuts got infected. At the school they developed a sort of splint to try and change his behaviour. We tried it at home too. He didn't scratch with his other hand. His face really looked better. Then the inspectors came along to the school and they said it wasn't right to use the splint, they should try something else. It didn't work and Nicki is scratching again. I can't stand him like that. I use the splint at home. Am I wrong? Could I be prosecuted? I am told that parents can get fined for hitting their children now. I don't hit Nicholas – but I might start if I have to 'bin' the splint (Father of Nicholas, who was injured in a road accident. There are three other children at home).

I let 'Paul' go to respite care. I don't want to but my husband insists. I really am scared he'll leave if we don't have some time. I've found out they use something called 'time out'. They put Paul in a room on his own and lock the door. It settles him down. I'm a bit worried by it. But I tried it at home and it worked! Then the lady at the respite care said she'd been told they could only do it if they didn't lock the door. Wonderful! Paul's out and off like a robot. They've got a member of staff to stand outside the door at 'Greenacres'. There's no reason to do that there. There's no spare person to stand outside Paul's door when he is at home, and I'm worried I will be accused of abuse. But what do I do? If he got out onto the road and had an accident, I suppose they'd get me for negligence! You can't win if you have a disabled child, can you? (Mother of Paul, aged 13, deaf/blind with learning disabilities).

Children with the most difficult behaviour are also the most likely to use services outside their local authority (with the cessation of admissions to long-stay hospitals such provision usually being made within the independent sector). A working party on learning disability and challenging behaviour convened by the Mental Health Foundation (reporting in 1994) noted that definitions of 'significant harm' in the context of control or treatment are extraordinarily complex. In a report on Challenging Behaviour and Learning Disabilities, Professor Christina Lyon (1994) stressed the importance of measuring controversial methods of care and control against the child's overall health and development and the involvement of appropriate professional advice in making such an assessment. She concludes that 'it would be foolish to say that there will not be circumstances when caring for children with learning disabilities presenting challenging behaviour may well be guilty of exposing the child to the suffering or the likelihood of suffering significant harm.'

She cites Volume 6 of the Children Act Guidance and regulations (*Children with Disabilities*) which in para 15.4 notes that when considering the need to request a court order for a child with a disability, all agencies (whether within the local authority or not) must have clear views on what would be the appropriate standards of health and development for the child in question. The use of court orders in place of earlier support and guidance for families is described as being 'against the principles of the Act'. The Guidance goes on to advise that 'children who require considerable amounts of personal care, who have few communication aids or who have severe learning disabilities will require very careful assessment ... All statutory and voluntary agencies are therefore required to ensure that their staff are aware of the inter-agency child protection procedures agreed by the Area Child Protection Committee in their area.'

Crucially, the Guidance goes on to acknowledge that 'it is possible that misunderstandings about the most effective management of some children with disabilities (in particular those with challenging behaviour) may occur without a clear understanding of the nature of the child's needs'. Currently there is general concern that Area Child Protection Committees are *not* aware necessarily of the treatment and control options for very disturbed children. Equally many disability-specific services have limited awareness of the wider range of child protection issues. Absence of mutual understanding can lead to cumulative difficulties as in the 1992 conviction of a Lancashire headteacher of a school for autistic children, where regular force-feeding (including regurgitated food) was routine with a group of very difficult children. Although a range of individuals were aware of the 'treatment regime', there were no formal complaints, largely because of confusion as to what was acceptable control and restraint and also because of difficulties in determining what would be appropriate methods of feeding the children in question.

Looking at the legality of parents' and carers' actions to control a child with severely challenging behaviour, Professor Christina Lyon (1994) proposes checklists to ensure that interventions are acceptable and that there is a clear rationale for the action in question. She proposes that any potentially damaging action should be matched against evidence that a comprehensive assessment has been carried out; that the behaviours – and any environmental, social, psychological or biological factors – have been spelled out and that proper consideration has been given to obtaining informed consent and to the integration of medicine within other concurrent treatments. She also makes connections with existing guidance, which may be utilised when there are arguments that force or control by parents have been excessive, noting that in some instances parents could argue that the use of medication or physical control or 'time-out' was not only the most effective method to manage a child but also *the least restrictive and detrimental alternative*. She comments that:

> understanding the context within which care and control is offered by professionals, carers and parents is particularly important both for those in official positions and for all of us who come into contact with such children and their families and carers ... They, and we ... may not fully understand the problems which caring staff and families actually face, nor the strategies which may ultimately have to be adopted to ensure that the child's welfare is treated as the paramount consideration, and that all reasonable steps are taken to ensure that the child's welfare is safeguarded and promoted (Lyon, 1994).

Messages for the future

The challenge for effective child protection procedures for disabled children is primarily that of reconciling the considerable expertise on disability issues in many professional services (with corresponding lack of awareness of child protection procedures) and the current local arrangements for child protection which frequently pay insufficient attention to the additional disability issues which may impact upon early diagnosis and effective intervention and which may under-estimate the contribution of disabled children to their own assessment and management. When a child is Black, or comes from an ethnic minority background, then race, religion, gender and culture must be given due consideration in assessment and planning. Misunderstandings (and allegations) about potential abuse can easily arise if there are stereotypical views of the family's life and culture. Equally without adequate interpreter and translation facilities, there may be no real shared understanding about the child and his or her family context.

Key issues for future discussion and development include:

- Greater interchange between disability and child protection services, with common training and greater awareness of their respective contributions to protecting children with disabilities.

- Utilisation of existing assessment arrangements for children with disabilities to avoid duplication and to ensure that any decision is made on the basis of the most up-to-date knowledge of child and family.

- Improved personal, social and sex education for children with disabilities and special needs. Overprotection will increase vulnerability as children become more independent in their local communities.

- Particular attention to the welfare and safety of children with multiple or complex needs or challenging behaviour. The work of Marchant et al. (1993) shows that such children can be assisted in communicating their experiences, but that they are particularly vulnerable and plans for such children should include clear arrangements for monitoring and regular review.

- Race, culture and gender issues in the context of disability.

- Many parents caring for a child with a disability receive little support. Pressures of everyday caring may result in some families accepting help which is inadequate. Or they may utilise inappropriate behavioural or treatment regimes. The implementation of policies for 'children in need' should state clearly how the local authority in question will identify and assess parents' needs and the range of services which will be available to meet them.

- Treatment, care and control may in themselves be abusive, particularly if a child has very challenging behaviour.

- We need to listen to the experiences of adults with disabilities who have been abused (Westcott, 1992; Sinason 1992). Their stories remind us of the cumulative and negative consequences of disability and abuse, in effect a double jeopardy. Most worryingly they indicate considerable reluctance by professionals to believe that disabled people can be abused and to acknowledge the particular isolation of those living in institutional care.

- There have been considerable doubts expressed about the ability of disabled children and adults (particularly those with multiple or learning disabilities) to act as reliable witnesses in Court. We need to explore further how such children can be helped to give evidence. Reluctance to prosecute because of anxieties about the achievable verdict may in turn lead some potential abusers to consider that disabled children are indeed safe victims.

In conclusion, the Children Act 1989 has provided us with a legal framework within which children with disabilities can be seen as 'children first'. However, the principle of integration and inclusion should not be allowed to conceal the fact that many disabled children need considerable support in order to lead lives which are indeed 'as normal as possible'. As Butler-Sloss noted in her introduction to the Cleveland Enquiry Report,

> *There is a danger that in looking to the welfare of the children believed to be the victims of abuse, the children themselves may be overlooked. The child is a person and not an object of concern.*

It is particularly easy to see a disability as separate to the child. But, if we see the person, our approaches to child protection and disability will become more effective.

BIBLIOGRAPHY

Audit Commission (1993) *Seen But Not Heard: Services for Children in Need*, London: HMSO.

Bradshaw, J. (1985) '75,000 severely disabled children', *Developmental Medicine and Child Neurology*, **27**, 25–32.

Craft, A. and Brown, H. (eds) (1989) *Thinking the Unthinkable: Papers on Sexual Abuse and People with Learning Difficulties*, FPA Education Unit

Department of Health, with the Home Office (1991) *Working Together under the Children Act 1989*, London: HMSO.

Department of Health (1991) The Children Act 1989 Guidance and Regulations, Volume 6, *Children with Disabilities*, London: HMSO.

Glendinning, C. (1983) *Unshared Care – Parents and their Disabled Children*, London: Routledge and Kegan Paul.

Hubert, J. (1991) *Home-Bound: Crisis in the Care of Young People with Severe Learning Difficulties*, King's Fund Centre.

Hubert, J. (1992) *Administering Drugs to Young People with Severe Learning Difficulties, Social Care Research Findings Number 18*, Joseph Rowntree Foundation.

Kennedy, M. (1989) 'The abuse of deaf children', *Child Abuse Review*, 3(1), 3–7.

Kennedy, M. (1990) 'The deaf child who is sexually abused – is there a deed for a dual specialist?' *Child Abuse Review*, 4(2) 3–6.

Part 1 Background to the enquiry process

Kennedy, M. (1990) 'Overcoming myths: the abused disabled child', *Concern*, Summer 1990, 4–5. National Children's Bureau.

Levy, A. and Kahan, B. (1992) *The Pindown Experience and the Protection of Children: The Report of the Staffordshire Child Care Inquiry*, Staffordshire County Council.

Lyon, C. (1994) *Legal Issues arising from the Care, Control and Safety of children with learning disabilities who also present severe Challenging Behaviour*, Mental Health Foundation.

Marchant, R. and Page, M. (1992) 'Bridging the gap: investigating the abuse of children with multiple disabilities', *Child Abuse Review*, (1)(3).

Marchant, R., Page, M. and Crane, S. (1993) *Child Protection Work with Children with Multiple Disabilities*, London: NSPCC.

Middleton, L. (1992) *Children First: Working with Children and Disability*, Ventura Press.

Office of Population and Census Surveys (1989) *OPCS Surveys of Disability in the UK*, London: HMSO.

Quine, L. and Paul, J. (1989) *Stress and Coping in Families Caring for a Child with a Severe Mental Handicap: a Longitudinal Study*, Institute of Social and Applied Psychology and Centre for Health Service Studies, University of Kent.

Report 3: *Prevalence of Disability Among Children.*

Report 5: *Financial Circumstances of Families.*

Report 6: *Disabled Children, Services, Transport and Education.*

Russell, P. (1992) *Future Challenges to Family-based Short Term Care: Opportunities and Challenges for the 1990s*, Council for Disabled Children, National Children's Bureau.

Russell, P. (1992) *The Children Act 1989 and Disability*, Highlight 109, National Children's Bureau.

Shah, R. (1995) *The Silent Minority: Physical and Mental Handicap in the Asian Community*, (2nd edn.) National Children's Bureau.

Sinason, V. (1992) *Mental Handicap and the Human Condition*, Free Association Books.

Sobsey, D. and Varnhagen, P. (1988) *Sexual Abuse and Exploitation of People with Disabilities: A Study of the Victims*. Unpublished manuscript.

Sullivan, P M., Vernon, M. and Scanlon, J. M. (1987) 'Sexual abuse of deaf youth', *American Annals of the Deaf*, 3, 256–262.

Westcott, H. L. (1969) *Abuse of Children and Adults with Disabilities*, London: NSPCC.

Westcott, H. L. (1991) 'The abuse of disabled children – a review of the literature', *Child: Care, Health and Development*, 17(4), 243–258.

Westcott, H. L. (1992) 'Vulnerability and the need for protection', in Gibbons, J. (ed.) *Family Support and the Children Act*, London: HMSO.

Wilkin, D. (1989) *Caring for the Mentally Handicapped Child*, Croom-Helm.

Part 2

Towards partnership with families

4

Building trust with families when making enquiries

David Shemmings and Yvonne Shemmings

Introduction

It is a tall order to expect family members who are the subject of allegations into child abuse and neglect to trust the professionals making the enquiries. Yet a wide range of disparate research findings indicates that such a relationship *can* be created, and sustained, provided professionals meet four conditions. These conditions are outlined in this chapter and the connection between them discussed.

Our emphasis, quite deliberately, is upon how professionals *demonstrate* their willingness and ability to work with families under these conditions. Such a focus, however, contradicts fundamental notions of the concept of 'trust': for many people, trust implies one person placing herself or himself unconditionally in the hands of another. From the research we offer an alternative metaphor in which to locate the concept as it relates to enquiries.

We then summarise the main research findings, and the key implications from recent legislation, concerning three ways in which trust can be demonstrated to family members: firstly, by offering to show them what is written in files; secondly, by involving family members at all stages of the enquiry process, especially before and during a child protection conference if one is judged to be necessary; and, thirdly, by explaining complaints and redress procedures to family members.

The findings indicate that professionals cannot yet claim to be offering family members truly participative relationships when making enquiries into allegations. We do not attempt explanations for this conclusion in this chapter; instead we concentrate upon its formulation by analysing the relevant literature and research.

Building trust when making enquiries: four key conditions

On the subject of family participation in child protection processes there exists currently a number of training packs (see Family Rights Group, 1991; Lewis *et al.*, 1992); research studies (Cleaver and Freeman, 1995; Farmer and Owen, 1995; Sharland *et al.*, 1993; Thoburn *et al.*, 1995); Department of Health guidance (DoH, 1995a); and other literature which is applicable to the subject of enquiries (see, for example, Biehal and Sainsbury, 1991). If these findings are combined with Carl Rogers' work on the core dimensions of effective communication within helping relationships, and also with the results of major research programmes undertaken in the United States in the 1960s by Robert Carkhuff and in the 1970s by Gerard Egan, then consistent patterns and themes emerge. From them we believe that it is possible to isolate four key conditions which account for most of the variation between successful and unsuccessful relationships with family members during the early stages of an enquiry process: firstly, workers must prove their 'openness and honesty' to family members in all their dealings with them; secondly, they must show 'even-handedness' when conducting enquiries; thirdly, they must demonstrate their 'answerability' for what they say and do; and, fourthly, they must demonstrate 'sensitivity' toward family members. Each condition is now discussed briefly.

Openness and honesty

It may appear self-evident to say that professionals should be open and honest with family members when conducting enquiries but being open and being honest are not the same. The difference is between dishonesty by omission (being 'economical with the truth') and dishonesty by commission (telling lies). Questions arise in professionals' minds about whether being dishonest by omission is justifiable sometimes if the interests of the child are thought to override the rights of family members. Such professionals may prefer to keep their 'cards to their chest' in the early stages. Whilst not necessarily lying to family members they are nevertheless not working in a truly open and honest way.

What effect might such a deception have? In some situations people under stress become highly attuned to the existence of discrepancies between the verbal and non-verbal behaviour in others. The conduct of enquiries into alleged child abuse or neglect appears to be one such situation. Thus, family members are likely to know intuitively when professionals are not being straight with them (see Cleaver and Freeman, 1995). To compound the problem, however, they are unlikely to reveal their unease to professionals, who, being ignorant of the true feelings underlying family members' reactions, will think that nothing is wrong and thus may perpetuate the deception.

Furthermore, from our experience of training professionals a problem exists which seems to be connected with an assumption on their part that openness and honesty will lead to a pleasant experience for family members. It is as if they are expecting either gratitude for their honesty, or immediate proof that their efforts are making it easier for family members, or both. Therefore, because in the charged and emotional context of enquiring into allegations being fully open and honest will often lead to fraught discussions, if their efforts are not rewarded quickly they may conclude that it is simpler 'only to be as open and honest as they have to be'.

As with the other three conditions, being open and honest is a necessary but not sufficient condition upon which to build a trusting relationship. Professionals have to be open and honest, not only about what they say and do but also concerning what they think. It is not enough for them to tell parents how they propose to conduct their enquiries and explain what information they will require: to build trust they will need to explain clearly how they then assess, evaluate and make sense of this information. The ability to substantiate their assessments is a critical skill in this process; it involves using plain language, being clear and specific, excluding irrelevant information and observations, and linking the information to subsequent conclusions and assessments (see Shemmings, 1991a; 1992).

Answerability

Arguably, professionals in the public sector are more accountable today than at any stage in the past. Whilst springing initially from the New Right as a way of forcing managerialism and consumerist ideology into welfare systems, nevertheless the advent of Citizen's Charters, increased access to information, the implementation of complaints procedures and the introduction of other institutionalised redress mechanisms, are all now embraced by academics and left-wing politicians. And naturally the increased accountability of professionals is welcomed by family members who become involved in formal child protection systems. These developments have not always been welcomed by professionals, however, who feel increasingly under pressure to perform more efficiently but with less resources available to meet an ever-increasing demand.

The research studies and the literature indicate convincingly that professionals who are willing to work in ways which demonstrate their answerability to family members are more likely to build trusting relationships, provided they embrace the idea that measures designed to increase accountability are human rights, not privileges within their gift.

Even-handedness

When enquiring into allegations of child abuse or neglect professionals need to display even-handedness at all stages. This requires them to be open to differing interpretations of how the allegation could be understood. Especially at the start of the enquiry process, being even-handed means reviewing actively (a) whether something abusive has actually happened and (b) that it must have been caused by the person, or persons, accused. The first step in the process of remaining even-handed is for professionals to examine carefully, and continuously, whether their assumptions and overall approach reveal prejudice or oppression.

In addition it appears from the studies that the ability to suspend judgement is a pivotal facility of professionals accomplished at demonstrating even-handedness (see Shemmings, 1992). It consists of avoiding rigidity in thinking, combined with fairness. If thinking becomes too rigid, flexibility can be re-established if a professional deliberately poses opposite scenarios to those which are in danger of becoming 'fixed' prematurely. This process minimises the problem of jumping to conclusions. It represents an attempt to bring to the present, hindsight acquired in the future.

Sensitivity

A parent who had been accused of abusing her child was quoted by a participant on a course we ran recently as saying that 'it's like the ability to give people "bad news" while cuddling them at the same time, but without the cuddle masking the bad news' (Shemmings and Shemmings, 1995). As researchers often find when interviewing people involved intimately in a phenomenon, her statement reached the heart of the matter: the first three conditions could be used in a caustic, even brutal, manner if workers forget that people subject to enquiries are *people*, who have a need, and a right, to expect to be treated sensitively. To achieve this, workers need to bring to the relationship accurate empathy, as well as positive regard, genuineness and warmth (Carkhuff and Berenson, 1967; Egan, 1990; Rogers, 1951). Not surprisingly, the sensitivity shown by professionals needs to be experienced by family members in direct proportion to the seriousness of the allegations made.

The relationship between the conditions

The above quote from the parent also highlights an additional feature concerning trust, the effects of which are likely to be magnified during the early stages of enquiries: because they are not mutually exclusive, the first three conditions overlap. Furthermore, sensitivity is best viewed as an envelope containing these conditions; for trust to be developed and sustained, sensitivity must always be shown. This is depicted in Figure 4.1. Whilst all the conditions have to be present, the arrows within each of the three discs illustrate the ideal relationship between the first three conditions, which is one of simultaneous occurrence; the aim is for workers to increase the area of the shaded segment. Therefore, whilst one of the three conditions may eclipse temporarily the other two, they, in turn, must be present in the background.

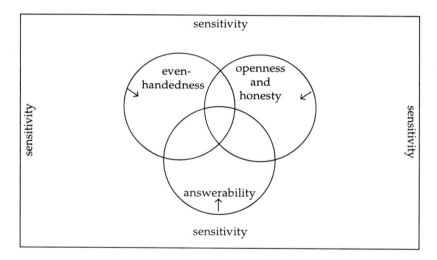

Figure 4.1. The relationship between the conditions

But why is it important for family members to be able to trust professionals when they are making enquiries? Does it matter if they do not? There are two main reasons why it matters considerably: firstly, it helps family members believe that the process will be conducted fairly; secondly, the success of any help and support offered to the family depends upon whether the professionals manage to convince those concerned of their trustworthiness. Failure to secure trust increases the likelihood that the relationship will be shrouded either in animosity and hostility, or that the family will approach

71

matters in a perfunctory manner. Neither outcome offers children much in the way of protection.

The discourse surrounding trust centres upon complex but well-established notions, both of faith and of surrender. To appreciate this we need only remind ourselves of typical 'trust-building' exercises created artificially during certain kinds of staff development programmes. For example, in order to simulate an experience of trust, sometimes individuals are encouraged to put their faith in a small number of colleagues by standing in their midst, closing their eyes and then 'falling' into their linked arms. The idea is that, by surrendering their physical well-being unconditionally into the hands of others, they will develop trust towards them. But whilst this concept may be appropriate in freely-chosen relationships based on equality, we argue that the 'Trust-as-Faith-and-Surrender' metaphor is entirely inappropriate and naive when applied to professionals making enquiries into allegations of child abuse and neglect. To expect family members to fall into the arms of state-sponsored workers is at best romantic and at worst patronising. We offer the concept of 'Demonstrable Trust' as a replacement for the 'Trust-as-Faith-and-Surrender' metaphor and we consider three specific ways in which it can be achieved.

Three ways of demonstrating trust when making enquiries

1. Sharing records and access to files: A brief summary of the legislation and research

A growing body of research has reviewed different aspects of sharing records: the implementation of policy and practice within social services in the United Kingdom (Braye et al., 1988a, 1988b; Butler, 1986; Doel and Lawson, 1986; Murray, 1985; Ovretveit, 1986; Shemmings,1991a; Thoburn, 1989) as well as in other countries (Munday, 1987); compiling records and recording practice in social service departments (Kinnibrugh, 1984; Raymond, 1988; Shemmings, 1991a), as well as in health settings (Baldry et al., 1989; Roth et al.,1980; Stein et al., 1979; Townes et al., 1967; Williamson, 1988); citizens' rights (Dolan, 1986, 1987, 1988; Frankel, 1984; Khan, 1983; Parsloe, 1988); and, finally, the views of clients (Doel and Lawson, 1986; Ovretveit, 1986; Raymond, 1989).

Overall the research concludes that poor recording occurs when professionals: fail to distinguish between fact and opinion; do not verify 'facts'; treat the file as a 'private diary' rather than as an official record (see Kinnibrugh, 1984); or when they do not substantiate what they have written. The conclusion drawn is that the best way for professionals to approach the task of recording is to offer to share their own case-notes, reports, assessments and correspondence with family members *as the work proceeds*. As one study showed, however, the problem is that a professional's idea of sharing records is often different to other people's: rather than *showing* the person referred to in the file what they had written, quite a large number of professionals interpreted 'sharing a record' as meaning *reading* from it 'in order to soften its impact' (Ovretveit, 1986). Partly to correct this, and partly to stress the benefits of adopting a more open and accountable approach to recording, Mark Doel and Brian Lawson at Sheffield University produced a training and staff development pack entitled 'A Paper Dialogue'. The approach to recording advocated is to see it as 'part of the work itself'. But herein lies a problem with such an approach if it is applied uncritically to enquiries in the early stages of the process: there is a danger that *an assumption will be made that some 'work' is taking place.* 'Work', however, is taken by many professionals to mean some activity aimed at helping people to change. Often this is not the case when professionals are making enquiries. Thus during the early stages of making enquiries, record-keeping is concerned with the rights of family members to see the information gathered and to understand how it will be assessed by professionals. We need to turn to the legislation to appreciate the rights of family members and the duties of professionals.

The main legislation covering access to information consists of: the Data Protection Act 1984 (dealing with computer-held records in all settings); the Access to Personal Files Act 1987 (covering manual records in social services departments, education and housing authorities); the Access to Medical Reports Act 1989; and the Access to Health Records Act 1990. Originally, neither the Access to Personal Files Act 1987 nor the Access to Health Records Act 1990 gave applicants retrospective access to information (the dates after which information can be seen respectively were 1 April 1989 and 1 November 1991). A more recent interpretation, however, has been made following a case considered by the European Court: if it is felt that seeing information recorded prior to these dates could help an applicant make sense of their own identity or their past, then it should be released (Judgement 2/1988/146/200, Strasbourg). Prior to this judgement, although official guidance recommended that it is 'good practice' to show an applicant information recorded prior to these dates – see LAC(89)2 – there was no legal requirement to compel the record-holder to make it available.

From the Department of Health's summary of the research studies (DoH, 1995b) we have seen already that approximately 80,000 of the 160,000 enquiries are viewed as needing 'no further action'. Therefore, a proportion (which some believe to be high) of the families concerned may not know that such enquiries have been made. If the existing Data Protection Principles (eight principles which outline the way in which data held on computers must be kept) were applied to manually-kept records it would appear that, unless it could be shown that to do so would lead to serious harm to a child, family members would have a right to know that enquiries had been made, as well as have a right to see any information about themselves. But, at the time of writing, it is not clear whether the data protection principles do apply to files completed manually. However, either the Access to Personal Files Act 1987 or the Access to Health Records Act 1990 will cover the rights of family members to see information about themselves if a manual record has been created, *but only if a family member asks.*

What can they see? The answer to this question is of interest not only to family members or other people referred to in files: it is of importance also for professionals seeking to demonstrate trust to those in respect of whom enquiries are being made. Professionals who practice openness, rather than simply talk about it, will use the records they compile as a vehicle to demonstrate their trustworthiness.

In agencies covered by the legislation i.e. social services departments, education and housing authorities, as well as in records kept by health professionals (if they are involved in the 'direct care of the patient'), an individual – referred to as the 'applicant' – seeking access to what is written must be allowed to see any information which refers to him- or herself wherever it is located, unless: the information about the applicant might cause serious harm to another person; it qualifies for exemption under the meaning of 'legal professional privilege'; it is covered by adoption legislation; or its release could prevent the detection of a crime. Applicants cannot see information about other people without their permission. Applicants may only see information about a child if it is judged to be in the interests of the child (i.e. access to it is not sought primarily to meet the interests of the applicant). Regarding information obtained from other people – usually referred to as 'third party information' – they are granted anonymity only, not confidentiality: the content of what they write will be available provided it does not reveal their identity. Before the introduction of the Access to Health Records Act 1990, health professionals were considered as 'third parties' in terms of their written communications in other professionals' records. Following its implementation, however, applicants can approach the health professional directly in order to seek access to the information about themselves.

In respect of challenging the accuracy of what is recorded, an applicant has a right of appeal. With regard to the Access to Personal Files Act 1987, the appeal ultimately is made to the local authority; with the Access to Health Records Act 1990 it is made to a court.

Finally, with the exception of adoption files (which must be held for seventy-five years) current legislation does not stipulate how long a file must be kept; neither does it specify a maximum period before information must be destroyed. At present this decision is made at the discretion of the record-holder.

During the past five years we have been involved in training over 5,000 practitioners and managers in participative practice. Although the legislation concerning access to records is complex, nevertheless the main implications for professionals are clear. We summarise them as follows during staff development sessions: firstly, assume that people will at some stage ask to see what you have written; secondly, when they do there is very little (if anything) that either you, or your colleagues in other agencies, will be able to withhold; thirdly, the best way to respond to this is to offer to share your records *without waiting to be asked*; finally, ensure that what you write about family members reflects what you have already said to them. At the end of this summary we ask participants to consider whether professionals should ever record anything which the person referred to would be surprised to read later.

2. Participation in child protection conferences: A brief review of research

The reader may wonder why participation in child protection conferences is considered to be part of the enquiry process. As the conference represents the culmination of a significant stage in the enquiry process, is it not too late to start thinking of participation? Yes; but two consistent themes emerge from the research: firstly, it is precisely the kind of practice that helps family members to feel that they have participated during the conference which needs to be introduced before and reinforced after the conference; secondly, families will not experience participation in the conference if they have not been involved right from the start.

There is also a third reason for discussing the relevant research findings on child protection conferences. This concerns the decision-making activity that takes place. But before dicussing them we need to reconsider our received ideas about the concept of 'decision'. A recent article by Robert Chia attempts a deconstructive analysis of this concept. He concluded that the:

> *... decision is better understood as a series of pre-definitive acts of punctuating the flow of human experience in order to facilitate sense-making and to alleviate our Cartesian anxiety. Decisions are not so much about 'choice' or 'intentions' as about the primordial 'will to order' whereby interlocking configurations of micro-incisions punctuating our phenomenal experiences contrive to construct and reinforce a stable but precarious version of reality* (Chia, 1994, p. 781).

He goes on to develop what he terms a 'becoming' theory of decision-making which is 'offered as an alternative to the "event" driven model of decisional theorising' (p. 781), but only after he has made the point that:

> *Understanding decision-making as an explanatory principle involves a recognition that it is the product of a post-hoc rationalisation process in which the cause/effect relationship established has been abstracted, reified and chronologically reversed. 'Decision-making' is a conceptual invention ... so as to appear as an 'event' preceding action* (Chia, 1994, p. 795).

His analysis contains important implications for professionals looking into alleged child abuse and neglect. Family members will assume that the key 'decision' (i.e. whether or not the child is considered safe enough with his or her parent or carer) is made in the conference. Anyone familiar with child protection conferences knows from experience, however, that this decision results from a complex social activity and, therefore, it is not an event but a process. This is where Chia's analysis is helpful. Applying it to making enquiries, his argument is that to encourage in family members the belief that the enquiry process culminates in a single decisional event – whether to place the child's name on the Register – misrepresents reality. In his terms, decision-formulation takes place both simultaneously and repeatedly in the minds of different professionals and at different stages during the decision-making process. Thus, even though parents, carers and children might attend and contribute to the conference, unless the professionals involved explain, substantiate and justify exactly how they assess risk, then in reality family members are likely to be excluded from most of the 'real' decision-making processes. Certainly, they will not be taking part in what Chia calls a 'becoming' process of decision-making.

Studies which have sought the views of family members who have been involved at different stages of the child protection process suggest that they are aware intuitively of the need to know how each professional's mind 'works'. For example, one parent said, 'It's sometimes the way they talk, it's hard to pin-point it. I don't think they were open and honest' (see Lewis *et al.*, 1992, p. 69). Recalling a different experience a mother commented:

She would say what she was doing as it happened, so we knew – though I'd have liked her to be more forthcoming at the beginning. I was very 'anti' her then. There was nothing she could have done to make it any easier. It feels like they put you under a microscope and they pick away at all the sensitive areas. To co-operate you have to open-up – no option. We couldn't put it behind us because she kept coming (Lewis et al., 1992, p. 70).

Was there anything which the professional – in this case a social worker – could have done to 'make it any easier'? In the sense of allieviating the mother's feeling of 'being under the microscope', perhaps not; but with regard to 'being more forthcoming' then the research points to many ways in which the process of making enquiries can be experienced as more participative by family members and in such a way as not to impede the progress of professionals trying to establish whether a child is safe enough. But to achieve these changes professionals need to put themselves under the microscope – in the sense of inspecting their values, attitudes and, in particular, any oppressive assumptions. They will need also to explain their assessments regularly with family members rather than expecting them to wait until the child protection conference. As far as possible, professionals should ensure that family members do not find out anything new in the conference, except in so far as information from individual professionals is used by the group to assess the alleged risk to the child.

Over twenty studies have been conducted into parents attending child protection conferences and they have been summarised by Ann Lewis (see Lewis, 1994). Each study had an impact on how participative practice developed within the local area in which it was undertaken. In addition, three studies have attracted a wider audience nationally (see McGloin and Turnbull, 1986; Shemmings and Thoburn, 1990; Shemmings, 1991b). Early on, however, the Department of Health was anxious to co-ordinate this policy and to this end it supported a training and staff development pack (see Lewis et al., 1992).

The findings from all of the studies are remarkably similar. They indicate that provided family members are involved at all stages in the enquiry process, then the effects upon the development of trust are likely to be positive. If, right from the start of the process, family members are treated in the manner depicted in Figure 4.1 then it permits the conclusion to be drawn that this trust will continue. And this, in turn, is likely to lead to beneficial outcomes for the child. For example, in the research conducted by June Thoburn and her colleagues, of the 73 children studied, whose parents or carers expressed a view about their own involvement, the outcome for the child was rated by the researchers to be 'good' in 83 per cent of cases when the parents had rated their own involvement as 'high' (see Thoburn et al., 1995).

From the main studies which refer specifically to attending the conference other key findings include: the importance of professionals explaining the purpose and conduct of the conference beforehand; providing family members with clear information about the conference in a form appropriate to their language and culture, and to take account of the needs of people with disabilities; ensuring that interpreters and translators are available when needed; making it clear that oppressive remarks will be challenged; telling family members who will be at the conference, and why; giving family members access to any reports and documents before the conference (and offering them a chance to meet the person chairing the meeting for 10–15 minutes beforehand); explaining the 'protocols' of the conference, i.e. seating arrangements, the order of the agenda for the meeting etc.; making sure that professionals communicate clearly their assessments and any complex ideas, without using jargon yet without being patronising; starting the conference by checking factual details (partly because it is important to get them right but also, because this information tends to be less controversial, it offers family members a way of becoming involved at the beginning of the conference); providing family members with practical ways of participating e.g. having a pen and paper available, being offered a glass of water etc.; and, finally, checking with family members their impressions after the meeting as well as clarifying what (if anything) happens next.

Few studies have considered specifically the involvement of children and young people in conferences, the exceptions being Liz Wilson's work on training for professionals (see Wilson, 1992) and two research studies – Steven Farnfield's at the University of Reading and David Shemmings' at the University of East Anglia – which currently are near completion. Additionally, Nicky Scutt, in conjunction with the NSPCC and the Youth Enquiry Service, has investigated the use of advocates when children attend conferences in Devon social services department.

More recently, interest has been shown to the concept of family group conferences (see Tunnard, 1994) which give families a far greater say and more involvement in the whole process of protection and how best to meet children's needs. At this stage it is too early to evaluate fully the results of a number of attempts to put the model into practice. However, although it offers new and innovative insights into participative relationships with families it is important to appreciate that the idea of family group conferences is not simply a different approach to the child protection conference: it represents a radical alternative to it by challenging many of the prevailing assumptions underlying 'a model of care and protection that, in the main, has held sway in the UK for 15 years' (Ryburn, 1994).

78

As part of its research programme into family support and child protection the Department of Health funded a major study by the University of East Anglia into family participation. June Thoburn, Ann Lewis and David Shemmings undertook research over a period of three years in seven English social services departments. After some contextual data is provided the relevant results are now considered briefly.

The study included 220 consecutive cases involving 378 family members, with more detailed information collected from an intensive study of 33 cases. The seven authorities were selected on the basis of their stated intention of implementing participative strategies and practice in all social work activity, including child protection processes.

The age-range of the children divided evenly between those aged under five, those between five and twelve and those aged twelve or over; 56 per cent were girls, and 44 per cent were boys. Black children formed 19 per cent of the study. Whilst the researchers rated 29 per cent of the allegations or actions as 'severe', i.e. including physical assaults leading to fractures or serious injury, life-threatening neglect, or penetrative sexual assault, with 11 per cent judged as resulting from excessive or repeated punishment, nevertheless the analysis left 60 per cent not being placed in either category. The researchers allocated the cases to one of three groups for analysis, based upon their rating of the likelihood of participation. 28 per cent were placed in the 'worst scenario' group and 27 per cent in the 'best scenario' group (leaving 45 per cent in the middle group). Outcome measures were devised (see Thoburn et al., 1995) which, for the whole sample, resulted in 65 per cent of children (n=215) being placed in the 'good' or 'moderately good' outcome group, and with 10 per cent in the 'poor' outcome group. In a quarter of the cases the outcome was considered by the researchers as constituting 'no change'.

Using Sherry Arnstein's analytic framework to reflect the hierarchical nature of 'participative' relationships – from full partnership at the highest level, to forms of placation or even manipulation at the other (see Arnstein, 1969) – and after comparing the views of family members concerning their own level of participation along with the views of the social workers and the research team, the overwhelming conclusion drawn from the research was that genuine partnership could only be considered to have occurred in 3 per cent of the cases, with only a further 16 per cent who were considered to have been genuine 'participants'. Most of the cases were classified in Arnstein's framework as having been 'involved', or 'consulted', or 'informed'. These concepts seemed to capture far better the experience of family members than did the notion of 'partnership'. Given the nature of what professionals are doing, perhaps these findings are not surprising. After all, who wants to be a 'partner' to someone who is trying to find out if their child is safe with them; and many professionals will admit that, with some adults who abuse children, they too find it difficult to cultivate and maintain feelings of 'partnership'. During the process of making enquiries partnership is possible but professionals would do well to aim initially for the more achievable goals of keeping people fully informed and helping family members to become genuine participants.

From the research undertaken at the University of East Anglia there emerged a wide spectrum of findings. Those which relate to making enquiries include: that the policy operated by the department or agency concerned – for example, an active policy of sharing records, giving out information on complaints procedures and making attendance at the conference as easy as possible for family members by providing help with transport or offering crèche facilities – affects significantly the amount of participation for family members ($X^2 = 50.27$; p <0.001); that attendance at the initial conference was associated significantly with being involved in the whole process of child protection ($X^2 = 49.07$; p <0.0001); that a higher proportion of family members whose social worker was Black were likely to be more involved than was the case when the social worker was White ($X^2 = 9.9$; p <0.01); and also that social work which was geared to a combination of support and good information, coupled with an open-minded and non-judgmental approach when making enquiries, was found to be related positively to higher levels of involvement. Surprisingly, it was found that 29 per cent of families allocated to the 'best' scenario group were considered *not* to have been involved in the process of child protection as a whole; and thus it is likely that they were excluded from the enquiry process.

Overall, therefore, what the agency does to facilitate better family involvement, alongside what professionals do when they are making enquiries, are the most likely predictors of a positive outcome, both in terms of levels of participation with family members and, more importantly in those circumstances when the child is at risk of abuse. The outcome for the child also is likely to be better if family members are involved. So perhaps the social worker in the earlier example, as well as her employer, could have 'made it easier' after all.

3. Complaints procedures: a brief review of the legislation and literature

The relationship between complaints procedures and the enquiry process is complicated. In the Children Act 1989 complaints procedures are referred to in Section 26 but they cover only Part Three of the Act; that is when services are received. The duty to make enquiries into allegations of alleged child abuse and neglect, however, derives from Section 47 in Part Five of the Act. Understandably, 'making enquiries' normally would not be considered to constitute a 'service' *per se*. Hence, from a legal perspective, unless they receive services under Part Three of the Act it would appear that, technically, family members about whom enquiries are made are not able to use formal complaints procedures. However, the current shift in policy, aimed at offering a more supportive approach to families, would suggest the use of a more flexible approach by extending to families the right to make a formal complaint (especially in the light of recent cases in which children have been judged to have been separated inappropriately from their family). Certainly the spirit underlying the guidance on complaints procedures issued by the Cabinet Office (1993) and the Department of Health (1991) heralds a pro-active approach.

In situations when services are provided as part of the enquiry process it appears that the right to make a complaint is less contentious. The problem, of course, occurs in situations when family members claim that the allegations are false, and thus an offer of services would be inappropriate. To this end, area child protection committees across the country are attempting at present to devise their own complaints procedures for child protection enquiries; but they are experiencing difficulties due to the multi-disciplinary nature of child protection work. For example, if a family member wants to challenge an assessment made at a child protection conference because s/he believes it led to an inappropriate registration, then to whom does s/he make the complaint: the agency employing the professional, the chairperson of the area child protection committee, or the person chairing the conference? Similarly, how does a person challenge the registration process in a meeting which involves so many different professionals?

Apart from two reports (see Lewis *et al.*, 1987; NCC/NISW, 1988) little research exists concerning the introduction of complaints procedures, not just in respect of family support and child protection but also in the field of health and welfare services generally. This is surprising because a key stratagem within the Conservative Government's approach to the public sector during the past ten years has been to transpose private sector management practice into the personal social services. This has meant importing from the commercial world the notion of a contractual relationship existing, not between 'professionals' and 'clients', but between 'service providers' and 'consumers', or even 'customers'. Although 'contracts' have been a feature of child protection for some time the suggestion has not yet been made that family members subject to enquiries should be referred to as 'customers'. One would have expected, therefore, an array of research studies on the subject of complaints procedures. Nevertheless there is a growing body of literature available. Unfortunately, like much of the literature on consumerism in health and welfare services, it tends to be rhetorical in nature rather than analytical and critical. But despite the problems identified, the guidance issued by the Department of Health and the Cabinet Office, and a report produced jointly by the National Consumer Council (NCC) and the National Institute for Social Work (NISW) both contain important tips for practice. The NCC/NISW report includes the following point, for example:

> Perhaps the best way of ensuring that clients are able to complain is to foster an atmosphere in which clients are able, however, young or vulnerable, to participate in decisions about their future . . . This openness is crucial. How can clients be expected to take seriously an invitation to complain when they are not given information about what they can expect of a social services department nor shown records that are kept on them; when they have no choice in decision-making about the kind of service that needs to be offered? (NCC/NISW, 1988).

The report goes on to list some of the reasons why some people do not complain including: fear that they will be ignored; an unwillingness to make a fuss; fear of retribution; not knowing how to complain; experiencing problems with communication; and a reluctance to 'trouble' people or persevere if initial attempts prove fruitless.

The Department of Health's *The Right to Complain* includes the following 'essential principles': 'a need for a climate which assures people that (their concerns) will be taken seriously' (para. 1.3), and 'Complaints procedures should be accessible to users, carers and representatives; understandable to staff; guarantee . . . a prompt and considered response; and provide a strong problem-solving element' (para. 2.1). When considering how best to respond to complaints, the guidance encourages professionals to consider carefully how *they* would prefer to be treated if making a complaint, which the Department of Health suggests includes: being listened to; having their concerns treated as important; and (if appropriate) being offered an apology, a solution, and the reassurance that the same thing will not happen again, either to the complainant or to someone else. In terms of the way family members want to treated when making complaints, echoes of the concept of mutuality can be heard (see Shemmings and Shemmings, 1995): they want professionals to 'do unto others as they would have done unto themselves'.

Conclusion

In a recent short article outlining the background to the idea of family group conferences, Murray Ryburn comments that 'lip service to the provisions of the (Children) Act can be accomplished without leading to what Jane Rowe (1989, p. 2) once called the "sea-change" in attitudes necessary if the Act's spirit of partnership and collaboration are to be realised' (Ryburn, 1994, p. 7). The findings reviewed in this chapter suggest that 'sea-change' is still the most appropriate phrase to describe what is required. Professionals have some way to go before they can be sure that, by actions rather than words, their efforts to build trust with family members during the enquiry stage will prove fruitful. Nevertheless the findings identify the kind of practice upon which they should concentrate. Although we consider true partnership still to be a tall order, if, in the light of the findings, professionals change the manner in which they conduct enquiries, then the prospect of building participative relationships with family members throughout the process looks more promising.

REFERENCES

Arnstein, S. R. (1969) 'A ladder of participation', *Journal of the American Institute of Planners*, Policy Studies Institute, London.

Baldry, M., Cheal, C., Fisher, B., Gillett, M. and Huet, V. (1989) 'Giving patients their own records in general practice: experience of patients and staff', *British Medical Journal*, **292**, pp. 596–598.

Biehal, N. and Sainsbury, E. (1991) 'From values to rights in social work', *British Journal of Social Work*, **21**, pp. 245–257.

Braye, S., Corby, B. and Mills, C. (1988a) 'Local authority plans on clients' access to social work records', *Local Government Studies*, March/April, pp. 49–57.

Braye, S., Corby, B. and Mills, C. (1988b) 'Progress on file', *Insight*, 29 April, pp. 22–23.

Butler, T. (1986) 'Opening up: the story of how client access to personal records was brought about in East Sussex', *Social Work Today*, 28 April pp. 11–13.

Cabinet Office (1993) *The Citizen's Charter Complaints Task Force: Effective Complaints Systems*, HMSO.

Carkhuff, R. R. and Berenson, B.G. (1967) *Beyond Counselling and Therapy*, Holt, Reinholt and Winston.

Chia, R. (1994) 'The concept of decision: a deconstructive analysis', *Journal of Management Studies*, **31**, 6, pp. 781–806.

Cleaver, H. and Freeman, P. (1995) *Parental Perspectives in Cases of Suspected Child Abuse*. London: HMSO.

Department of Health (1991) *The Right to Complain*, Social Services Inspectorate, London: HMSO.

Department of Health (1995a) *The Challenge of Partnership in Child Protection: Practice Guide*, London: HMSO

Part 2 Towards partnership with families

Department of Health (1995b) *Child Protection: Messages from Research*, London: HMSO.

Doel, M. and Lawson, B. (1986) 'Open records: the client's right to partnership', *British Journal of Social Work*, 16 (4), pp. 407–430.

Dolan, P. (1986) 'Protecting personal privacy', *Community Care*, 24 July, pp. 18–19.

Dolan, P. (1987) 'An extention of social rights', *Social Work Today*, 23 March, p. 6.

Dolan, P. (1988) 'A right to privacy or a right to know?', *Insight*, 15 January, pp. 8–9.

Egan, G. (1990) *The Skilled Helper*, (3rd edn), Brooks-Cole, Monterey.

Family Rights Group (1991) *The Children Act 1989 – Working in Partnership with Families*, London: HMSO.

Farmer, E. and Owen, M. (1995) *Child Protection Practice: Private Risks and Public Remedies*, London: HMSO.

Frankel, M. (1984) 'Benefits for everyone in file access bill', *Community Care*, 25 October, p. 12.

Khan, A.N. (1983) 'Confidentiality of children's files', *Justice of the Peace*, **147**, 23, pp. 356–358.

Kinnibrugh, A.D. (1984) *Social Work Recording and the Client's Right to Privacy*, University of Bristol, School of Advanced Urban Studies (Occassional Paper 12).

Lewis, A. (1994) *Chairing Child-Protection Conferences*, Avebury: Gower.

Lewis, A., Shemmings, D. and Thoburn, J. (1992) *Participation in Practice: Family Involvement in Child Protection (A Training Pack)*, University of East Anglia.

Lewis, N., Seneviratne, M. and Cracknell, S. (1987) *Complaints Procedures in Local Government*, Centre for Criminological and Socio-Legal Studies, University of Sheffield.

McGloin, P. and Turnbull, A-M. (1986) *Parent Participation in Child Abuse Review Conferences: A Research Report*, London Borough of Greenwich, Directorate of Social Services.

Munday, B. (1987) 'Client access to personal records', *Eurosocial Reports*, 30, Vienna.

Murray, K. (1985) *Client Access to Records*, University of Glasgow, Department of Social Administration and Social work.

National Consumer Council and the National Institute for Social Work (1988) *Open to Complaints*, NCC/NISW.

Ovretveit, J. (1986) *Improving Social Work Records and Practice: Report of the BASW/BIOSS Action Research Project into Social Work Recording and Client Participation*, BASW publications.

Parsloe, P. (1988) 'Social services: confidentiality, privacy and data protection' in Pearce *et al.* (eds), *Personal Data Protection in Health and Social Services*, pp. 28–91, Croom-Helm.

Raymond, Y. (1988) A study of consumer opinion of a shared recording policy introduced by a local authority social services department, unpublished dissertation, University of East Anglia, Norwich.

Raymond, Y. (1989) 'Empowerment in practice: users' views on their records', *Practice*, July, 1989.

Rogers, C, R. (1951) *Client Centered Therapy*, Houghton-Mifflin.

Roth, C.H., Wolford, J. and Meisel. (1980) 'Patient access to records: tonic or toxin?', *American Journal of Psychiatry*, **137**, pp. 592–596.

Rowe, J. (1989) 'Chance of a life-time', *Adoption and Fostering*, **13**, 3, pp. 1–2.

Ryburn, M. (1994) 'Planning for children here and in New Zealand: A comparison of the legislation', in Tunnard, J. (ed.) *Family Group Conferences: A report commissioned by the Department of Health*, Family Rights Group.

Sharland, E., Seal, H., Croucher, M., Aldgate, J. and Jones, D.P.H. (1993) *Professional Intervention in Child Sexual Abuse*. Summary of final report to the Department of Health.

Shemmings, D. (1991a) *Client Access to Records: Participation in Social Work*, Aldershot: Gower.

Shemmings, D. (1991b) *Family Participation in Child Protection Conferences, Report to Lewisham Social Services Department*, University of East Anglia, Norwich.

Shemmings, D. (1992) 'The use of language' in *Participation in Practice: A Reader*, Thoburn, J. (ed.), University of East Anglia, Norwich.

Shemmings, D. and Shemmings, Y. (1995) 'Defining participative practice in health and welfare', in Jack, R. (ed.) *Empowerment in Community Care*, Chapman and Hall.

Shemmings, D. and Thoburn, J. (1990) *Parental Participation in Child Protection Conferences: Report of a pilot project in Hackney Social Services Department*, University of East Anglia.

Stein, E.J., Furedy, R.L., Simonton, M.J. and Neuffer, C.H. (1979) 'Patient access to medical records in a psychiatric inpatient unit', *American Journal of Psychiatry*, **136**, pp. 327–329.

Thoburn, J. (1989) 'Implementation of a shared records policy: an example of co-operation between social work educators, managers and practitioners', *Issues in Social Work Education*, **8**, 2, pp. 137–148.

Thoburn, J., Lewis, A. and Shemmings, D. (1995) *Paternalism of Partnership? Family Involvement in the Child Protection Process*, London: HMSO.

Townes, B.L., Wagner, N.N. and Christ, A. (1967) 'Therapeutic use of psychological reports', *Journal of American Academy of Child Psychiatry*, **6**, pp. 691–698.

Tunnard, J. (1994) *Family Group Conferences: A report commissioned by the Department of Health*, Family Rights Group.

Williamson, V. (1988) 'Patients first', *Social Policy and Administration*, **22**, 3, pp. 245–258.

Wilson, E. (1992) *Children/Young Person's Attendence at Child Protection Conferences, Resource Pack*, Bath/Wansdyke Pilot Project.

5

Suspected child abuse and neglect: are parents' views important?

Hedy Cleaver and Pam Freeman

The jury heard that the baby lay in a pram in the corner of his parents' bedroom, tied into his sodden baby clothes and facing the wall, and was ignored and had no stimulation for hours on end. Eventually, he developed ulcers and a nappy rash which covered 35 per cent of his body. Infection took over, followed by blood poisoning. Crying and miserable, in his last hours the baby lapsed into a coma and died from pneumonia. (The Independent, 18 April 1994).

The widely reported case of Maria Colwell in 1974 was to open the flood gates on press reports of severely abused and neglected children. National coverage of child deaths or serious injuries continued with examples such as Jasmine Beckford, Kimberly Carlile and Doreen Mason. Such cases raised both public and professional awareness that parents can and do inflict pain and suffering on their children. A recent study suggests that approximately 230 children die each year as a result of parental abuse or neglect (Wilczynski, 1994). The awareness that parents hurt and harm their children is highlighted by the fund-raising campaigns of the NSPCC and other pressure groups. Their strategies keep the image of suffering children in the forefront of public consciousness. Similarly much of the recent professional literature has focussed on abused and neglected children.

The continuing catalogue of hurt and injured children raises the question of why, in cases of suspected child abuse, there is a parallel concern for parents' rights. The Cleveland and Orkney cases were clear illustrations of this opposing position. They showed a public scandalised at what appeared to be unnecessary interference and intrusion into family life; and of over-zealous social workers. The Department of Health's (1995) child protection practice guide aims for a more balanced position by emphasising the reasons and principles of working in partnership with parents. But many would claim that, when making enquiries into cases of suspected child abuse, sympathy for the parents' point of view should be the least of professionals' concerns.

This chapter argues strongly in favour of attending to parents' perspectives during the initial enquiry. It is based on data from a three-year study which explored both the incidence of suspected child abuse and the experience of families caught up in the process (Cleaver and Freeman, 1995). The research identified 583 cases of suspected abuse by scrutinising all reports to police, probation, health visitors and social services, in a single geographical area during one year. The main body of the work was a two-year prospective study which tracked the experiences of 30 families from the moment child abuse was raised.

The importance of understanding parents' perspectives

The research findings show that establishing whether or not a child has been or is at risk of abuse, at the outset of a case, is far from easy. In the majority of cases injuries were rare and less than five per cent of children required hospital treatment. Most of the suspected abuse was minor and in many cases the situation remained unclear. Social workers assessed risk and made decisions in situations where there was much suspicion and little evidence. It is open to debate whether the system is successful in identifying those most at risk. Indeed, Gibbons and colleagues (1995) suggest under a quarter (21 per cent) of investigated cases needed protective intervention. Thus large numbers of families, where children appear not to be at risk of significant harm, are entering the child protection system.

To raise the spectre of child abuse has long-term negative effects on families. The extent of the problem is illustrated by extrapolating nationally the finding that 29 per cent of suspected child abuse cases which involved an interview with parents, resulted in a child being registered (Cleaver and Freeman, 1995).

When responding to a report or suspicion of child abuse, social workers attempt to assess both the present circumstances and future risk to the child. Their judgements are influenced by the way they see families. Our study found that this was predominantly in terms of the category of suspected abuse, such as those used in *Working Together* paragraph 6.40 (DoH, 1991). For example, families suspected of physical abuse were viewed differently from those suspected of sexual abuse or neglect. When this perception is combined with the way parents react at the moment the suspicion is made apparent, it fashions the way a case develops. Farmer and Owen (1995) found that when the suspected abuse is minor and the circumstances are far from clear, professional judgements about children's welfare are determined increasingly by parents', and in particular by a mother's, co-operation. Unco-operative mothers trigger the instigation of a child protection conference even when concerns are relatively minor. However, families can be categorised in different ways and, if this is done in terms of their domestic circumstances, it allows the current concern to be set within a wider perspective (Cleaver and Freeman, 1995).

The decision to register a child usually reflects a greater degree of concern but not necessarily a greater need for protection. Gibbons and colleagues (1995) found only 34 per cent of high risk substantiated cases were registered compared to 23 per cent of low risk substantiated cases. Nevertheless, even when there is a greater need for protection, parents' perspectives cannot be dismissed because in the majority of cases children remain at home. The research found only 51 of the 583 children suspected of having been abused were separated from their parents. When separation was considered essential practically half of the children rapidly returned home. It is clear, therefore, that in the majority of registered cases professionals will need to work with parents to ensure the future well-being of the child.

But what of the remaining families caught up in the system? The data indicates that attending to the parents' perspectives when the child is not registered is equally important. Two thirds of families, where there were suspicions of child abuse, were assessed by professionals to be in need of some help. Of the 583 cases, where suspicions of child abuse were seriously considered, only one fifth resulted in no further action. Although most of the non-registered cases needed services, what they got was monitoring or a referral for further investigation. Nonetheless, from the professional's perspective this meant a continued need for contact with these families.

Putting into practice the principle of working in partnership with parents at the initial stages of a child abuse enquiry is a formidable task because, in the majority of cases (70 per cent), suspicion fell on the parents or carers. But who was suspected varied with the type of abuse. For example, our research found mothers and fathers (male and female carers) came equally under the spotlight for physical abuse but in cases of neglect and emotional abuse mothers (female carers) bore the brunt of responsibility. In suspected sexual abuse men dominated the stage although fathers, male kin and mothers' partners shared the limelight with unrelated men.

Non-family members accounted for half of those under suspicion. But outsiders were rarely strangers and over 90 per cent of unrelated suspects were well known to the family and/or victim. Nonetheless, the majority of parents were unaware of what was happening to their children.

Thus, the findings reviewed so far suggest three reasons for considering parents' perspectives in cases of suspected child abuse. Firstly, parents' reactions to the allegation is one of the main ways professionals assess the future risk to the child. Secondly, in the majority of cases parents are the chief suspects. Finally, in the majority of cases families are in need of services, but alienating them at the outset may prevent many from seeking future help. This leaves a final question unanswered: do parents' perspectives matter in terms of outcome?

Outcome for the 30 study families was explored by comparing five areas of family life, prior to the enquiries being made, with their situation two years later. This exercise revealed that when parents and professionals held a common understanding of events certain aspects of family life were likely to improve. For example, although practical help alone improved families' living situations or their physical and psychological health, in other areas, such as family relationships, parenting skills and child development, a shared understanding was the key to improvements. Parents were less likely to take heed of counselling or accept proffered services if they disagreed with the original diagnosis or the need for any subsequent intervention.

The data was fairly conclusive in showing that parents' perspectives are important. Apart from a few exceptional cases, outcome on all aspects studied improved when material support for families coincided with parents and professionals holding corresponding perspectives of events. Significantly, when this happened the finding was that the child was likely to be living at home and protected against future abuse.

How can the views of accuser and accused be brought closer together when at the outset of an enquiry parents and professionals were in warring camps? An accusation, all in a day's work for professionals, is a cataclysmic life event for parents. Although a small number of parents experienced an element of relief that things were finally out in the open, the majority believed they had already been judged and condemned and reacted with anger and fear. But however inauspicious was the start, the research identified key moments in an enquiry which offered both sides the opportunity to reassess and change their views. These occurred at the point when suspicions were first raised with parents, during meetings or case conferences or when fresh evidence manifested itself. At these moments, offers of practical help or a change of worker, for example, would warm the cold hostility of some parents. Similarly, professionals changed their attitudes towards suspected families. In some cases there were renewed concerns and suspicions subsequently were confirmed. In others professionals came to appreciate more the positive aspects of certain families which resulted in a reassessment of their original concern. Nevertheless, even when a good working relationship was forged between social worker and parent, a long-term wariness of professionals was a frequent legacy of the initial enquiry.

The evidence cited would suggest that the argument for a better understanding of parents' perspectives is a strong one. Unless this is achieved parents' behaviour will be misinterpreted and misunderstandings will persist. Furthermore, unwarranted large numbers of families will continue to be drawn into the child protection system because much of the early risk assessment is based on interpreting parental reactions to social work enquiries. As a result valuable time and resources will be wasted. The research offers a number of insights into what affects parents' perspectives when suspicions are first broached.

Influences on parents' attitudes and behaviour

How the concerns of possible child abuse are raised initially with families sets the tone for any subsequent intervention. It was found that most parents accepted that serious suspicions of child abuse always should be looked into, but they considered that in their own particular case the supposed incident was minor or the accusation was malicious. Parents' trust in professionals was violated by what was perceived as a precipitate action and the intervention was resented. As a result the family shrank from voluntary co-operation.

The research found that being confronted with suspected child abuse was a far cry from the social interactions most families encountered. Faced with the allegation many parents reported expected emotional reactions such as fear, shame, guilt or powerlessness. In contrast, however, a few described quite unexpected emotions such as excitement, jealousy and a desire for revenge.

Fears and anxieties were acute and wide-ranging. Parents were afraid of losing their children, were frightened of losing their reputation within the community or their livelihood and were worried that the suspicion would destroy their family. Sometimes parents' fears were less obvious. A few sat in a coma of anxiety during the interview worrying that other skeletons well hidden in the back of the closet would be revealed, such as a past history of drug abuse, a present fiddle over the social security or undeclared earnings.

Parental reaction to these powerful emotions fluctuated. For example, anger could alternate with self-blame and self-deprecation. Remorse would occur with hostility, which was directed towards the social worker or members of their own family. Rational responses are difficult to predict when people are under extreme duress. The problem is exacerbated because families are not homogeneous. Individual family members hold different perspectives and apply idiosyncratic coping strategies.

At this point in the enquiry, professionals are wrapped up in their efforts to ensure the safety of the child and are aware that any mishandled abuse case could haunt them for dereliction and incompetence. Social workers who raise the possibility of child abuse were met frequently with verbal abuse, hostility and silence, instead of a client's smiles and gratitude. Under this degree of stress interpreting parents' reactions can be a difficult task; does a mother's denial and vehement defence of her partner indicate collusion, repudiation or is it a way of coping?

The study explored both the psychological and sociological dimensions of the experience in order to gain some understanding of parents' reactions and behaviour when faced with suspected child abuse. The term 'psychological dimension' depicts influences such as self-image, emotional well-being and people's perceptions of one another. The 'social dimension', on the other hand, refers to externally-driven influences, such as the power wielded by professionals and the way private information about the family is made public.

The psychological dimension

When faced with a suspicious professional asking probing questions, parents must make snap judgements about role and competence, based upon the outward appearance of the agency representative. But the style of clothing sported by the professional signals different things to different people. One parent may perceive the social worker's casual dress as an indication of a sympathetic and approachable person whereas, to another, it suggests disorganisation and unprofessionalism. Clothes are a personal statement, but a uniform may trigger a generalised reaction. For example, the police commonly are seen as authoritarian and powerful, and nurses and health visitors as concerned and sympathetic. The role of social workers is unclear and as a result their arrival raises anxiety and bewilderment. When parents are confronted with an agency representative, their perception of what is likely to happen has already been moulded by prejudice and long-held assumptions.

The face-to-face enquiry offers a chance for participants to challenge pre-established images and such an opportunity has to be appreciated and seized upon. Most people in unaccustomed or fraught situations fall back upon orthodox ways of self-presentation. As a result, for one young couple with a history of growing up in care, drug abuse and homelessness, the unheralded arrival of the drug squad late one evening did little to dent their already well-established view that 'the police are out to get us'.

One need only to picture, on the one hand, a uniformed policeman invading the home of this semi-destitute teenage couple and threatening to take away their child and, on the other, a helpless baby being rescued by an honourable guardian of the law from squalor, degradation and amphetamine poisoning, to understand the significance of different perspectives.

The difficulty at the initial stage of any enquiry is that professionals also hold preconceived ideas about the parents they suspect of child abuse. As a result they may judge parents' responses as deceptive, even when they are being honest. Many parents reported that during the early interviews they felt trapped because everything they did or said was given a hostile or sinister interpretation.

Professional judgement may be confounded further because parents under suspicion could exhibit unease or reticence, even when telling the truth. When this occurred professionals were left feeling that they had not discovered everything. Indeed, whether or not the precipitating incident was true mattered little to how parents behaved at the initial interview. Very few parents feel entirely happy about every aspect of their parenting.

The situation is complicated further because at this stage parents' emotions may be very complex and loyalties divided between suspected perpetrator and supposed victim. The enquiry into a 14-year-old male baby-sitter suspected of sexually abusing a five-year-old girl serves as a good example. In this case the mother's reaction would have been confusing for any professional trying to establish the level of risk to the child. Although concerned for her daughter, she was also disbelieving of the allegation and strongly defended the boy who was the son of a long-standing friend.

To understand and interpret parents' reactions may be confounded further because in some cases parents hold a hidden agenda. The research found that a few mothers took the opportunity offered by the enquiry to rid themselves of a violent husband or, occasionally, an unwanted child. But, more commonly, they hoped for better housing or respite care. It is important for workers to gain insight into the possible hidden agendas of parents and children because where families feel they have gained something, no matter how tenuous, their perspective of the social workers' intervention improves.

A suspicion of child abuse, irrespective of its validity, influences profoundly both parents' perception of self and of other family members. Naturally, parents attempt to cope with the enquiry and to massage their bruised emotional well-being. To do this they may use a number of strategies. For example, to fight off feelings of low self-esteem they can blame others, particularly social services, and cast themselves in the role of someone 'hard done by' by reeling off a catalogue of adversity. The fact that the majority of families drawn into the system were struggling with a multitude of problems makes adopting such a strategy easy to understand. Alternatively parents may seek to blame circumstances beyond their control, such as chronic illness or poorly maintained and over-crowded accommodation. But regardless of the strategy they adopt, the majority of parents reacted with understandable outrage. It may be difficult for professionals, working daily with extreme distress, violence, illness and exploitation, to comprehend just how great an affront suggestions of abuse can be to one's self-image as a parent.

Parent's perspectives of their present encounter are also coloured by any previous experience of social services. A prior knowledge of the service helped them to both interpret the signals they received from social workers and to decide on the most effective strategy to adopt. Innocent parents on the other hand based their knowledge of social workers' role on media reports. As a consequence, when social workers knocked at their door, they had little idea of what was happening or how best to react. A few parents initially met social work enquiries with co-operation, believing that the misunderstanding would be resolved quickly. However, if this did not happen they felt trapped and became increasingly cautious. Irrespective of any prior knowledge of social services, the commonly held assumption was that social workers 'take away your children'. This dreaded expectation of what could happen in the coming months influenced parents' attitudes to their present predicament and led many to take up very defensive positions.

Even for the most socially skilled parent, being confronted with suspected child abuse is an extraordinary situation in which the rules of behaviour are unknown. Being cast into the role of the accused inhibits parents from trying to understand the professional's point of view. In the majority of social encounters, where power is more equally balanced, each player seeks to understand the perceptions of the other and adjust their behaviour and responses accordingly. But when faced with a suspicion of child abuse, parents find it difficult to exchange views or challenge child care assumptions. For example, to ask searching questions about suspected physical abuse hardly creates an atmosphere for an open discussion about the use of corporal punishment.

This inability to explore professionals' views and beliefs forces parents to make rapid assumptions about the professional's likely response to any information they wish to impart or discuss. They must gauge quickly the consequence of adopting a particular strategy; a problem which is exacerbated because the outcome of taking up one stance rather than another is rarely clear. Hence, saying as little as possible at this stage was often seen as the best tactic.

The social dimension

An exploration of the research data showed that 22 of the 30 parents in the study were disadvantaged. These families were on the margins of society in that their health was poor, their housing inadequate and they were beset with financial difficulties. In general, the other problems they faced were well in excess of any abuse issue with which they were confronted. Their ability to interact with child protection professionals suffered accordingly. To most parents professionals appeared to be all powerful. Not only did they seem to hold all the cards, they also controlled the rules of the game. Parents believed that the child protection system itself set the style and pace of the enquiry, made judgements based on undisclosed criteria and decided on courses of action, regardless of their views.

Whilst all the professionals are engaged in the same primary task of protecting children they bring different priorities to the case depending on the agency they represent. The health visitor is concerned primarily with the health of the mother and child and has no hesitation in undressing and physically examining a baby where there are concerns for its welfare. The police see their prime function as gathering evidence to gain successful convictions. The social worker's role, however, is less straightforward because s/he has to balance a requirement to protect the child with a need to support the child and its family. As a result, when social workers raise suspicions of child abuse, parents often receive woolly and ambiguous messages. As one mother said, 'I didn't know what she was trying to tell me'.

The way suspicions come to light was also found to influence parents' attitudes to the enquiry. Situations in which a parent sought help were construed and experienced differently from those in which parents had the enquiry thrust upon them. When a parent or child broached concerns about a child or disclosed abuse it gave them a measure of control. They retained the power to decide when to talk, whom to talk to and what to reveal. There was seldom any cathartic revelation and information was more likely to be leaked gradually in order to test professional responses. But when parents or children asked for help their trust was destroyed if they found themselves the object of suspicion; similarly, it was damaged if they lost control of events or if professionals failed to respect or involve them in the decision making. In an enquiry professionals are not the only witnesses to the unpicking of private lives. Other family members usually sensed what was happening and brought their anxieties to bear. A strong sense of betrayal was a common perspective among those compelled to acknowledge that abuse may exist in their family.

Situations in which a social worker or health visitor raised the suspicion of abuse with parents were experienced differently. Parents were totally unprepared and saw the initial interview as a confrontation, with the professional cast in the guise of the accuser, and they themselves forced into the role of the accused. The accusation, and this is how parents perceived social workers' enquiries, challenged their personal integrity and undermined their sense of reality and control. It was as if the door had been opened to a room in which everything said and done assumed a surreal and sinister quality. At the end of the interview the door stayed ajar and the contents continued to spill out. Irrespective of the outcome, parents had to struggle to pick up the pieces and integrate what had happened into their normal view of the world.

How might the situation be improved?

The child protection system tends to fall between two stools. On the one hand there is a desire to be specialist, to deal only with the problem of child abuse and to divert those families who have other difficulties to more appropriate provision. On the other hand there is an attempt to be generic, to see abuse in its wider context and to respond to the many needs that exist within the majority of families drawn into the system. Consequently, at the moment, the process is neither sufficiently focused nor sufficiently eclectic to deal with the issues which child abuse enquiries raise. As a result some professionals and many parents are confused about the function of the child protection system.

Nevertheless, the present arrangements have considerable strengths. The obligation of child protection is placed on a range of professionals. Unfortunately there seems little attempt to match the service provided with the particular situation of the families involved. When suspicion of abuse is first raised with parents the interaction needs to be handled with great sensitivity. Although the Children Act 1989 places the responsibility on the local authority to decide what action to take in order to safeguard or promote the child's welfare, social workers are not the only professionals able to make the initial enquiries. Section 47 (1) states that local authorities 'shall make or cause to be made, such enquiries as they consider necessary . . . .' which suggests that the exploratory visit to parents can be delegated to other professionals. This raises the question of whether it would be possible to link certain professionals with the requirements of particular families.

The scope may be limited for professionals to influence positively the psychological dimension of parents' perceptions and attitudes during the first stages of an enquiry. However, simply by keeping in mind the enormous burden many parents already carry, by offering practical help and focusing on the strengths that exist within families social workers can moderate parents' sense of invasion.

In contrast, the social dimension is more amenable to change. The research suggests a number of improvements. Firstly, offering more information. This is essential because parents who enter the child protection system are unaware of the complex topics that are likely to be explored. They are entitled to know what are the issues, why they have surfaced, and what is (and what is not) regarded as acceptable behaviour. They also need to know the most likely outcome of the case; in almost all cases this will mean telling parents that their child will *not* be taken away from them. In short, professionals should aim to be honest with parents, even when it may not entirely suit their strategy.

Not only is there a need for greater information but it must be readily comprehensible and usable to all families. A full and carefully worded explanation during the interview may not be enough because in times of stress what is said may not be understood, can easily be forgotten or not 'heard'. A greater use of written material and video or audio recordings to reinforce verbal communication would help to avoid misunderstandings. In addition, if parents were given a copy of the notes taken during interviews it would remind them of what was said and agreed. Commitments by both the family and social worker could be followed up more easily.

Parents may have difficulty communicating when English is not their first language, if their hearing or speech is impaired or if they have severe learning difficulties. Initial contacts with other professionals prior to any visit may enable better preparation, for example though mobilising a signer or interpreter. To use a family member, friend or neighbour may be expedient but it can have disadvantages. They may filter or interpret what is said, or in some cases their presence can inhibit or frighten the speaker.

There are particular circumstances in which all parents feel bereft of parenting skills and believe they have failed their children. Nevertheless, at that or any other moment they would rightly resent any general charge that they are *bad* parents. Therefore allegations should be expressed in specific terms and tempered with a clear admission that definitions of good parenting practice do not exist. It may help all involved in an enquiry to bear in mind that 'good parenting' is often elusive and that there is much trial and error in bringing up children.

Another possibility highlighted by the research, which could influence social workers' perspective of parents, was to get them to reflect more deeply on their actions. For example, one experienced social worker noted that, 'if you ask yourself, "what are your motivations for doing this?" at each point in an enquiry, you make life easier for yourself in the long run'. Several managers thought that inexperienced workers needed regular reminders to reflect on how they would feel if their child was the focus of suspected child abuse. Others considered it important to advise staff to consider what type of threat they, as workers, represented in terms of gender, class, 'race' and status, and what they could do to reassure particular parents. Although personal characteristics are not changed easily, being aware of the problem and discussing it with parents and children can go some way to allaying fears.

Finally, the data suggests that there is much room for improvement with regard to acknowledging and respecting parents' rights. Parents have a right to know how the suspicion arose and what has been said about them. Because many realised that their reaction to social workers could have far-reaching consequences for their family, they wanted to know what was relevant to the enquiry. For example, what information about their personal lives can they keep private and what has to be revealed? In cases where parents disagree with a particular professional's judgement they could be offered the option of a second opinion. In instances when the parent loses all faith and believes the relationship with the social worker has disintegrated they could be offered a new social worker.

Needless to say, each of these suggestions has resource implications and might extend what already is a lengthy and difficult process. Equally their implementation may result in fewer complaints, which also can be very time-consuming and costly. The argument for a better understanding of the parents' point of view is overwhelming. Indeed, the research shows that when practical help is combined, with professionals and parents holding a common perspective of events, the relationship between parents and children improved, there were improvements in parenting skills and children living at home were more likely to be protected.

REFERENCES

Cleaver, H. and Freeman, P. (1995) *Parental Perspectives in Cases of Suspected Child Abuse*, London: HMSO.

Department of Health and Social Security (1991) *Working Together; A Guide to Arrangements for Inter-Agency Co-operation for the Protection of Children from Abuse*, London: HMSO.

Department of Health, Social Services Inspectorate (1995) *The Challenge of Partnership in Child Protection: Practice Guide*, London: HMSO.

Farmer, E. and Owen, M. (1995) *Child Protection: Private Risks and Public Remedies*, London: HMSO.

Gibbons, J., Conroy, S. and Bell, C. (1995) *Operation of Child Protection Registers*, London: HMSO.

Wilczynski, A. (1994) 'The incidence of child homicide: how accurate are the official statistics?' *Journal of Clinical Forensic Medicine*, **1**, pp. 61–66.

6

Partnership from the child's perspective

Murray Davies, Paul Gerber and Jeannie Wells

Lack of partnership

What has emerged from the research is that a substantial number of children and young people have no confidence whatsoever in adult support of any kind. They talk to 'no-one' ... Many children are adamant that there are no solutions, but believe there could be a lot more understanding (Butler and Williamson, 1994).

They don't really listen. And then they don't believe you. My mum is mentally disturbed. And because I wouldn't talk to them – I mean, I've always kept people at a distance, that's just the way I am – they thought I was disturbed, like mum. When I told them about being raped they put it down to my imagination. Why should I imagine that? But he's owned up now. But no-one believed me. Social workers don't listen. They see what they want to see. They don't want to know (Butler and Williamson, 1994).

The views of children, voiced in these quotations, show their lack of trust in adults and, from a child's perspective, suggest that there may be little upon which to base partnerships.

It was in the late 1980s that the Report of the Inquiry into Child Abuse in Cleveland was published, and revealed some of the distance between adults and children. This report highlighted 'Samantha's story' and the pain of her abuse by her father from four years old to 19 years old. Samantha raised six points for action, all important, and one of which highlighted the need for confidentiality, '. . . I needed to feel that what I said was very secure. I could not trust many people'. The Report also emphasised that, 'There is a danger that in looking at the welfare of the children believed to be victims of sexual abuse, the children themselves may be overlooked. *The child is a person and not an object of concern*'. Since this report, there is little evidence of significant progress in discovering and responding to the wishes and feelings of children in a way that establishes effective partnerships between children and adults, and in which children are involved in decisions affecting their lives. The Children Act Report, for example, presents a very gloomy picture.

> *It was not the general practice of staff to ask children how they felt about decisions affecting their daily life or their future, and their views were not routinely recorded on case files. There was also a wide disparity in the levels of skills and experience of staff working with disabled children. This demonstrated the importance of a comprehensive training programme for a workforce of fieldwork staff carrying a wide range of child care duties, and disability workers who carried responsibility for children* (The Children Act Report 1993, HMSO, 1994).

The same report also comments on the significant numbers of children on child protection registers, or being 'looked after' by local authorities who were not allocated social workers. It is very difficult to see how the welfare of the child is paramount in such circumstances. Partnership, from a child's perspective, becomes quite meaningless.

In 1993 the Social Services Inspectorate examined casework management arrangements in a sample of English authorities which had reported significant difficulties with unallocated child protection and/or children being looked after. A case was deemed to be 'allocated' when a named social worker was appointed as the key worker and undertook social work aspects of the child protection plan, and a child 'looked after' if a named social worker had been appointed to undertake all the legal requirements. Five local authorities in the sample had levels of unallocated child protection cases which exceeded ten per cent. Not only were departments failing to meet their statutory responsibilities, there was little foundation for any partnership, little planning in relation to children's needs, little account taken of a child's wishes and feelings, and little involvement by the child in any ongoing work to deal with the circumstances that led to the abuse.

Further information about the current state of partnerships with children is provided in the following extracts from the Social Services Inspectorate Report: *Evaluating Child Protection Services* (DoH, 1993).

> *Social workers and their managers generally recognised the importance of the principle of ensuring that the welfare of the child is paramount. Nonetheless, there was a worrying number of cases where clearly the child's welfare had ceased to be the primary concern . . . . Interviews with children were not always undertaken. This was because they were too young or because of assumptions about their feelings made by the social workers, which were not supported by the evidence. Little attention had been given to the involvement of other staff, such as family centre workers, with skills to help young people understand what was happening . . . In one authority, social workers did believe that they had given due consideration to the wishes and feelings of the children, but when young people were*

interviewed, they felt that social workers did not always know how to talk with them . . . While social workers placed importance on interviewing children at an appropriate pace and consistent with their age and understanding, practice in general was not always of that quality. Social workers still had concerns about their lack of skills in involving and interviewing children. It is a matter which needs to be resolved . . . Even where there is evidence of ongoing work with children, limitations about the extent of their involvement, the information available to them, and the extent to which they can influence, direct or control what is happening is very limited.

Commitment to partnership

Developing partnerships with children takes time, commitment and skill; it does not just happen. Children remain suspicious about adults. To remedy this situation a considerable investment in developing partnerships is required from professionals. But such professionals face competing demands, not least resulting from the administrative and organisational context in which they operate. In investigations of child abuse (which for many children will be their first contact with a social worker) children often are totally unaware of the organisational context of the workers interviewing them. Parents may have some idea of this context, as well as of the process of gaining information. Care-takers will be the main providers of 'finding out' what has happened, but it is likely that friends, relatives, and peer group will be equally uncertain. Many children report during the therapeutic process that they have no idea who it was who first saw them, let alone where they came from or why.

Attempts to resolve perceived deficiencies in current legislation by trying to define, and redefine, 'good child-care practice' via memoranda and statements of standards can never achieve the aims of respecting and responding to the wishes of children. It is not difficult to understand that there will be uncertainty, confusion and emotional cost to children experiencing this level of response.

Careful listening

The key requirement in understanding children's expectations is careful listening and hearing, features often absent from adult agendas, but essential if the administrative bias is to be redressed. A part of the problem which needs to be addressed is that children do not expect to be listened to, and yet professionals know that listening is the most important way of acknowledging that a person (who may be a child) exists in his or her own right.

Consultation and listening to the views of children in different settings, reveal important new information and perspectives. They demonstrate that children's perceptions as users and recipients of services are influenced by different considerations to those of the professionals who provide them, reinforcing the danger of relying only on adult and professional views (Davies and Dotchin, 1994). Children demonstrate that they do have views about the dangers they face, what they consider to be harmful and the nature of the help they want. They doubt adult commitment and adults' ability to understand, with the result that there are probably large numbers of children 'at risk' about whom adults never get to hear.

For some children – especially for Black children, and for disabled children – there are additional requirements which must be heard and responded to. Black children feel more distant from the predominantly White-orientated services which are available to them, which often are not presented to them in a way that makes them accessible. For disabled children the perception that they are less capable, and less able, has a disempowering effect. They need to be listened to; they are also anxious about the ability of adults to understand, and the isolating effects of labelling which limits opportunities.

At present the formal child protection processes and protocols exist largely for purposes other than helping children with solutions to their difficulties. The child's view of the problem is seldom established; certainly the child's view of a proposed solution is rarely on the agenda.

Partnership in decision making

Principles of participation are based on the assumption that participants in any process actively receive correct and vital information and simultaneously contribute *their own special knowledge* to it, thereby shaping and customising it.

Granting or withholding consent to the proposed actions of others which will influence one's life is seen as a fundamental human right in the adult world. Penalties can be imposed when there is a failure to respect another adult wishing to withhold consent. In fact a failure adequately to seek consent may lead to hostility and litigation. Rights are exercised by adults only when they have sufficient power, and access to it, and feel confident enough that they will not be victimised and end up worse than when they started. These are lessons for working with children.

The lack of respect for this fundamental right is based on the cultural belief that children are unable to make informed choices, which at the same time justifies withholding or distorting information of critical importance to young people. Considered too immature to make decisions on the one hand, they are expected to have the confidence of adults in seeking information, redress, explanation and choice on the other (which in fact many adults do not have, particularly at times of stress and vulnerability).

In terms of rights, opening the way for children to be consulted more fully in defining their interests leads to a rethinking of childhood. Taking consent seriously is one means of attempting this. Consent is not an event but a process of selecting options, negotiating them, and accepting or rejecting them, then making an informed choice and becoming emotionally committed to it. Consent can only happen when there is an absence of force or coercion. It is about deciding one's own best interests and preferences; it determines whether children can decide which rights they prefer to have, or whether adults choose for them.

This highlights an important dilemma in child protection. It means being clear about when and why adults intervene to protect children from harm, and then being able to explain this to them. Children can be encouraged to make decisions and to take part in procedures affecting them, within parameters set by adults. The decision about the degree of consent rests in the main with adults and organisations, and this is how the procedures and processes are framed. Shifting the balance of power means involving children in thinking through how their opportunities to give consent are enhanced rather than diminished.

In a study by Alderson on children's consent to surgery, patients aged between eight to 15 years old, and the adults caring for them, were interviewed (Alderson, 1992). They were asked at what age they thought children were able to understand their proposed treatment, and around which age they could be trusted to make wise decisions about it. The replies from each group – patients, parents and professionals – ranged from early childhood to early adulthood and revealed as much about the respondent as they did about ages of competence. Alderson points out that, 'Young children's complex awareness of material and moral concepts, and the potential value of consulting them, are becoming more widely recognised'. She also suggests that the general public is unlikely to adopt more liberal views, 'As long as some child care professionals continue to preach discredited theories, and generalise about children's supposed inabilities' (Alderson, 1992).

Parental responsibility

Most adults 'feel' that they have to protect children without necessarily having any real knowledge about why or how they might do this. They are influenced heavily by political, social, environmental and cultural sources which give a framework of reference about how all of us might behave.

Ownership of children by parents was enshrined in English law a hundred years ago. Child protection law ensured that children could be removed from their care and control if the treatment of the child was bad enough. 'Bad enough' has been defined differently at different times. Definitions have been influenced by different belief systems in different cultures. Whilst there is a recognition in all cultures that young children are 'dependent' in some way, cultures vary greatly in determining at what age children are expected to assume 'adult' responsibilities. Therefore 'childhood' can be seen as a social construction, as can the degree of protection and care afforded by the adults. Partnership between adults, children and the State has been affected variously by such constructions.

In England and Wales the Children Act 1989 seeks to strike a balance between opportunities for children to be heard in the decisions which affect their lives, and the rights of parents to exercise their responsibilities. In practice there is a tension between parental rights and responsibilities and the rights of children. The modern function of parental rights appears to be 'to permit parents to discharge their duties to children' (Bainham, 1988). This highlights the question of 'whether the promotion of children's welfare is the same as the protection of their rights' (Bainham, 1988). It can be argued that it is not the right of children to take their own decisions which is upheld, but the right of adults (including professionals) to take decisions on their behalf. The right of protection gives the wider society a duty to support children from exposure to harm, exploitation and other hazards associated with childhood by giving them a right to advocacy and information.

Adults do have clear responsibilities for the protection and welfare of children. A parent must make an infinite number of decisions and judgements every day in respect of a child. The Convention on the Rights of the Child acknowledges this responsibility. Article 5 states that governments must 'respect the responsibilities, rights and duties of parents . . . to provide . . . appropriate direction and guidance in the exercise by the child of the rights (in the Convention)'. However, it also recognises the potential conflict in the exercise of those responsibilities by asserting that they must be carried out 'in a manner consistent with the child's evolving capacity'. In other words, adults do not have unfettered rights to act on behalf of children. The Convention places further constraints on the powers of adults with responsibility for children by requiring that, 'In all actions concerning children, whether undertaken by public or private social welfare institutions, courts of law, administrative authorities or legislative bodies, the best interests of the child shall be a primary consideration' (Article 3). This principle provides a test against which adults need to evaluate their decisions and actions in respect of those children; however, it is by no means a straightforward or unproblematic principle to apply.

Apart from the Children Act 1989, the concept of the welfare of the child is absent from English law. Even within the Children Act 1989 there is no obligation on parents to act in their children's best interests. Children's welfare is not central to decisions made throughout society. Clearly many professionals working with children – teachers, nurses, doctors, for example – would argue, with justification, that they operate on a day-to-day basis with that principle as central to their work. However, because they are under no legal obligation to exercise their responsibilities within the framework of a 'best interests' principle, children have no means of ensuring that their interests are heard nor any means of redress in the event of a failure to do so.

The competence of children

Wherever boundaries of 'childhood' are drawn, there is broad consensus that children are more vulnerable comparatively than adults, thus requiring special measures to protect and promote their needs. And it is their need for protection which is used to justify the continued resistance to giving children more control over decision-making in their lives. Children are perceived as lacking competence to take responsibility for their own lives and therefore are viewed as vulnerable and in need of protection. Because they need protection, adults are invested with powers to act on their behalf; because children are denied the powers to make decisions and to participate fully in them, they are rendered more vulnerable to the authority of adults.

Children are vulnerable because of their dependency. As such, they are exposed to a host of risks and hazards. But children and young people are given little voice or opportunity of expression about how they perceive, cope and act, on a daily basis – and without adult assistance – with such experiences. The abuse of children continues to be viewed in terms of isolated experiences resulting from behaviour on the part of a small number of aberrant adults. Since many of the other hazards of childhood are denied by an adult-dominated society, inappropriate assumptions are perpetuated about the competence and knowledge of children and young people.

Arguments which view children as not rational, and unable to make reasoned and informed decisions, imply that there is little sense in giving children rights since they are incapable of exercising them. Children are said also to lack the wisdom that comes from experience and therefore they will make mistakes in choices. So in denying them the right to make decisions for themselves, society, it could be argued, is merely attempting to protect them from their own incompetence.

As Franklin (1989) highlights, children reveal a competence for rational thinking, and for making informed choices, with the information that is available to them. Children make rational decisions all the time about how they conduct themselves in an adult-dominated world. They can explain, justify and remember things in much the same way as adults, while at the same time, having little information about the general and specific constructs of wider society.

An examination of the competence of a three-year-old to recall, describe and contextualise her abuse and abduction has been recorded graphically by Dr David Jones (1987). It reveals a high level of competence that indicates the need for more research into the developmental abilities of children under five years who have been deemed 'incompetent' by virtue of their age.

Franklin (1989) also explored age limit arguments on children's rights and found them incoherent. In the UK a child reaches the age of criminal responsibility at ten, is sexually adult at 16, eligible for work at 16, but not politically 'adult' until 18. These age limits also vary across societal histories and cultures.

A popular view is that children will make too many mistakes if they are allowed to have rights. Yet adults are allowed to make (sometimes catastrophic!) mistakes and learn from them.

Respecting young citizens

Radical changes are required in the manner in which children and young people are perceived and how their needs are better understood. To promote these changes in adults, children must be empowered through participation in, and partnership with, the formal structures. New routes for the child's voice to be heard and represented independently are critical first steps in respecting children's citizenship and the rights thereby accorded.

The UN Convention on the Rights of the Child 1989, and the Children Act 1989, both provide a fresh impetus for children to participate more actively in decisions affecting their lives, and then challenge established adult and professional views, practices and prejudices. Whilst this points to children having the right to be consulted about decisions which affect them personally, the Children Act 1989 only requires that children's views should be taken into account (rather than that they should be observed).

Listening to children, and hearing what they have to say, is at the root of developing effective human rights for children. This process values the views of children, but is not achieved easily or accepted universally. It challenges the protectionist view that it is not fair to involve children in difficult decision making, particularly because they may be involved in considering some painful or upsetting outcomes. The protectionist view would avoid the exposure of children to further 'unnecessary' pain.

Listening requires a commitment from practitioners who already may be trying to juggle with competing demands on their time. Also, as children are a relatively 'powerless' group, it is easier to exclude them. This attitude feeds into professional arrogance, particularly for those professionals defined as 'experts' in specific areas of practice, who may believe and act as though they 'know' what children require. It may be threatening to acknowledge a need to find out views and opinions directly from children.

The reservations of children about adult support, centre on whether they believe that adults are capable of understanding their experiences and concerns. Adults are described as imposing their own views on a situation, breaching confidentiality, and responding inappropriately by trivialising or over-reacting (Butler and Williamson, 1994). This research reported on desirable professional intervention and included careful listening, availability, and a non-judgmental and non-directive attitude. Children wanted less pressure, patient explanation, and an outline of options and suggestions, together with the time and space to give them their full consideration. 'I want my own choices – otherwise my life might be ruined by someone else's mistake' was a view expressed by one young person, and which reflected a common view (Butler and Williamson, 1994).

Whilst children want professionals to be sympathetic, supportive and optimistic, they want straight-talking, realism and reliability, and not as it is sometimes seen – 'bullshit and false promises'. Trust and confidentiality also were crucial. Information shared in confidence with professionals should be treated with absolute confidentiality. If professionals cannot help then they should say so; children should be consulted before matters are taken further – it should be their choice if matters go further. Butler and Williamson (1994) found that many young people gave accounts of trust being breached, thus causing them to have little confidence in professional support.

The dilemma for professionals is whether they can respect and respond to such information from children, and then adjust practice and procedures accordingly. It is argued here that there are a number of ways to proceed.

1. Children are more vulnerable when they have no power, no information and no access to information. So it is important to explore, with young people, their information needs and to create opportunities for access to and discussion about such information. Children who are more informed are likely to be less vulnerable. They should have information about the child protection system and the possible outcomes and options to increase choice.

2. Children use 'helplines' as a way of discussing issues, receiving information and maintaining control. Therefore exploring what is valued in helplines could be extended in face-to-face contact so that the child retains control and confidentiality and makes informed decisions. Children should have an opportunity to explore their own understanding of the challenges and hazards which confront them, and to develop their solutions (which may involve the statutory network and courts).

3. Venues for discussing issues with children tend to be adult-orientated. There is a need to create child-centred environments by listening to the views of children about current venues and being actively supportive in changing them.

4. The antidote to abuse of power is confidence in the right to be heard, which has to be supported with those rights being upheld. Children who are more aware of their rights are less likely to be abused, it is argued; so a greater focus on children as individuals is advocated, and thus the current child protection system needs to become more child-centred and child-initiated, recognising the need for different responses to different circumstances. An analysis of how systems need to change to accommodate this needs to be undertaken, as well as time spent on finding ways to involve children in this process.

5. Children have a right to know the hazards of childhood and contribute to all the processes to help avoid them. There is a need to identify clearly hazards known by children (not as remembered or perceived by adults) and then to seek ways for children, in partnership with adults, to develop their ideas about how to share this information, so as to devise prevention programmes.

6. Confidential counselling and information services – easily available and as of right – should be established on a local, drop-in basis with the responsibility on professionals to report suspected abuse but modified in line with young people's wishes. Children should be aware of the status of the information they give and be informed properly so that they can have the opportunity to withdraw from the process, if necessary.

7. Schooling has a part to play in enhancing young people's knowledge of the adult world and in providing opportunities to discuss, debate and learn, in partnership with teachers, about their protection needs and about strategies to enhance and promote their strengths.

8. All children involved in child protection enquiries and legal proceedings should have, as a right, independent and high quality legal advice and representation from the beginning. Victim and witnesses should receive high quality, specialised victim-support. Reducing the trauma of a court appearance enhances credibility and assists in the process of psychological adjustment. Child witness support programmes should be available using trained specialists with an understanding of child development and the effects of trauma, to support and advise the child before the trial. Concerns regarding coaching about evidence could be reduced greatly if the support programme were overseen by a legal representative of the court. Such support programmes can be extended to provide support and advocacy to children participating in case conferences or case review meetings to promote their participation in decisions affecting their lives (see Scutt, 1995).

9. Participation in policy- and procedure-making groups in organisations can lead to the development of child-centred procedures and services. Current procedures do not take sufficient account of the child's perspective. For change to take place there needs to be a commitment to the benefits of devolving power to children.

10. The development of children's rights services promotes the voice of the child and provides information to children about their rights, enabling them to complain, seek redress and to participate in civil liberty activity as it affects them.

11. Methods now exist to establish children's expectations of services, and then to monitor performance of services against these (see, for example, Davies and Dotchin, 1994). This approach could be

extended to all children's services so that children's views and wishes are reflected properly in the design of services, so that there is a greater sense of ownership and a greater willingness to use them.

12. Written agreements involving children need to include the empowerment and participation of children. The requirements of child protection procedures and practice during the initial investigation and assessment of a suspected case of child abuse can leave children feeling powerless, as well as feeling that they have not participated in decision making. This sense of powerlessness can be perpetuated when written agreements describe the work which practitioners and children will be engaged in, but where important decisions (and even some less important ones) are made by the practitioner. Set formats for agreements can make flexibility difficult and do not provide sufficient contributions either to respect children's wishes and feelings, or to shape what happens in ways which divert attention towards organisational needs. Participation demands more than arrangements to take part in existing organisational structures and processes; it requires more flexibility in order to listen to the wishes and feelings of children and their carers, and then to agree arrangements which respect them.

13. Information about services and leaflets rarely indicate outcomes, or the likely horrors and difficulties. For example children are not usually aware that defendants will see all papers and reports. Adults expect this information and get legal advice. Most children do not have their views expressed because Guardians ad Litem and child care panel lawyers often are reluctant to interview children and young people or to allow them unreservedly to express their views to the court. Experience suggests that a large amount of information in reports about children are 'adult' views and 'adult' interpretations of children's behaviour.

Conclusion

There are probably no institutions or agencies that believe the present arrangements make adequate provision for the protection of children. Nonetheless what we see is a continuing failure to address change towards an acknowledgement of the rights of children. Policy issues concerning the allocation of resources to young people and their families for preventative work, rather than protective and investigative intervention, need to contain effective processes to hear the voices of young people in their definition and application.

Section 5.23 of *The Challenge of Partnership in Child Protection: Practice Guide* (HMSO, 1995) upholds the view that children should have 'a clear explanation of both the purpose and process of interviews' and that this should 'include information about their rights during the process'. To change the current attitude of partial child participation requires not only the giving of information but also a radical change in the context of child protection practice. 'Protection services' need not mean the withholding of information and rights to 'protect' children's 'innocence'. Emerging research, such as Davies and Dotchin (1994), shows that involvement by young people can prevent inaccurate 'labelling' and wasted resource provision which may currently be targeted inappropriately because of lack of information. If young people are deprived of information, like adults, they will probably fill the gaps with mis-information. This does not enhance prevention or protection in child abuse.

Unless the rights of children are promoted, and unless their participation is accepted at a level consistent with adults, then adequate responses will not be developed for vulnerable children. There is a need for a more child-centred and child-initiated system. Adults can feel threatened and fear losing their power and control by allowing child-centred views rather than adult-centred ones. For change to take place, children need to feel empowered; there are opportunities for all adults to begin this process in a wide range of settings.

BIBLIOGRAPHY

Alderson, P. (1992) 'Rights of children and young people' in Coote, A. (ed,) *The Welfare of Citizens*, IPPR/Rivers Osram Press.

Bainham, A. (1988) *Children, Parents and the State*, Sweet and Maxwell. Modern Legal Studies.

Bala, Nicholas, Prof. (1993) *Child Sexual Abuse Prosecutions: Children in the Courts*, Queens University Ontario, Canada.

Butler, I. and Williamson, H. (1994) *Children Speak*, Harlow: Longman.

Butler-Schloss (June 1988) *Report of the Inquiry into Child Abuse in Cleveland*, London: HMSO.

Davies, M. and Dotchin, J. (1994) 'Improving quality through participation' in Cloke, C. and Davies, M. (eds) *Empowerment and Participation in Child Protection*, Harlow: Longman.

Dezwirek Sas, Louise *et al.* (1993) *Three Years After the Verdict*, London Family Court Clinic. Ontario.

Department of Health (1993) *Evaluating Child Protection Services: Findings and Issues*, Inspections of Six Local Authority Child Protection Services, Social Services Inspectorate Report.

Department of Health (1994) *The Children Act Report 1993*, London: HMSO.

Part 2 Towards partnership with families

Department of Health (1995) *The Challenge of Partnership in Child Protection: Practice Guide*, London: HMSO.

Franklin, B. (1989) 'Children's rights: developments and prospects'. *Children and Society*, 3:1, 50–66.

Freeman, M.D.A. (1983) *The Rights and Wrongs of Children*.

Home Office with Department of Health (1992) *Memorandum of Good Practice on Video Recorded Interviews with Child Witnesses for Criminal Proceedings*, London: HMSO.

Jones, D.P.H. (1987) 'The evidence of a three year old child', *Criminal Law Review 1987*, 667–681.

Lansdown, G. (1995) in Cloke, C. and Davies, M. (eds) *Participation and Empowerment in Child Protection*, Harlow: Longman.

Scutt, N. (1995) in Cloke, C. and Davies, M. (eds) *Participation and Empowerment in Child Protection*, Harlow: Longman.

Spencer, J.R. and Flin, R. (1990) *The Evidence of Children: The Law and the Psychology*, London: Blackstone.

The Convention on the Rights of the Child, Adopted by the United Nations General Assembly (1989), London: HMSO.

Part 3

The enquiry in progress

7

Child abuse referrals: what? why? and how?

David Cooper

Introduction

Child protection is an uncertain science in a confused world. Debates about childhood, parenthood, family life and the role of the State, fuelled by the instant power of the media, form the turbulent backdrop to allegations of child abuse. This chapter will consider the starting point of such allegations when they become translated into referrals to local authority social services departments (SSDs).

What are the social and psychological contexts for referrals? Can we understand them better by considering what happens to referrals once they are made? Who are the informants, what are their motives, why and how do they say what they say and how are their 'messages' dealt with by 'intermediaries' and then by SSDs? Broadly speaking, the child protection system resembles a perforated funnel and two key questions arise: how is information selected in the first place for entry into the funnel and what subsequent filtering takes place as the referral descends through the funnel? This chapter will consider the first of these questions.

The context of referrals

Analysing messages

The construction of, handling and response to, referrals can be seen as a message process. There are senders, transmitters and receivers involved and individuals (who may also be members of organisations) can occupy more than one role in this process. The metaphor is not a simple one in that the initial sender, the informant, may in turn have received other messages. Even the receiver system which is ultimately the SSD can be broken down into more than one element, as referral-takers pass on messages to their supervisors. All participants in the message-processing bring their own contexts into play and these will range from a one-to-one relationship to a large statutory organisation. More widely, everyone will act within current social and political climates.

Useful frameworks exist to help make sense of this complex process whereby child protection referrals arise and are handled initally. An ecological model (Cooper, 1993, Chaps 4 and 6) defines individuals as active members of different social systems in child abuse events. Secondly, ethnomethodology offers rich insights into the details of everyday communications and the hidden assumptions that underlie them. I shall also draw on social psychology and attribution theory, in particular, in exploring how we judge other people's behaviour.

Ecosystems

At a broad level, individuals are part of an over-arching macrosystem which contains society's beliefs, values and norms. Disseminated through a potent media, whether it be the tabloid or serious press, TV news reports or documentaries, and reinforced by government reports, our present macrosystem conceives of child victims threatened by paedophiles, brutal fathers and neglectful mothers; these victims need rescuing by an efficient emergency service of police and social workers. Sometimes these agencies see too little and children die or are abused further; sometimes they see too much and innocent families are damaged. This is a very potent system and colours child protection referrals from beginning to end; even those who abuse are not immune to it. The analysis is further complicated because, in our multi-cultural society, the dominant White system has too often proved either unwilling or ill-equipped to appreciate differences in child-rearing practices for example (Fitzherbert, 1967).

At the same time individuals exist in microsystems which encompass daily experiences and can apply equally whether it be a child and parent or two social workers in a team. Finally, the model conceives of exosystems, groupings which have power over an individual but which s/he cannot penetrate easily. In child protection terms these would be the official agencies which make decisions about children, but other individuals and agencies can become associated with these exosystems and therefore less permeable by families. The value of the ecological model is that it helps to locate individuals and to describe their behaviour both as active contributors to, and objects of, social processes. In terms of messages this suggests that 'facts' will reflect system allegiances and priorities.

Relevance and ethnomethodology

What actually happens within such systems? Wattam (1989, Chap. 2) has developed the useful concept of 'relevances'. In her analysis of child sexual abuse referrals she makes the point that we need to understand how people decide consciously or otherwise what is relevant to them in sending or receiving messages. Thus children may offer their own 'version' which may or may not fit the expectations or requirements of social workers. They in turn possess not just a personal, or professional, but also an 'organisational relevance' (p. 31). This may mean that the social worker, intent on getting 'good' evidence, may pay too little attention to apparently vague statements by a child. Conversely, descriptions of events which do not hold great importance for the child may, to her/his surprise, be treated very seriously.

Wattam draws on ethnomethodology in her account. Garfinkel's (1967) classic studies suggested that everyday communications are based on unspoken, 'taken-for-granted' assumptions and rules which may be difficult for outsiders to understand. The context includes the past, present and future and so, in terms of alleged child abuse, messages require skilled interpretation from others; if there are cultural and language differences, the problem is further compounded. What people say, what they mean, and why now rather than at some other time, requires more than mere 'accurate' recording on referral forms.

Attribution theory

A central purpose of the current child protection enquiry process is to allocate responsibility. This is implicit in the Children Act 1989 terminology and from the very beginning of a referral it is crucial. It is not just events that are reported on but, either explicitly or implicitly, the laying of blame. The extent to which various people in the message process lay blame can be considered by reference to attribution theory in social psychology. Brigham (1991, Chap. 2) has a useful summary of the way we selectively organise and perceive events; the crucial element is the extent to which we explain things either as the result of circumstances, or attribute them to individuals, or a combination of both. 'Schemas' are employed, often as shortcuts, to fit things into patterns that are based on our previous experiences of people or events. Our judgements will operate along three dimensions: 'locus', i.e. whether the blame is internal or external to a person; 'controllability', i.e. the extent to

117

which the person could control what happened; 'stability', i.e. whether the person's behaviour was typical or not. Essentially, if we consider that behaviour in a situation was internal and stable then we are more likely to blame that person for the events in question.

Once attribution is underway there is a tendency to concentrate on a person's 'central traits' and to commit the 'fundamental attribution error' (Brigham, 1991, p. 78). This consists of underestimating the power of environmental forces on other people, and is more common where observers lack detachment and have an over-simplified perception of situations; it is also more likely the further away they are from the object of their perceptions. In the world of alleged abuse, where the difference between accidental and deliberate action is central, these concepts help to interpret the often complex perceptions and motives of those involved in the referral message process. Enquiries in the current climate of child protection can become preoccupied with 'clear facts', 'good evidence' and 'getting it right', yet the reality is that the great majority of referrals are not clear-cut and interpretation is at a premium.

Referrers in action

Children

Children are a variable source of referrals. They may exist in an abusive situation without complaining because it is part of their everyday, 'taken-for-granted' experience. They may not feel as distressed as outsiders would expect and Browne and Finkelhor (1986) have suggested that the impact of sexual abuse may be worse sometimes on older children simply because they have become aware of the social shame of being 'different'. In 'system' terms there is a conflict between the family and a wider system (for example, at school) and the experience is painful but also is a stimulus to complain. At other times, however, children find it too difficult to cope with this threat to family communication and will suppress allegations; they may also be getting benefits from the relationships despite the abuse and will be risking too much by any revelations to outsiders. It is simplistic always to talk of children being 'afraid to tell', even though this is undoubtedly a serious factor in some cases, rather it may be a tortuous matter of cost and reward. O'Hagan (1989, pp. 72–3) has warned of the dangers of premature removal of children from their families, which has provoked suicide and even murder at times as extremely intense feelings have been exposed and impeded.

Children have their own priorities which their version of events will reflect. What may appear to others as particular acts of cruel abuse may be less upsetting to a child than slow cumulative neglect and indifference from another source. What about children 'telling lies'? To say that they never do is clearly as extreme as saying they always do! Research is not straightforward because of obvious methodological difficulties but there is now an increasing number of studies into the more formal aspects of children's testimony (NCB/Barnardos, 1991); these suggest that the key factor may be the child's relationship with those around her/him at the time of questioning. Again, a child may be too close to a carer and too much influenced by 'central traits' – 'my dad is a good person for me' – to acknowledge particular acts of abuse. Here the 'fundamental attribution error' operates in reverse.

It becomes obvious that a child who is under pressure or fear will communicate differently, just as adults do. There is a general problem of child abuse allegations which are unsubstantiated; these seem to be more likely where there is some conflict within the family (Wakefield and Underwager, 1988, Chap.12; Hughes, 1993, p. 8; Thorpe, 1994, p. 58) and it is not difficult to imagine the emotional and cognitive dilemmas for children torn between disputing parents. The teachers' union, NASUWT, has expressed concern recently about the devastating effect on its members of abuse allegations by children (*Guardian*, 5 October 1993, p. 6). The Union points to the rise in such allegations, and questions what percentage of them are false or at least seriously exaggerated. This is difficult to estimate because only a small proportion of cases provide strong enough evidence to justify prosecution anyway. What may be happening here is that the school exosystem is now more easy for children to penetrate as discipline eases and against the background of a macrosystem which has made sensitivity to abuse more common. This encourages children to talk more than they may have done previously to their teachers. At times this will lead to a welcome disclosure of abuse but it can also create other situations as children form new and perhaps ambivalent relationships with them which could mirror those within their families.

Children are at the centre of abuse and they are thus central figures in every sense. Their position in terms of referrals is the most complex because they have the most to gain but also the most to lose. Their lack of power, particularly when they are very young, means that they are enmeshed in dangerous family communication contexts and this may be why they find it difficult to tell their stories easily; conversely, they may attempt to achieve power by making false or inflated allegations. They need to be taken seriously, as *Working Together* recommends (DoH, 1991, para. 5.11.1), so that their complex needs can be heard in a way that is sensitive, unprejudiced and no more 'legalised' than necessary. Theirs is not always a simple world which can be conveyed in simple messages.

Parents

In the referral process parents should be considered first together, and then separately, because they share a common context but can also diverge sharply as individuals. Taken together they are important both as referrers (especially mothers) and as key contributors to messages and communications.

The nature of the parents' or carers' relationship will influence referrals about child abuse particularly if one of the partners is suspected. The problem of unsubstantiated allegations has been noted and this will be aggravated if a relationship has broken down. Conversely, too close a relationship, with all its shared communication assumptions, may delay or prevent disclosures of actual abuse. Faller (1988, p. 269) has argued that the non-abusing parent offers better protection to the child the more independent s/he is from the abusing partner. Yet if the child protection system is too menacing it may strengthen parent solidarity and resistance. The parents are always at the focus of child protection and, like their children, may have understandable doubts about being investigated. Even if the suspected abuser is outside the family it is still the assessment of parent 'performance' which determines outcomes.

Mothers occupy a special position that has been frequently explored in feminist literature. Analysis of child abuse referrals reveals an over-representation of low-income, single parent (usually the mother) families but with the male father-figure contributing significantly to the abuse (Corby, 1993, pp. 64–74; Thorpe, 1994, Chap. 10), and in the more 'classless' field of sexual abuse males are even more prominent as abusers. There will be many psychological, political and practical reasons why mothers do not initiate referrals when they may have better evidence than anyone else. Milner (1993) argues that women have additional reasons for keeping quiet, apart from a fear of domestic violence: conventional views of the mother's primary caring role can mean that the focus of child protection work and concern will fall on her, whereas the father will be harassed less because a lower standard of involvement is applied. Allegations of neglect, emotional harm or collusion by the mother may then be added to the original referral if she appears unco-operative.

Whilst the overall residual responsibility and vulnerability of mothers is a striking feature of the great majority of families who become known to social workers, fathers have to face their own challenges in allegations. The

120

dramatic growth in alleged abuse in general and sexual abuse in particular in the last 15 years has created another 'taken-for-granted' communication context that also illustrates attribution theory, namely that men as a group *do* carry responsibility. This has been a central plank of feminist theory and Milner's article is a good recent example; the blame is laid more on 'central traits' and less on the mitigating effects of circumstances. In terms of attribution theory, the 'locus' of the event is alleged to be internal, it is 'controllable' and it is 'typical'. Milner gives a case example and while she devotes some space to exploring the environmental pressures on the mother, the father is dismissed simply as 'alcoholic' (p. 59).

Men may be wary of making or being involved in allegations. Notwithstanding Milner's otherwise valuable analysis, a heavy focus can also fall on fathers and the modern abuse discourse is replete with perpetrators, rescue and prosecution. Women now initiate the majority of divorce applications and receive residence orders more often (Hoggett and Pearl, 1991, pp. 223–7) which leaves an increasing number of men attempting to establish themselves in new families. Despite the historical advantage of patriarchy this is an inherently vulnerable position; men may in their turn prefer not to upset a newly established relationship even if they see abuse and will be less able than they should to make appropriate attributions. Conversely, where they are unable to establish close relationships with stepchildren they may be less understanding and thus more critical about their behaviour; this can lead to family disputes, abuse and/or allegations.

For parents then, mothers and fathers, alike and differently, referrals present difficulties. They arise from varying contexts, and messages may hold a number of meanings. Children are only a part of their priorities and this helps to explain why apparently precise allegations are sometimes denied vehemently by a non-abusing parent. As the last section of this chapter argues, child protection enquiries can be a blunt instrument that exacts a heavy price for its benefits; for this reason the role of parents in referrals always needs very careful and sensitive assessment.

Wider family and neighbours

Many of the above dynamics apply here. As a source of referrals, extended family and neighbours are important because they combine ongoing knowledge of the nuclear family with a degree of detachment. Official child abuse Inquiries have at times criticised workers for not paying enough attention to complaints from such sources and this was vividly shown in the case of Maria Colwell. However, the validity and reliability of their messages may depend on their relationship with the family. If their everyday communication with the parents and child breaks down then allegations need to be treated with caution. In her study of sexual abuse referrals Hughes reported a small number of unsubstantiated cases 'in context of neighbour or family friction' (Hughes, 1993, p. 8). Thorpe (1994, p. 55) noted similar problems in his study of child protection referrals in Western Australia.

At the same time, relatives and neighbours may be too involved with the family to report when they might. This may also reflect shared cultural values so that abuse is not accepted as such. Relatives and neighbours may therefore stand together with the parents against the exosystem of the child protection agencies. However, if they do then make allegations it may be a very serious sign that a family has offended local mores and it is not just a passing squabble. Interpreting such messages is difficult because of the uncertainties in the context; one way is to develop close local contacts through voluntary networks. These can help to monitor and interpret what is said about families over time rather than in an 'all or nothing', 'event-specific' way that is the nature of official enquiries. In other words, the fluidity of the relative or neighbour system needs to be matched by a similar filtering system which is then available to official agencies.

A feature of abusing families is that, as their problems grow, they tend to become more isolated (Crittenden, 1988, Chap. 7; Gibbons, 1990, Chap. 7). The intervening layer of relatives and neighbours is therefore vital as a barometer of stress as long as it is read with skill and caution.

Intermediary agencies

Here I include workers in a variety of settings ranging from informal groups and voluntary agencies to teachers and medical staff. They occupy the position of being both receivers and senders of referral messages. At the more formal end, *Working Together* (DoH, 1991) emphasises the overriding duty of, for example, doctors, health visitors and teachers to report suspicions of child abuse. The reality is less simple. Even in the USA where mandatory reporting laws exist, workers' professional dilemmas are reflected in varying levels of compliance. This appears to be partly because, for them as for family and neighbours, the child protection system can make heavy demands (Hutchison, 1993).

All intermediary workers and agencies have their own contexts, their own everyday communication assumptions, and an abuse allegation will disrupt these to some extent. Voluntary agencies operating in the ill-defined area between State and family face special difficulties. Their ability to help families will depend on acceptance and trust and the more formal and legalistic the enquiry system becomes, the more the dilemma grows. Rather than there being a sliding scale of knowledge and opinion, which is the feature of informal contacts, there is a pressure for clear attributions. Despite this, voluntary workers have a distinctive part to play in influencing messages particularly if social workers can appreciate the constraints they face. A strong voluntary sector is an essential element in the referral process; it offers the capacity for setting messages in richer contexts.

Medical staff play a key part in referrals because much of the defining of abuse requires their particular expertise; there is not space in this chapter, however, to do more than comment on the main features of their contexts. A medical model of abuse has been and remains influential, though now it has been overlaid with a legal one (Parton, 1991). Partly this stems from the excesses of the Cleveland affair where a torrent of sexual abuse referrals streamed from paediatric diagnoses. Although media attention focused on clinical matters the Inquiry criticised the referrals because they took little or no account of wider non-medical contexts and thus fell into the child protection error of 'all-or-nothing' messages. Little filtering, interpretation or challenging of 'facts' seems to have happened and the paediatricians drew on narrow schemas to explain events, investing medical 'facts' with more validity than they merited.

The extent to which medical staff work within the community will influence their approach to making referrals. Paediatricians are specialists but also largely hospital-bound workers; they are therefore more likely to make referrals, but within a narrow context. General practitioners, on the other hand, are more reluctant participants in the enquiry process (Burns, 1991, p. 35) but may have a wider frame of reference. More generally many doctors may have difficulty in seeing abuse in middle-class families because of their socialisation and training (Dingwall *et al.*, 1983).

Health visitors and nurses who work within the community occupy a position mid-way between their hospital colleagues and social workers, and their professional associations have regularly pointed out the dilemma this poses. With a foot in the camps of primary as well as secondary prevention they, more than most, have to wear two hats; the benefits, though, more than compensate for the difficulties. They can talk effectively about local child-rearing patterns; they are active contributors to child protection discussions but with a professional identity distinct from social workers or the police, and they enjoy frequent, well-understood entry to the local community.

Teachers deserve special comment. Schools occupy a unique position because of their daily contact with children and Gibbons (1993) recorded them as the most frequent source of referrals outside the family. They are represented on area child protection committees but their context is not as 'welfarist' as that of health and social services staff. The demands of the national curriculum, the financial pressures of opting-out and the lack of pastoral or counselling staff all mean that schools are not set up automatically to contribute to child protection processes; nor do they find it easy to attend in-service courses along with other workers.

Their real strength lies in their opportunity to make comparisons about children. They will have soundly-based views of how individuals should be performing and where there are deviations this will be noticed, as will fluctuations in a particular child's behaviour and moods. Their contact through time also permits an averaging-out of impressions which is the hallmark of Garfinkel's accurate understanding of messages. A further value of teachers is their knowledge of children's friendships and rivalries; this offers useful information if statements are made about one child by another or if there is an epidemic of similar allegations.

Despite these advantages, the system position of teachers is a complicated one. At times they may seem to children and their parents to be hostile outsiders to be avoided at all costs; at others, and because of a general lessening of formal discipline, children may develop close personal relationships with teachers and begin to send them a variety of messages. Some of these may become false allegations that say more about inappropriate entanglements than actual events. Some, on the other hand, may include vital information that may not otherwise have emerged about abuse in the family. The use of the 'designated teacher' system in schools is necessary so that any allegations can be handled more consistently. The NASUWT debate, referred to earlier, saw this filtering as essential to protect both children and teachers; from a legal viewpoint it might be argued that this could reduce children's rights because schools might be tempted to hush up unpalatable facts or make interpretations better left to social workers or the police. However, the opposite risks of denying teachers some professional discretion in contextualising messages would ultimately be much more serious if we thereby forfeited their genuine co-operation.

Official receivers of messages

Child abuse allegations and other concerns about children eventually arrive on the desks of local authority social workers as the legally responsible welfare agency. Police have a similar duty to investigate suspected crimes.

A striking feature of modern child protection is the extent to which the two agencies routinely collaborate. This section concentrates on the SSD because the civil law under which they must act extends beyond and is far less clearly defined than criminal law. Having said that, another feature of child protection, and one which runs throughout this book, is the way the style of the latter has permeated the former. This has a crucial effect on the way referrals are received.

Wattam's 'organizational relevance' is strong in SSDs. Successive child abuse Inquiries have demanded ever more prescription in child protection procedures. The *Memorandum of Good Practice* for the interviewing of child witnesses (Home Office, 1992) is a recent example of this. In Garfinkel's terms any communication within an SSD will be based on certain assumptions that draw on the past – 'we have been criticised a lot' – as well as the future – 'if we get this wrong we will be criticised again'. Thus there can exist a psycho-legal schema that underpins social workers (as well as others). Social work has also been heavily influenced by feminist thinking and particularly its concern with sexual abuse which has shown an enormous growth in reported levels in the last 15 years. Nowhere is attribution theory more apt than in this field with its strong emphasis on laying blame, rescue and the punishment of abusers. Race and culture are also key contexts for SSDs to consider. MacDonald (1991), for example, regrets that the question of children's background receives only selective attention in the 1989 Children Act and the continuing under-representation of Black workers can produce partial or inappropriate responses to requests for help in Black families (Ahmed, 1990). Conversely, an unthinking desire to appear anti-racist may prevent White workers from challenging Black families who may be abusing their children (Corby, 1993, p. 152).

Do social workers respond equally to all allegations of abuse? In 'pure' message terms, sexual abuse or severe physical ill-treatment may seem clearer for both senders and receivers because of the emphasis on distinctive events. However, the less easily measured experience of neglect can be just as damaging to children (Crittenden, 1988; Gillham, 1994, pp. 98–111) and this should be considered in the light of my earlier comment about allegations from relatives and neighbours which may not be followed up. Thorpe (1994, pp. 192–202) argues that the child protection system works best in a small minority of sharp-edged extreme cases where the messages are relatively clear and which are amenable to the collection of firm evidence and the prosecution of firm rescue policy and practice. Where it is less appropriate in its methods and less successful in its outcomes is in the more common situations where individual blame is less easy to attribute. In her analysis Milner (1993) claimed that too many families which had become child protection cases had earlier asked for help with services to little avail; is this an example of the power of different messages to draw different responses from the state receivers?

The message takers

The final part of this section considers who actually takes referrals in SSDs. The term 'social worker' may in fact be misleading for several reasons. Firstly the experience of the frontline worker may vary considerably. Despite the Government's public concern about child protection work it has been surprisingly casual in insisting that this difficult work is done by the right staff. It has not even managed to give the weight of regulation to CCETSW's recommendation that only qualified and experienced social workers should have responsibility for child protection (Cooper, 1993, pp. 79–81). In many SSDs the vital message-taking and interpreting may be done by new staff or – although this is harder to verify – by unqualified workers.

With the influence of community care changes and budget cuts, SSDs are now employing a large number of staff under various names such as 'community care worker', 'information officer', 'customer care officer' or 'referral co-ordinator'. While this is not to suggest that such staff are left on their own to decide on the status of referrals, their presence in the message process is important. While they may share the 'organizational relevance' of social workers they will not have their 'professional relevance' to the same extent. Gadsby Waters (1992) has shown in her study of supervision in child protection, that the monitoring of policies and procedures may be much more vigorously pursued than professional supervision or personal support. Given the current pressures on staffing budgets it is vital that front line workers in child protection are the strongest, not the weakest, link in the chain. The first response to the referral message is such that it can become part of that message and that has important implications for children and their families.

Overall, the SSD must make some sense of referrals. They do so in a difficult macrosystem which prefers some messages to others and which demands an almost impossible combination of prescription and flexibility, procedures and professional judgement (Jamous and Peloille, 1970). The right amount of sensitivity is difficult to achieve and maintain and perhaps there is some merit in police policies of moving staff regularly to avoid staleness or burn-out. Dale and Davies' (1986) widely quoted concept of worker 'dangerousness' pictured workers who were not hearing the message of abuse; the term can equally apply to those who hear too much or the wrong things. Whatever the symptoms and causes, the role of the official message-taker cannot be overemphasised; while the SSD is at the end of the message process, its influence reverberates back along the line through intermediaries to the senders.

The family in the referral

This last section addresses perhaps the most difficult part of the whole referral question. Later chapters will explore what happens to the family as a child abuse enquiry unfolds when in many ways the problems, though difficult, are simpler to identify. At the very beginning there is a fundamental legal problem: if information is received that a child may be at risk should it be shared immediately and fully with the family?

A traditional police view might be that people under suspicion have only as many rights as do not impede the proper conduct of the enquiry. Where children are concerned there is a clear duty under the Children Act 1989 to offer them protection and hold their welfare paramount; in other words, the interests of parents must come second. In practice, however, it is the 'transactions' (Gillham, 1994, pp. 109–110) between parents and children which hold the key, so any separation of one from the other is rarely appropriate. Parents now attend child protection conferences more often, though not always through the entire proceedings, and are given far more information than previously; the position has its flexibility and it appears to work (Burns, 1991, pp. 173–5). The *Working Together* guidelines also emphasise the participation of parents in enquiries. This suggests that even if parents are suspected of abusing their children they occupy a special position as alleged offenders; it is now common for specialist police teams to deal with cases where intra-familial abuse is suspected while CID handle other criminal investigations.

The consequences of routinely excluding the family are serious. In a study of the impact of enquiries Farmer (1992) reports that events can accelerate very quickly and soon leave families feeling powerless and swept along. PAIN has ample case material to confirm the way attitudes are hardened by the legal demands of the enquiry and communication becomes polarised. Once parents are under suspicion they become legal 'untouchables' and intermediary workers may become wary of talking too freely with them for fear of compromising evidence. Even where suspicion falls elsewhere the family may be viewed as unreliable in the enquiry because they are emotionally involved! Malucchio *et al.* (1986, p. 146) add to this the interesting observation that, as the exclusion and sense of powerlessness grows, parents may project blame onto the investigators, or the referrers, and then withdraw from parental responsibility. These are, however, largely practical and legal considerations and do not address the moral justice question. A child abuse allegation, even if the alleged perpetrator is an outsider, is an assault on the family's integrity and they deserve as much information and respect as possible.

Dilemmas remain. In very serious allegations no-one should suggest that premature information is given to the family or anyone else which is likely to threaten the child's immediate physical welfare or which will destroy irreplaceable evidence. The identity of informants is protected in law and *Working Together* emphasises the importance of confidentiality between agencies. Although partnership is a central theme of current law and guidelines these do not provide any ultimate answers about involving the family, especially at the beginning of the process – and perhaps they cannot. In some cases false and even malicious allegations may be made. Should the family be told immediately or, where the matter can be resolved by sensible low-key enquiries, would it be better not to approach them provided that the decision to take no further action is clearly recorded and the case closed? These are dilemmas that cannot be resolved by law alone; good practice and a moral appreciation of the rights of parents as well as children are also required. This may seem imprecise and unsatisfactory but perhaps all that can be said is that the family's position becomes more difficult with every minute that elapses after a referral is received. Full communication should be the rule and exceptions to it should be recorded, with their reasons, in SSD case files.

Summary

This chapter has explored the various, distinctive and intertwined contexts for child protection referrals. There is much uncertainty about what is, or what should be, treated as a valid referral; all within an enquiry and investigation system which works less well when 'facts' are not clear – the most common feature of many referrals!

The various contexts of those who participate in the allegation message process have been explored, whether they be senders, receivers or both. A number of models have been used to illuminate the sources, motives and processing of messages concluding with a discussion of the vital role of SSDs and their frontline staff. Finally, the difficult but crucial question of the position of the family at the beginning of the referral has been considered. It could be said that we always start as we mean to go on. This makes it essential that our understanding of how and why allegations of abuse arise is both wise and efficient.

REFERENCES

Ahmed, B. (1990) *Working Together for Children's Welfare: Partnership and the Children Act 1989*, Conference Report, Michael Sieff Foundation, Surrey.

Brigham, J. (1991) *Social Psychology*, 2nd edn, New York: Harper Collins.

Browne, A. and Finkelhor, D. (1986) 'Initial and long-term effects: a review of the research', in Finkelhor, D. *et al.* (eds) *A Sourcebook on Child Sexual Abuse*, Newbury Park, California: Sage.

Burns, L. (1991) *Partnership with Families: a study of 65 child protection case conferences in Gloucestershire to which the family were invited*, Gloucestershire County Council.

Cooper, D. M. (1993) *Child Abuse Revisited*, Buckingham: Open University Press.

Corby, B. (1993) *Child Abuse: Towards a knowledge base*, Buckingham: Open University Press.

Crittenden, P. (1988) 'Family and dyadic patterns of functioning in maltreating families', in Browne, K., Davies C. and Stratton, P. (eds) *Early Prediction and Prevention of Child Abuse*, Chichester: John Wiley.

Dale, P. and Davies, M. (1986) *Dangerous Families: Assessment and Treatment of Child Abuse*, London: Tavistock.

Department of Health (1991) *Working Together under The Children Act 1989*, London: HMSO.

Dingwall, R., Eekelaar, J. and Murray, T. (1983) *The Protection of Children*, Oxford: Blackwell.

Faller, K. (1988) *Child Sexual Abuse*, Basingstoke: Macmillan.

Farmer, E. (1992) 'The impact of child protection interventions: the experiences of parents and children', in Waterhouse, L. (ed.) *Child Abuse and Child Abusers*, London: Jessica Kingsley.

Fitzherbert, K. (1967) *West Indian Children In London*, London: Bell.

Gadsby Waters, J. (1992) *The Supervision of Child Protection Work*, Avebury.

Garfinkel, H. (1967) *Studies in Ethnomethodology*. Oxford: Basil Blackwell.

Guardian (1993) *Child Abuse: The Harshest Allegation*, 5 October 1993, p. 6.

Gibbons, J. (1990) *Family Support and Prevention*, National Institute for Social Work, London: HMSO.

Gibbons, J. (1993) *Operation of Child Protection Registers*, Summary Report of DoH Project.

Gillham, B. (1994) *The Facts about Child Physical Abuse*, London: Cassell.

Hoggett, B. and Pearl, D. (1991) *The Family, Law and Society*, 3rd. edn, London: Butterworths.

Home Office with Department of Health (1992) *Memorandum of Good Practice on Video Recorded Interviews with Child Witnesses for Criminal Proceedings*, London: HMSO.

Hughes, S. (1993) *Study of Referrals of Child Sexual Abuse (Hereford area)*, Herefordshire County Council.

Hutchison, E. (1993) 'Mandatory reporting laws: child protective case finding gone awry?' *Social Work*, **38**, pp. 56–63.

Jamous, H. and Peloille, B. (1970) 'Professions or self-perpetuating systems? Changes in the French university-hospital system', in Jackson, J. (ed.) *Professions and Socialisation*, Cambridge: Cambridge University Press.

MacDonald, S. (1991) *All Equal Under The Act?* London: Race Equality Unit.

Malucchio, A. N., Fein, E. and Olmstead, K. (1986) *Permanency Planning of Children*, London: Tavistock.

Milner, J. (1993) 'A disappearing act: the differing career paths of fathers and mothers in child protection investigations', *Critical Social Policy*, Issue 39, Autumn 1993.

Part 3 Enquiry in progress

NCB/Barnardos (1991) *Children As Witnesses*, Paper No. 104.

O'Hagan, K. (1989) *Working with Child Sexual Abuse*, Buckingham: Open University Press.

Parton, N. (1991) *Governing The Family*, Basingstoke: Macmillan.

Thorpe, D. (1994) *Evaluating Child Protection*, Buckingham: Open University Press.

Wakefield, H. and Underwager, R. (1988) *Accusations of Child Sexual Abuse*, Springfield, Illinois: C.C. Thomas.

Wattam, C. (1989) 'Investigating child sexual abuse – a question of relevance', in Blagg, H., Hughes, J. and Wattam, C. (eds) *Child Sexual Abuse*, (NSPCC), Harlow: Longmans.

8

Categorising referrals about children: child protection or child welfare?

David Thorpe

Very shortly after completing a study on children in care in a Scottish child welfare agency, the author travelled to Western Australia to direct a study on behalf of the National Committee of Social Welfare Ministers and Administrators. The research was used to design a computerised child protection information system. Both the Scottish and Australian research (Bilson and Thorpe, 1987; Thorpe, 1994) focused on child welfare careers and used data extracted from case records.

One of the last case records to be examined in the Scottish study described a case very similar to one of the first Australian records which was looked at a few weeks later. The Scottish case concerned two female children aged seven and ten years old, living with their single female parent. Their mother had a problem with alcohol. She had bouts of very heavy drinking. The record describes the girls returning home from school late one afternoon to discover that their mother was lying unconscious on the settee with a near-empty bottle of whisky by her side. The girls walked out of the house and went down the road to their maternal grandparents who arranged for the mother's emergency admission to hospital. An application was made to the child welfare agency for the grandparents to become registered formally as foster parents and as a consequence they received foster parent grants and the children were recorded formally as having voluntarily entered care, placed with relatives. Their stay in care lasted several weeks until their mother was discharged from an alcohol treatment facility and returned home. The reason for the children entering care was recorded both statistically and on file as 'parental ill-health'. In the research, the children were placed in a category of cases which came under the heading of 'general misfortune'. Social work

131

activity recorded on the file consisted of child welfare, police and health checks on the grandparents, two interviews with them and a series of interviews, primarily by medical social workers, with the mother as she made rapid progress. After restoration, the case was closed with some follow-up visits. It was seen to be a successful and appropriate use of the agency's statutory obligations and resources.

The Australian Case was very similar. The ages of the children differed slightly from that of the Scottish children. The relatives in this case were an uncle and aunt and the mother's condition was less serious – she had merely fallen asleep in front of the fire after drinking about half a bottle of wine. The children stayed in care, placed with relatives, for only a few days before their mother came home after a brief stay in an alcohol rehabilitation unit. One aspect of the social work service was similar to that of the Scottish case: the approval procedure for relatives as foster parents, the completion of documents (with the mother formalising the admission to care) and the agency payments to the relatives. Other aspects of the service however were utterly and completely different. The reason centred upon the initial categorisation of the case as 'child protection', as the relatives' request for them to be approved as foster parents was interpreted as an allegation of neglect. Instead of one social worker being involved, two went to the house. The referral form, formally commented on and signed by the team manager, simply said 'Neglect investigation' and then named the two social workers assigned to the task. The report of the investigators, after having checked out a wide range of factors – including mother/child relationships, domestic conditions, the reactions of all parties to the investigation and the mother's health and personal history – concluded with the expression 'Neglect substantiated'. The mother was asleep when she should have been awake and available to her children. She was asleep because she had been drinking, therefore she was culpable.

Different versions of these stories now abound in child welfare agency case records right across the developed world, especially the English-speaking part of it. Indeed, in the very recent past a social work student repeated a similar story to the author. In this case the concerns were about a single male parent with an alcohol problem caring for a seven-year-old boy who shortly after the 'investigation' went to live with his mother. There was, however, absolutely no evidence that he had neglected the child – but he did have an alcohol problem. The agency was in England (not Scotland or Australia) and the report of the enquiry formed part of the student's contribution to her practice teacher's placement report.

The recent increase in child protection work

Child protection services in the English-speaking developed world currently are faced with major problems in dealing with allegations of neglect, and physical and sexual assaults on children. The numbers of allegations made and the consequent scale of investigative activity has continued to increase year on year since the late 1960s and early 1970s (Besharov, 1985). Many commentators date these increases from the time when the 'battered baby syndrome' was first brought to professional attention in the early 1960s and when the media brought the problem of physical and sexual assaults on children to the attention of the public in the early 1970s (Parton, 1985). It was not until the 1980s, however, that the implications of these increasing referral rates became a matter for concern. Writing in 1985, Besharov commented that,

> Until the late 1970s it was necessary to continue the expansion of reporting programmes and child protection agencies. Public and professional awareness needed to be increased and greater reporting needed to be encouraged. Now, however, the level of child protective intervention into private family matters has reached unprecedented levels. Moreover much of the present high level of intervention is unwarranted and some is demonstrably harmful to the children and families involved (Besharov, 1985, p. 556).

It is not difficult to understand why a parent's health problem can be reinterpreted as an act of neglect. It depends very much on the training of the intake or duty social worker, the formal guidelines issued by the agency as to how an allegation of 'abuse' or neglect differs from a request for help and, overwhelmingly, upon the ideological orientation of the hidden culture of practice within the agency.

The problem of the broadening definition of 'child abuse'

In the spring of 1994, a 'flyer' was issued by the *International Journal of Child Abuse and Neglect*. In that small leaflet, under the heading of 'aims and scope', are two key sentences.

> Child Abuse and Neglect, *the International Journal, provides an international multidisciplinary forum on all aspects of child abuse and neglect including sexual abuse, with special emphasis on prevention and treatment. The scope extends to all those aspects of life which either favour or hinder optimal family interaction* (ISPCAN, 1994).

If this international body, with its journal and global formal and informal network of professionals, in health, education, child welfare, legal and law-enforcement agencies, is defining 'child protection' concerns so broadly, then the potential for interpreting any enquiry made of a statutory child welfare agency as an allegation of 'abuse' or neglect, is limitless. Again, 'The scope extends to all those aspects of life which either favour or hinder optimal family interaction'. Of necessity, agency guidelines are prescriptive. As has been demonstrated, they allow the individual worker a high level of discretion in the initial categorisation of cases.

One of the consequences of the use of the word 'abuse' to describe the object of child protection's attention is, of course, that many of the investigations triggered by appending that descriptor to cases draw complete blanks. In defining a case in this way, the orientation of the social worker is inevitably forensic. She or he will interpret the primary purpose of the first contact with the client as that of searching for evidence of 'abuse'. Since the term itself 'reflects the transformation of the original concerns [of child protection] to embrace virtually any problem which may have an adverse impact on a child that can possibly be attributed to some act of commission or omission of an adult' (Dingwall, 1989, p. 28), then, superficially at least, it should not prove too difficult to suggest that 'abuse' or neglect exists in every family which is investigated. However, it is ironic that, despite the opportunity presented by the term 'abuse' to increase endlessly the statistics of child 'abuse', in reality approximately 65 per cent of all enquiries fail to confirm or substantiate the original allegation. Besharov (1985) comments that in the USA, 'more than 65 per cent of all reports of suspected maltreatment – involving over 750,000 children per year – turn out to be "unfounded" '. He then goes on to draw attention to the consequence of this and offers some explanation as to why such high 'unfounded' rates exist: 'Of course some degree of over reporting is to be expected, as the law requires the reporting of "suspected" maltreatment. However, the present level of over reporting is unreasonably high and is growing rapidly. There has been a steady increase in the number and percentage of "unfounded" reports since 1976, when approximately only 35 per cent of reports were "unfounded" ' (Besharov, 1985, p. 556). The 'unfounded' rate of 65 per cent in the United States matches research findings in Australia (Thorpe, 1994) and South Wales (Denman and Thorpe, 1993).

All of this suggests that, theoretically at least, it should be possible to reduce the numbers of child protection enquiries, but *with the caveat that this must be achieved without creating a risk that children who have already been harmed, injured or neglected will not receive protection from further harm, injury or neglect in so far as such protection is possible.*

Researchers and commentators in the United States generally prefer tighter legal definitions. As Giovannoni and Beccerra say 'Many assume that since child abuse and neglect are against the law, somewhere there are statutes that make clear distinctions between what is and what is not child abuse and neglect. But this is not the case. Nowhere are there clear-cut definitions of what is encompassed by the terms' (Giovannoni and Beccerra, 1979, p. 2). However, the context in which arguments for tighter legal definitions are made is that of the United States, where all states have mandatory reporting laws which oblige specific groups of professionals (e.g. teachers, doctors, dentists etc.) to report children whom they believe have been 'abused' to state child protection agencies. It is interesting to note that, despite the fact that mandatory reporting laws did not exist in either South Wales or Western Australia, 'unfounded' reports were in the same proportion as those in the United States.

Receiving referrals: professional choices

The stories at the beginning of this chapter suggest that the way in which referrals about the welfare of children are handled at the very first stage of contact with an agency is a crucial defining moment. It crystallises the direction and orientation of the agency and determines the next event, which is the agency's response. That response can either be an enquiry, usually procedurally-determined and involving other agencies and professionals, or it can be one in which the needs of a family are explored. The former activity triggers a forensic gaze, a search for evidence that something has happened or appears likely to happen. The latter activity, very much in contrast to the gathering of evidence (the agency's legal agenda) is driven instead by the client's agenda, which is more negotiable. In many instances, a visit – whether for reasons of child protection or child welfare – may not even be necessary although the conditions under which a 'no visit' decision is made need to be explicit since the worker and agency remain legally accountable for their actions.

Research findings from the United States

In the United States many child welfare agencies have written 'screening' policies to deal with allegations, while others have informal policies. In 1987, a study was made which compared those agencies using written policies with those which had unwritten policies. The researchers reported that 'At least half of both groups (administrators and supervisors) reported screening out reports when the perpetrator is not a caregiver; when no specific act of abuse or neglect was alleged but the parent's behaviour was described as "not good for the child"; and when the problem reported was not appropriate for the CPS (Child Protection Service) and should be referred to another agency. Examples of parental behaviours that led to screening out included addiction to drugs and illegal or immoral behaviour. Truancy was an example of a complaint that would be referred to another agency, in this case the school system' (Downing *et al.*, 1990, p. 363). In this study, however, the researchers were unable to determine how far written or unwritten policies actually affected levels of investigatory activity.

Hutchinson (1989) studied 228 allegations in a child protection agency in the United States. She concluded 'that the typical child maltreatment report is filed by a non-mandated reporter and involves neglect of a school-age child by a single parent. This typical case stands in contrast to the "battered child syndrome" that stimulated current legislation – a supposedly classless phenomenon of a badly beaten child detected by medical professionals' (Hutchinson, 1989, p. 14). While Hutchinson was able to determine some factors which precipitated enquiry decisions (such as the source and nature of allegations) these were not necessarily good predictors of whether or not a case was substantiated. In a large study of 100 county child protection agencies, Wells *et al.* (1989) discovered that 'the primary reasons for screening out reports may be categorised as follows: Characteristics of the perpetrator; the complaint does not describe a specific act of child abuse or neglect; the problem is within the province of another agency; repeated unsubstantiated allegations; there is not enough information to proceed; the family already receives services; the case is not in the jurisdiction of the agency that received the report; or information that invalidates the report is obtained' (Wells *et al.*, 1989, p. 47).

The difficulty with these American studies is that they dealt primarily with agencies whose sole task was to investigate and service only child 'abuse' cases. In Australia and the UK, state and local authority child welfare services have legal responsibility for child protection and child welfare. In other words they do not necessarily have to make a 'no visit' decision. They can choose to deal with a referral as being a welfare *or* a protection matter. The cases described at the beginning of this chapter suggest that there may be three options available in response to allegations: a visit to assess a case for welfare services; a visit to investigate an allegation of 'abuse' or neglect; or a decision not to investigate the allegation. These decisions depend not only on who makes the allegation and what the nature of the allegation is, but also, as will be shown, it will depend on how the allegation event is handled and the way in which the intake or duty social worker interacts with the referring agent. This may be a crucial factor in responding to child welfare referrals.

The picture at local levels – monitoring referrals in an agency

One practical and feasible way of beginning to explore this issue is to look at patterns of referral and the results of enquiries in a department. In reality, this is how the task of creating screening and gatekeeping procedures can begin – by conducting research at a relatively local level. For the purposes of this chapter, a 100 per cent sample of child protection referrals made to one agency will be used to analyse statistically some of the complexities involved. The study made in Western Australia was used in the design of a computerised child protection information system. The main purpose of the system was that it should have the capacity routinely to monitor and evaluate child protection work (which inevitably includes ways of analysing all the issues surrounding allegations and enquiries). 655 case records were used in the Western Australian research to produce a set of data fields and data items which would structure the database for the child protection information system. Five data fields (Area, Allegation, Result of Investigation, Source of Allegation and Context of Allegation) are used to produce tables and charts for this chapter. They have been chosen in order to demonstrate how local agency workers and managers can go about the task of assessing the need for and nature of gatekeeping criteria in child protection, using their own data.

Table 8.1 produces a mean distribution of child protection allegations of 32.75 per area during the four month sampling period, the average percentage distribution being 5 per cent per area of the 655 allegations. Two areas stand out as having below average and above average numbers of referrals. These are area 8 (with only one recorded referral) and area 20 (with 82). In fact, because of a number of factors, including a complete change of staff working in a range of very remote rural locations, it proved impossible to reconstruct the allegations made to area 8 during the retrospective study; no diaries or records existed from which staff could recall whether or not they had decided to categorise a case as child protection or as something else. In complete contrast, area 20 produced twice as many allegations as virtually any other office, a matter which immediately should alert its workers to re-examine their system of categorisation. In this instance it may have been worthwhile having the social workers in area 16 (a geographically adjacent office with similar demographic population characteristics) examine referral

Table 8.1. Area – four month frequency distribution of child protection allegations

Area	Number of allegations	%
1	28	4.3
2	34	5.19
3	23	3.51
4	26	4
5	47	7.17
6	21	3.2
7	42	6.41
8	1	0.15
9	28	4.3
10	31	4.73
11	40	6.1
12	25	3.81
13	30	4.6
14	46	7
15	42	6.41
16	33	5
17	16	2.44
18	23	3.51
19	37	5.65
20	82	12.52
	655	100

Average number of allegations per area = 32.75.
Average percentage of allegations per area = 5 per cent.

categorisation procedures in area 20, and vice versa, in order to compare the averages. A rapid comparison of the two areas produces the information given in Table 8.2.

Table 8.2 confirms that, in this example, high rates of 'child protection case' categorisation leads to low rates of confirmation after an enquiry. It also appears to place a number of cases in the 'at risk' category. These are enquiries in which no evidence of a child being harmed or injured was found,

Table 8.2. Results of enquiries into allegations of 'abuse' or neglect in areas 16 and 20

Area	Allegations	Substantiated (%)	At risk (%)
16	33	14 (42%)	0 (0%)
20	82	23 (28%)	12 (14.6%)

but in which social workers believed that they had identified factors in the situations of families which placed children 'at risk'.

Table 8.3 examines what happened after investigating the different types of allegation for the 655 allegations of 'abuse' and neglect.

Table 8.3. Allegations and results of enquiry

	Allegation type					
	Physical 'abuse'	Emotional 'abuse'	Sexual 'abuse'	Neglect 'abuse'	Unknown 'abuse'	Total
Investigated	147	14	143	309	42	655
Substantiated	48	5	65	88	15	*209
	(32.6%)	(35.6%)	(45.4%)	(28.4%)	(35.7%)	(31.9%)
'At risk'	23	3	15	53	3	109
	(15.6%)	(21.4%)	(10.4%)	(17.1%)	(7.1%)	(16.6%)

* This row only adds up to 209 (i.e. only 31.9%) because 7 cases had a different substantiation from the original allegation.

Table 8.3 shows that, of the 655 allegations, 209 were substantiated (31.9 per cent) and a further 109 (16.6 per cent) were classified as being 'at risk'. In seven enquiries, while social workers were unable to confirm allegations, they found evidence to substantiate other forms of 'abuse', bringing the total of substantiated cases to 216. The highest rate of substantiation was for allegations of sexual assault where nearly half of the enquiries (45.4 per cent) confirmed that an assault had taken place. Allegations of physical assaults were confirmed in just under one third of cases (32.6 per cent) and just over one third of emotional 'abuse' allegations were substantiated (35.7 per cent), although the numbers were small. Neglect allegations appear to be the least likely to result in confirmation (28.4 per cent).

The next question to ask of a local child protection service relates to how the source of allegations affects substantiation rates. Table 8.4 looks at the sources of allegations and the likelihood of substantiation after an enquiry.

Table 8.4 shows that those social workers who interpreted three referrals as allegations from the person believed responsible for 'abuse' or neglect placed them in the 'at risk' category. What in fact these cases reflect are very stressed and confused parents who *believed* they had injured or neglected children, but in reality had not done so. The next three highest sources of 'unfounded' reports are anonymous, friends/neighbours and other (non-parental) relatives. Indeed, these three sources between them accounted for nearly one third of allegations (202 cases, or 30.8 per cent). Of these 202 enquiries,

Table 8.4. Sources of allegations of 'abuse' and neglect and results of enquiries.

Source	No. of allegations	Numbers substantiated	Numbers 'at risk'	Numbers not substantiated	Percentage not substantiated
Person believed responsible	3	0	3	0	100
Anonymous	37	2	2	35	94
Friends/neighbours	100	12	17	88	88
Other relatives	65	16	15	49	75.3
Day care	4	1	2	3	75
Dept officer	35	9	15	26	74.2
Social worker	11	3	2	8	72
Parent/guardian	84	20	5	59	70.2
Non-govt.	19	7	2	12	63
School	88	34	17	54	61
Hospital health centre	50	22	10	28	56
Not stated	13	6	0	7	53
Other	46	22	3	24	52
G.P.	15	8	1	7	46.6
Sibling	7	4	0	3	42.8
Police	55	32	12	23	41.8
Other health professional	11	9	1	1	9
Child	12	9	2	1	8.3
Total	655				

allegations were substantiated in only 30 instances (14.85 per cent). This finding suggests that there may be extensive scope for gatekeeping allegations which are made from these sources. Departmental officers and social workers in other settings also had low substantiation rates. Since these were professionals who could be held accountable through the enquiry process, once again there may be scope for clarification at the point of referral. Parents' and guardians' allegations were confirmed in only 29.8 per cent of cases.

The most reliable sources in Table 8.4 were the child, health professionals (including general practitioners) and siblings, whose referrals were more likely to be confirmed as 'abuse' or neglect than not; while schools, health centres and hospitals were very much in the middle range of reliability. Some of these professional groups also generated substantial numbers of 'at risk' cases. Schools and the police particularly were prominent in that respect.

Figures 8.1, 8.2 and 8.3 show allegation by type, source and result of enquiry. They do not deal with allegations of emotional 'abuse' or those allegations classified as 'unknown', since in the former case there were only 14 such allegations and of course in the latter case allegations could not be defined. The figures are much easier to understand than a three-way cross tabulation. They illustrate what can be made of allegation data at local levels.

Figure 8.1 deals with allegations of physical abuse and shows that the three major sources were schools, non-parental relatives and friends/neighbours. The second two sources, however, did not prove reliable, whilst schools were a significant source of reliable allegations (12 out of the 48 substantiated cases). Even then, however, the rate of substantiation from this source was just over one third (12 out of 31 allegations). Child victims and health professionals proved highly reliable, while the police, siblings, anonymous callers, non-government welfare agencies, persons believed responsible (PBR) and day-care centres were not accurate sources of allegations of physical 'abuse'.

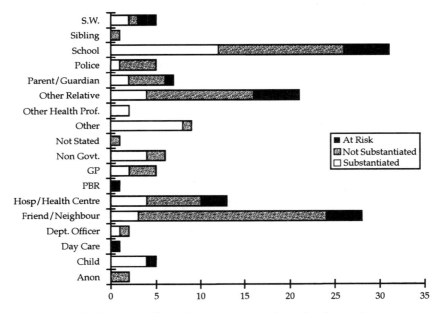

Figure 8.1. Physical 'abuse' allegations, source and result of enquiry

Figure 8.2 looks at allegations of sexual 'abuse'. The largest sources of referrals were parents/guardians, schools and the police. The police were good sources of reliable reports of sexual assaults and schools also were reasonably dependable. Parent/guardian allegations were substantiated in 15 out of 30 cases whereas hospitals and health centres proved reliable in only 5

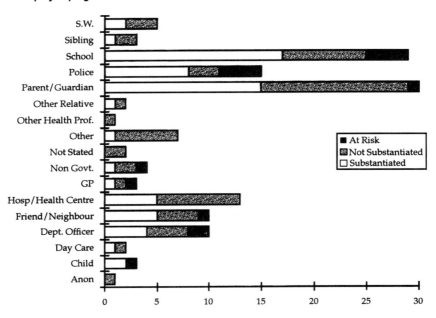

Figure 8.2. Sexual assault allegations, source and result of enquiry

out of 13. In this instance, friends/neighbours score the highest substantiation rate of any allegation category – 5 out of the 10 allegations of sexual 'abuse' from these sources were substantiated after enquiry. In contrast, anonymous callers proved completely unreliable in this allegations category, while other health professionals were totally reliable.

Figure 8.3 illustrates the sources of neglect allegations and the results of enquiries. The major sources of neglect referrals shown in Figure 8.3 were friends/neighbours, non-parental relatives, anonymous callers, parents/guardians and the police. It can be seen that parents/guardians were totally unreliable (they even scored low on 'at risk' categorisations) while in response to allegations of neglect by friends/neighbours, investigations confirmed only 4 out of 59 (a substantiation rate of 6.7 per cent). On the other hand, police, hospital/health centre and GP referrals for neglect tended largely to result in substantiation, as did referrals by siblings. Since the scale of allegations of neglect was so large (309 in total), again Figure 8.3 suggests that a great deal of unnecessary enquiries potentially could be avoided if intake and duty social workers are able to look at initial case categorisations and focus carefully on conversations with callers.

The final issue raised in this chapter relates to the relationship context in which allegations arise. During the research in Western Australia it was

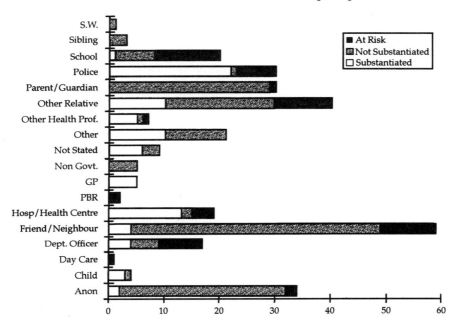

Figure 8.3. Neglect allegations, source and result of enquiry

discovered that many allegations made by non-professionals arose within the context of conflicts between family members (including custody/access disputes). Others came about as a consequence of conflicts between neighbours. Indeed approximately one fifth of allegations occurred where these disputes existed. When the methodology of the Western Australian study was used in a UK local authority, the pattern was very similar (Thorpe, 1994; Denman and Thorpe 1993). Figure 8.4 shows how these contextual patterns relate to the results of enquiries.

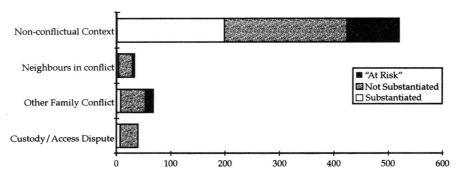

Figure 8.4. Contexts of allegations.

By comparing the results of enquiries which took place in conflictual contexts with those which were non-conflictual, Figure 8.4 shows that conflictual contexts were much more likely to produce a 'not substantiated' outcome for the enquiry than those situations which were conflict free. As Thorpe comments:

> ... *conflict between people who shared legal responsibility for children or came from the same family, or knew each other as neighbours, provided the contexts for approximately a fifth of allegations. Moreover, investigations do not generally substantiate the allegations. It would suggest that in a significant minority of cases official child protection activity has now become one channel whereby these differences of opinion and concerns about the care of children are dealt with and that within the definitional boundaries of these two agencies (one in Western Australia, one in the UK), more often than not they are not matters to be considered as far as child protection is concerned* (Thorpe, 1994, p. 58).

The analysis of a number of issues surrounding child protection referral events in one agency leaves many points to ponder. Firstly, it is clear that area, allegation type, source, results of investigations and contexts can be explored reasonably thoroughly by means of four tables and four charts. This does not involve a lot of work, and it can be replicated easily in any locality which collects child protection data on these five, simple variables. Secondly, the results point to those aspects of the process which lend themselves readily to the introduction of formal or informal gatekeeping procedures, depending on referral source and the nature of the allegations. The important thing is that the production of this information offers a starting point for further analysis and discussion at intake and duty officer levels.

Thirdly, it suggests that in negotiating and constructing cases as 'child protection referrals' an opportunity exists for social workers to exercise discretion in the way in which they conduct telephone conversations. These conversations with relatively unreliable sources could be structured to include the elicitation of information on the following lines:

1. Can the caller identify a specific action or inaction which has caused harm or injury to a child?
2. Does the caller have any 'interest' in the child? (legal, kinship etc.)
3. What action does the caller think the agency ought to take; e.g. the provision of services to help someone look after a child and, if so, what kinds of services; the removal of children; issuing a warning?
4. Does the caller know what will happen when a child protection enquiry gets under way?
5. Is there any action the caller can take (other than making the allegation)?

6. Are there ways in which the caller can continue to be held accountable in some way to the agency for having made the allegation?

This list merely represents a starting point, but it encompasses all the matters raised by the results of research in the United States. The intention however should not be to *discourage* referrals; rather, it should be to give an opportunity to those who make allegations to develop personal or agency responses which do not necessarily trigger a formal child protection enquiry. They may need time to reflect on whether or not an enquiry is required – for example they could be encouraged to make contact with the person or persons about whom they are making allegations in order to get them to seek help. If, in the caller's view, they either cannot make that contact or, after it has been made, there are still concerns then they should come back to the child welfare agency. Ways of involving sources of allegations in the work and making them more accountable have to be devised if child protection allegation rates are to be contained yet exclude, as far as possible, the risk of leaving children who have been seriously harmed, injured or neglected without protection.

Successful gatekeeping in child protection is a realistic possibility; how else can one explain the variations over time, and between localities, which demonstrate different ways of dealing with referrals? (Ways moreover which appear to result in excluding or including cases from investigation). The conversational mechanisms which accomplish the tasks of inclusion or exclusion in child protection have not yet been researched fully; but there exists, as this chapter has shown, a practical way of explaining some of these issues at local level by means of creating four tables and four figures and by reading the text of case records.

REFERENCES

Besharov, D.J. (1985) ' "Doing something" about child abuse: the need to narrow the grounds for state intervention', *Harvard Journal of Law and Public Policy*, 8, 3, pp. 539–589.

Bilson, A. and Thorpe, D. (1987) *Managing Child Care Careers*, Glenrothes: Fife Regional Council Social Work Department.

Denman, G. and Thorpe, D. (1993) *Family Participation and Patterns of Intervention in Child Protection in Gwent: a Research Report*, Lancaster: Lancaster University Department of Applied Social Science.

Dingwall, R. (1989) 'Some problems about predicting child abuse and neglect', in Stephenson, O. (ed.) *Child Abuse and Public Policy and Professional Practice*, London: Harvester Wheatsheaf.

Downing, J.D., Wells, S.J. and Fluke, J. (1990) 'Gatekeeping in child protective services: a survey of screening policies', *Child Welfare*, LXIX, no. 4.

Giovannoni, J.M. and Becerra, R.M. (1979) *Defining Child Abuse*, New York: Free Press.

Hutchinson, E.D. (1989) 'Child protective screening decisions: An analysis of predictive factors', *Social Work Research and Abstracts*, September 1989.

ISPCAN (1994) *Child Abuse and Neglect*, New York: Pergammon.

Parton, N. (1985) *The Politics of Child Abuse*, London: Macmillan.

Thorpe, D.H. (1994) *Evaluating Child Protection*, Milton Keynes: Open University Press.

Wells, S.J., Stein, T.J., Fluke, J. and Downing, J. (1989) 'Screening in child protective services', *Social Work*, **34**, 1, pp. 45–48.

9

Planning an enquiry into allegations of child abuse and neglect

Lyn Burns and Tony Young

This chapter takes as its start point the referral of alleged abuse to the Social Services Department and considers the way in which the enquiry is planned. It begins by examining the development of the concept of planning in child care practice and then considers the issues facing the workers involved in undertaking child abuse enquiries. The context is thus set for an examination of the different stages in planning the enquiry. The primary objective of the enquiry is, of course, to establish whether the child is at risk; however, the way in which the child and the family are involved in the process is a crucial factor in developing a partnership for any further involvement with the statutory agencies which may be necessary.

The context in which enquiries into allegations and concerns about child abuse are made is set out clearly in legislation: the Children Act 1989 and the associated guidance e.g. *Working Together*. In 1992 the *Memorandum of Good Practice* was issued governing the joint interviewing of children by police and social workers. These requirements are incorporated into the Procedures produced by each area child protection committee (ACPC).

The concept of 'planning' and its development in child care practice

The central importance of 'planning' in all good social work practice has gained growing acceptance among professionals and is clearly underpinned by legislation, research and Department of Health Guidance. The key role of planning is perhaps nowhere more obvious than in the process of making detailed arrangements for the future care needs of children who are being looked after by local authorities. Where the local authority believes that it can only secure a child's safety and best interests by recourse to court proceedings, the Children Act 1989 requires the social worker to produce detailed written plans which show that s/he has anticipated the development of the child's needs and has projected future plans to meet them. Plans are scrutinised by the Guardian Ad Litem and the court, and it is unlikely that a care order would be granted unless these plans are sufficiently comprehensive. Whilst previously it was enough, in order to secure a care order, simply to show that the child's needs were not being met sufficiently, the Children Act 1989 now requires local authorities in addition to demonstrate to the court the adequacy of its plans for the child's future.

Thus, although care planning was important before the 1989 Act, the Act made it imperative in proceedings. Beyond that it consolidated the concept as a primary social work tool in relation to all children who are looked after by the local authority – whether as a result of proceedings or as a result of a voluntary agreement with parents. Equally, the requirement on local authorities to promote the welfare of children in need demands clear planning if services are to achieve this end. This is particularly important (see Gormley 1994) given the current imbalance between child protection enquiries (safeguarding activities) and prevention and family support (promotional activities).

Planning, crisis-management and initial enquiries

On the surface, planning as a concept might seem to be at odds with the dynamics of crisis-management. Planning, after all, involves carefully considered assessments, deliberation and exploring options and is oriented around fine-tuning; by contrast, crisis-management is characterised by the need to respond quickly on the basis of at best partial information and is oriented around the need to expedite solutions.

On closer examination, however, it is clear that the concept of planning is equally critical to effective crisis management in general and to initial enquiries into allegations of child abuse – commonly regarded as the archetype of 'crises' – in particular. Indeed, crisis management must visualise alternative patterns of events and plan for contingencies accordingly. Effective initial investigation demands of professionals a highly developed skill which combines the imperatives of planning and of crisis-management; the concept needs to be developed in both the literature and in practice.

Statistics show that three out of four child protection enquiries result in no further action, which leads to the view that too many families are being investigated (Noyes, cited in Sedgwick, 1994). Even when children are in the system there is no guarantee that it will ensure their safety; Farmer and Owen (1995) found that 30 per cent of children in her study were not protected by the registration and child protection planning system, and this led her to propose that the same 'broad brush' approach may not work in all cases.

In the context of such findings, and in view of the national debate about the balance of child protection versus children in need, it is even more important that child protection enquiries are conducted properly. From the family's point of view, effective planning will ensure that an initial enquiry is conducted professionally, fairly, and with due regard to the rights of the individuals involved. A number of research studies confirm the importance of involving the family at the earliest possible stage. In Gloucestershire, for example, it was found that families who had not been involved in the initial stages of an enquiry and initial child protection conference had a 'them and us' view throughout the process, whereas those parents who had been involved understood the process; and they felt involved even when they did not agree with the outcome (Burns, 1991). Most children continue to live with their family even where the enquiries confirm a basis for concern (Burns, 1991; Shemmings and Thoburn, 1990). This being so, it is important that the process does not damage the working relationship between the parents and the professionals. Effective planning is therefore an essential conceptual tool for maximising parental involvement and minimising likely obstacles to future partnership.

The debate about the stage of an enquiry at which the parent/s should be informed was highlighted by the Cleveland Enquiry (DoH, 1988) – although the recommendations of the Report did not reduce the tension of the debate. However, the publication of the Report marked the beginning of an increased awareness of the role of parents and the need to involve them in the process. Discussion focused on the involvement of parents in child protection conferences, and it was noted that the Social Services Departments which already involved families in other work within the Department (e.g. planning for children in care) had an ethos which facilitated the involvement of parents in conferences. The subsequent work undertaken by many ACPCs in advance of the implementation of the Children Act 1989 enabled problems to be aired and strategies devised to overcome them. For example, many professionals were concerned that they would not be able to say all they wanted in a conference if the parents were present (NSPCC, 1990). However, as McGloin and Turnbull pointed out in one of the early studies of parents attending review conferences, when parents perceive that the professionals are being honest and open then trust can be built. Likewise where parents perceived that they had been involved in the decision making they were more likely to be committed to the subsequent plans (McGloin and Turnbull, 1986). Given the issues at stake, we would argue that professionals who have concerns *should* be prepared at all times to communicate these directly to parents because it is in both the short and long term interests of children and their families.

Therefore planning is pivotal to effective and ethical child protection enquiries. We have identified five elements which are common to all child protection enquiries and planning is critical to each: 'evidence' and the rights of parents; the risk of abusive enquiries; working together – co-ordination and partnership; focusing on the child; and transparency.

'Evidence' and the rights of parents

The rights of parents to control and care for their child as they see fit can only be circumscribed when a local authority has evidence that their behaviour may be exposing the child to 'risk of significant harm', as defined by the 1989 Children Act. When such evidence is available, the local authority can only intervene to limit those rights in direct proportion to the degree of risk identified. The professionals involved need to be conscious that parents have rights at each stage of decision making in the course of the enquiry, and that parents have the right to be consulted and to have their permission sought. This is of course complicated, either when one or other parent is identified or suspected of the abuse and of a crime, or when it is suspected that both may be involved. Again, professionals must rely on evidence to support any decision to impinge on parental rights.

The process must protect inherent parental rights and do so without allowing a parent to conceal any part which they may have had in the abuse. Achieving this, however, is far from easy. Cleaver and Freeman (1995) for example, found that a suspicion of child abuse affects profoundly the family's perception of themselves, and this in turn can influence their preparedness to work in partnership with the professionals. In an intensive study of 61 children from 30 families, referred to a local authority because of concerns about child abuse, they found that parents felt 'guilty until proved innocent'. It is commonly the case that, unlike the criminal law, where the assumption is 'innocent until proven guilty', the conduct of initial enquiries of child abuse allegations must presume neither guilt nor innocence. This is an important distinction. The enquiry should seek equally information which either confirms or refutes the allegation and this neutrality inherent in the nature of an enquiry must be conveyed clearly to families at all times throughout the process. When we consider that children are very often unable to convey their own views, because of age, disability and/or their dependent position, the importance of this is reinforced. Corby (1987) and Burns (1991) both found that at least 70 per cent of children who are the subject of case conferences are under the age of nine. Whilst parents may be able to account for an event quite plausibly, the investigating social worker cannot always rely on a child's agreement with such an explanation. The worker should take no explanation at face value but, rather, should adopt an open position in relation to any account. No judgement can be made until the process is concluded and all the information is considered.

The complex balance of rights, as between parents and children or between one parent and the other, clearly is subject to shifts as information unfolds in the course of an enquiry and will have a direct impact on the management of the process. There will be, for instance, implications for the timing of initial enquiries and the order in which each parent should be informed that the enquiry is taking place. Thus, because in these circumstances parents have the right to refuse to give the local authority an opportunity to speak to the child about an allegation, the social worker will need to decide whether it is advisable to seek their permission when the child is at home with the parent or, say, at school. For example, parental refusal during the child's school hours gives the local authority time to take measures to protect the child from parental contact prior to interviewing the child; this may be important, both to protect the child and to prevent a parent from interfering in the child's evidence. By contrast a decision to seek parental permission when the child is at home with the parent may meet with refusal and consideration will again need to be given to protecting both child and evidence, perhaps in the face of angry and aggressive parents. In these circumstances, there will be less scope for real partnership with parents. This does not preclude partnership, but in order to keep open the possibility of partnership it is important to remember the need to explain the reasons for decisions. In any event the need is obvious to plan the sequence and to anticipate responses to foreseeable developments.

The impact of parental rights and of the legal context on the conduct of enquiries cannot be underestimated. The detailed process of an enquiry needs to be *planned* scrupulously in order to minimise the potential conflict between the rights of parents and the interests of children without infringing the former or failing to protect the latter. This in turn will facilitate provision of information to support decisions for action should it be necessary further on in the enquiry process. Burns (1991) found that parents who understood the reason for a decision about their child could accept it even if they did not agree with it.

The risk of abusive enquiries

If the Cleveland Enquiry emphasised the importance of observing and protecting parental rights, it demonstrated even more clearly the potential which the process of making enquiries has for inflicting significant harm on children and on their families.

Just as the sequence of a planned enquiry will have identified the stages at which various powers may have to be invoked, so the plan will need to incorporate ascending threshold criteria for deciding the level of intrusion in the child's life. For instance, an allegation or even substantial prima facie evidence of child sexual abuse cannot of itself justify vaginal or anal examination. It is not uncommon to hear it suggested, when the only clear evidence of abuse is verbal, that a medical examination is necessary for the purposes of corroboration even when it is unlikely that the evidence would identify an abuser. This is highly debatable. It is important that, in the course of planning, those responsible for conducting the enquiry have identified clearly the threshold criteria for seeking a medical, which will of course depend on individual circumstances.

Only effective planning can ensure that the tendency towards 'cascading' (from initial information gathering through to the identification of prima facie evidence, to video interviewing and beyond to medical examination) is checked at every stage. There is little doubt that each stage potentially is more abusive to the child than the previous one. Planning guards against the inherently abusive nature of this process. It ensures that if the information collected at any point suggests that the allegation is not substantiated, then the enquiry can be halted. Effective planning will minimise the risk of 'system abuse' (Amphlett, 1992).

Working together – co-ordination and partnership

The need for planning is self-evident when we look at the range of individuals and activities potentially involved in the conduct of an enquiry. Only a well co-ordinated plan can manage such complexity. In addition to the social worker, an enquiry can involve the police, health visitor, family doctor, paediatrician, solicitors, siblings and extended family, school teachers, translators and various other specialists. Planning is essential to determine quite simply who is going to do what, when, where and how, and to identify the stages at which information is pooled and reviewed, and when decisions are made. A lack of professional co-ordination has been found to be destructive and confusing to families (Marneffe *et al.*, 1985). Whilst it is certainly the case that the introduction of the *Memorandum of Good Practice* when fully implemented, has enhanced the joint working practices of the police and social workers, the role of the other professionals already involved with a family, or needing to be involved because of the nature of the allegation, must also be considered. A number of studies point to the importance of co-ordination, particularly in allegations of sexual abuse where repeated interviews and/or medicals can be perceived as being traumatic in themselves (Glaser and Frosh, 1988). The need to achieve effective co-ordination and communication throughout the process is set out clearly in *Working Together* (DoH, 1991). In addition it is always important to remember that, even in the midst of a distressing enquiry, partnership with parents is still possible and the process needs to take account of the future relationship between parents and agencies. Even in the face of parental opposition to an enquiry, it is vital to identify, jointly and clearly, those areas where we can work in agreement and those where we differ. If planning fails to take account of this potential, the opportunity for avoiding conflict may be lost and any consequent parental opposition may, in turn, compel a greater level of intervention than the identified abuse would have justified. In short, if we are to avoid resorting to interventions simply in order to deal with secondary issues of parental anger and antagonism, it will be important at the planning stage for professionals to agree an 'attitude' which strives to take parents with them wherever possible.

It has to be acknowledged from the outset that the enquiry can itself cause such feelings (Cleaver and Freeman, 1995). Whilst for the professionals involved child protection is an everyday occurrence, for the family, who are at the centre of an enquiry, it is not; it may even be their first contact with professionals in this context. Thus it is not surprising that many parents feel powerless when confronted with an initial allegation. Quite simply, first impressions are extremely powerful in shaping the relationships between parents and professionals (Brown, 1984). A wholly negative first experience for parents will entrench initial antagonism. Equally, even where parents believe themselves to be wrongly 'accused', they may recognise the legitimate role of the professionals if they see that the process has been managed properly, with due regard paid to their rights and the nature of their relationships within the family. Those parents who have had previous experiences of the child protection system will bring these experiences to a new enquiry – positive or negative – and this will clearly affect the ability of family and professionals to work together (Burns, 1991). Cleaver and Freeman (1995) concluded that professionals should pay attention to the views of parents because they are changeable and responsive to skilful negotiation. When the way in which the event is seen by the parents and the professionals corresponds closely, then the child is more likely to be protected against further abuse.

Focusing on the child

In the course of conducting an initial enquiry it is all too easy to focus on the nature of the alleged abuse and to become concerned with managing the complexity of the process or with the longer term implications of various outcomes. Moreover, because of its complexity and the potential for autonomous activity among those involved, the process can take on a life of its own, appearing to drive events and decision making rather than being driven by the needs of the child.

The social worker's proper concern for the child can obscure his or her awareness of the requirements of the process and of procedures. Equally, the danger for the supervisor and for those managing the enquiry lies in the possibility, inherent in their role, of becoming too concerned with 'process' at the expense of recognising the child's needs as they develop in the course of the enquiry. This is similar to the cascade effect, in the sense that it is possible to become trapped into following a procedure simply because it is in existence. Experienced social workers will readily prompt their manager if they believe this to be happening but since not every social worker is sufficiently experienced or confident, and the manager is to all intents and purposes in control, this offers no safeguard against being overzealous. In addition, managers are under pressure particularly to demonstrate adherence to procedures because of their responsibility for the success or otherwise of the enquiry. It is important therefore that the plan provides explicit safeguards and ensures that the enquiry maintains its focus on the needs of the child.

Thus the plan needs to incorporate structured and regular intervals at which the enquiry is refocused on the needs of the child. Whilst we would not embrace the *Memorandum of Good Practice* in its entirety, its approach to planning clearly identifies such stages at which the question of terminating the enquiry in the interests of the child should be considered and this model is to be commended.

Child-centred enquiries mean determining in advance questions such as: Who might be the best person to interview the child? Which venue or environment will put the child at ease for the conduct of the interview? Whether or not s/he will need the presence of a relative? What kinds of cues might suggest to the interviewer that the child is under stress because of the interview? Is there a need for play or similar materials and for approaches which 'speak' to the child at their level and age of understanding? And so on. These are only some of the many questions which must be addressed in detail and in advance, in the course of planning an initial enquiry.

Transparency

The Memorandum also offers useful first principles in relation to transparency. By transparency we mean simply the need for professionals to be able to justify to themselves and others, both at the time and later, why they took certain decisions at each stage. This will include writing down the main issues for investigation and recording key information, and their reasoning, as they exist as helpful tools for professionals at the time and may provide essential information and/or evidence at a later stage.

The pre-enquiry planning meeting is the crucial vehicle for exploring the above issues and sets in train a disciplined approach to recording both the planning itself and any subsequent action in such a way that the process is clear to everyone. Good planning conveys clarity, but at the same time is dependent upon it.

Planning the enquiry in practice

Having considered the issues involved in the planning of the enquiry, we now move on to look in detail at the practicalities. The over-riding theme is that good practice involves up to seven stages in an enquiry, each of which needs careful planning.

We believe that those undertaking child protection work should be qualified and experienced child care social workers who have undertaken training in child protection.

Clarity about the purpose of enquiry

It may appear to be obvious that the purpose is always to establish whether a child is at risk of abuse, or has been abused, and if so, what is the likelihood of further abuse. There is wide acknowledgement that there are many influences which potentially can impede the ability of those involved to keep this objective at the centre of their concern. Workers and managers have to remain alive to these dangers; indeed this is precisely why the process demands a highly developed level of skill and professionalism. In order to keep these dangers in check, throughout the enquiry the worker and the manager must:

- ensure that the *child* remains the focus of the enquiry;
- check value judgements by professionals;
- be aware of the dangers of tunnel vision in professionals;

- ensure that workers do not view suspected abuse through the norms and values of their own background and that differences in understanding which derive from cultural difference do not distort professional perceptions.

Preliminaries

At the point of referral the child protection register and the internal records should be consulted to check whether the child/family/alleged abuser is already known. If there is a social worker involved already the referral should be discussed with him or her (and/or his or her manager). Where the referral concerns a situation in which the independence of the Social Services Department could be said to be compromised (e.g. where the allegation concerns a member of the department's staff) consideration should be given to asking the NSPCC or another area office to undertake the enquiry.

Validation of referral

The aim of this stage is to consider whether it is possible that the allegation is true or whether there are alternative explanations for the incident or cause for concern. Those with responsibility for child protection work must be fully conversant with the requirements of the Children Act 1989, which defines the basis for an enquiry as:

> Where a local authority . . . have reasonable cause to suspect that a child who lives, or is found, in their area is suffering, or is likely to suffer, significant harm, the authority shall make or cause to be made such enquiries as they consider necessary to enable them to decide whether they should take any action to safeguard or promote the child's welfare (Section 47, 1, 6).

The validation stage is therefore a critical part of the process; without it a referral of concern could lead to an unlawful enquiry (Thorpe, personal communication).

The information gathered in the course of initial validation will form the prima facie evidence which justifies a fuller enquiry. It is essential to the planning of the next stage. There are three steps:

1. To talk with the referrer in more detail, ensuring that the information obtained is factual or based on substantiated opinion, and not speculative. Is it possible, for example, that the referrer is either deliberately or unwittingly making assumptions about a family because of differences in lifestyle or attitudes to bringing up children?

It is important to establish whether the referrer has talked to the parent(s) about the concern, and if so, what was the outcome of this.

2. To look at what information is known already about those involved. The accuracy of this should be checked, where possible, so that relevant facts can inform the enquiry.

3. To see if there is a less intrusive means of checking out the allegation, e.g. is the health visitor already planning a visit to a baby referred for crying for long periods? Is a child anonymously reported to have bruises due for a PE lesson today?

It is only at this point, therefore, that the need for a full enquiry can be considered properly. A generalised concern should never, on its own, give rise to an enquiry. If the outcome of these three stages suggests that there is a reasonable cause for concern, an enquiry should be undertaken. If there appears to be no cause for concern the manager should consider whether any further action is appropriate, for example, by informing the parents that an allegation was received and then offering a service to address any difficulties identified during the enquiries.

Planning the interview

If at the end of the validation stage there is a need for an enquiry, the first and most important consideration is whether the available information suggests that immediate action is necessary to protect the child. If it does it may be appropriate to involve the police, either to accompany workers or to be on standby. Except when a child is in immediate physical danger, it is essential that the timing of a removal from his/her home be agreed after consultation with the relevant professionals. The likely effect of the stress of the enquiry and the timing and manner of a removal from home should not be overlooked when attempting to gauge the immediate safety of a child.

Once the child's safety is assured the planning of the interview commences and this can be conducted in a structured way by means of a 'planning meeting'. This could be as little as a meeting between the social worker and his/her manager, or a highly formalised meeting between a number of professionals, depending on the complexity of the situation. In any event, the conduct of enquiries cannot be planned 'on the hoof' and we would suggest that at this point a structured meeting takes place which reviews the evidence, agrees ground-rules and identifies stages for undertaking the enquiry. The key decisions taken at this stage should be recorded. It is important to ensure that the planning meeting remains a tool for planning the enquiry and does not become a pre-case conference in which conclusions are reached.

The meeting should undertake the following:

- Use the available relevant factual information to provide background detail and to set a context to the cause for concern.

- If the allegation is of child sexual abuse or involves a serious physical allegation, then involve the police.

- Plan who will explain to the child and family what is happening and why; who will be involved and the reason; what may be the possible outcomes of the enquiry; and when (and where) the discussions will take place. The way in which the family are involved at the beginning of the process sets the scene for the future: most children who are the subject of child protection referrals live with their family and continue to do so. It is important to give family members information leaflets which outline the local procedures and practice, and which describe the legal aspects of the child protection system and provide details of the complaints procedure (PAIN, 1991; NSPCC/Family Rights Group 1992).

- Consider the issues of first language, culture, gender, disability and class and the way in which these may affect the enquiry. Take into account the child's developmental age and level of understanding when planning the interview. When interpreters are used, ideally they should have undertaken training in the child protection process.

- Decide on the order of interviews. For example should the parent/s be seen before or after the child?

- When the workers are of different cultural backgrounds from the child or family, ensure that advice is available from people with a knowledge of the background, traditions and beliefs of the culture of family members (bearing in mind issues of confidentiality).

- Take account of the issues arising from the different roles of the social services (primarily, the welfare of the child) and the police (primarily, to secure evidence for criminal proceedings).

- Consider how to ensure that a joint enquiry is conducted with the welfare of the child paramount, e.g. it need not be a police officer who takes the lead role when interviewing.

- Ensure that arrangements are made for interpreters.

- Ensure that family members are aware that they can seek independent advice about the enquiry. An indication of what advice should be obtained and likely sources should be given. For example, it is important to suggest choosing a solicitor who is a member of the child care panel.

- Depending on the nature of the allegation, consider whether more than one worker should be involved. In a child sexual abuse enquiry, the worker who collects the child or carer for interview could be the one who offers the supporting role.

The information gathered so far may raise the question of whether or not a medical examination is necessary – either for the purposes of evidence or for treatment. Even if the main reason for seeking a medical is evidential, forensic accuracy is not the only consideration. Remembering that the focus is always on the child, the need for sensitivity, choice of personnel and venue will be very significant. Similarly, the most ethical approach will consider the least intrusive means of gathering medical information, e.g. monitoring by a health visitor, school nurse. Or it might be that a regular medical appointment is due, which could provide information or an opportunity to obtain an opinion on the cause for concern. The plan should clarify how much say in this the child should have and ensure that the range of options allows for preferences in respect of gender and culture. It is also important to consider ways of ensuring that the child is not subjected to repeated medicals; this is especially important with allegations of sexual abuse. Whilst it is important for parents to be able to seek their own medical opinion, this should be in the child's best interests and not be abusive to the child. It is possible to conclude that a medical examination should not proceed even if a qualified medical practitioner suggests that it should. For example, a child who has alleged that a parent has sexually abused him/her should not undergo a second medical examination to assist the parent's defence in a criminal proceeding. It may have been more appropriate for an independent second medical opinion on behalf of the parent to have been obtained by another doctor's involvement in the initial examination. If a medical is appropriate then the question of who gives consent must be considered (taking into account the wishes and feelings of the child). This being so, it is important that the worker seeks agreement from the parent about who makes the examination.

Reviewing the progress of the enquiries

Once the outcome of the initial interview is known it should be considered alongside the existing information. A further planning meeting may then be needed, dependent on the outcome of the previous stage. Whilst it will have been appropriate to have working hypotheses about the outcome (so that resource implications can be explored) this is the point at which the work so far is reviewed and further plans made when needed – it is necessary simply to pause and consider original hypotheses again, in the light of the interview. Again the focus of the planning is the welfare of the child. The following should be considered:

- If access to the child has been frustrated, consider possible reasons for this which may include: Does the parent or carer understand why it is important that the child is seen, and how it may be to their benefit? Are there alternative means of checking the referral which might be more acceptable to the parents and still allow the best interests of the child to be met (for example, a later appointment with child's preferred GP)? It is important to explain (in a non-threatening way) that there may be a possibility of court action if parents refuse access.

- Has the child received clear information about the enquiry in an understandable way? Again, workers need to take into account the age and level of understanding of the child and provide as many opportunities as possible for questions. It may be appropriate to consider other forms of communication (for example, using play or stories). The child's actual (as opposed to anticipated) performance in the interview may provide pointers here.

- Has the child been given the opportunity to speak freely? Was an accompanying adult acceptable to the child (rather than it being someone else's idea)? Did the interview highlight possible areas of conflict (for example, if the child divulged a family secret)?

- Has the worker ensured that family members are clear about the cause for concern. It is very easy for families to become caught on a 'merry-go-round' controlled by professionals who assume that the family know what is happening. Workers will need to remember that this is a time of stress for the family – even if they accept responsibility for an incident – so they will probably not absorb all that is said to them. Try and ensure that positive feedback is given. e.g. their level of co-operation with the enquiries. (This is discussed further in Chapter 10 on the use of recorded agreements in enquiries.)

What further action should be taken?

This is the point to consider 'what next?' In doing so all the available information should be reviewed and discussed with a senior or manager. The key question is whether, having considered all of the information, the allegation is substantiated. If so, a professional assessment is made about the likely future risk to the child who is the subject of the allegation, and to any other children in the household. There are then two avenues to follow: securing the future safety of the child and obtaining further evidence of abuse so that planning can begin to reduce future risk.

If on balance it appears that the child's safety cannot be assured by remaining in the current situation, then other options need to be considered. Removing a child into a local authority placement with people who are strangers should be the option of last resort only (Children Act 1989; Ryan 1994). It is appropriate to discuss with family members or carers the reason if there needs to be a change, in order to gain their co-operation as well as to seek their ideas. For example, is there a relative or friend who could come and stay in the household or have the child to stay? Is it possible for the person allegedly posing the risk to leave for a while? The Social Services Department is empowered to assist with the costs (Children Act 1989, Schedule 2, section 5). The worker should provide a clear timescale for family members in these circumstances, since such measures will have implications elsewhere (for example, in respect of the other responsibilities of a relative). The parents should also be made aware of the implications for them of their chosen actions in the next stages of the process. This is important because at this point in the process the parents may not perceive themselves as being part of a voluntary partnership.

When an application for an order is necessary, it is important to check again that all possible options for a voluntary partnership have been explored. At this stage the worker also should ensure that family members continue to be aware of their right for independent legal advice as well as their right to seek a second medical opinion.

Following initial enquiries

Once the safety of the child has been secured, planning still continues in order to pave the way for the next stage of the child protection process: risk assessment and the child protection conference. Even though the family may not be in agreement with professionals, we discussed earlier the importance of enabling them to participate in the process designed to protect their child by ensuring that they understand fully the reasons for any decisions made by the local authority. A further opportunity exists at this point if the worker informs the family of their rights and encourages them to seek an independent legal opinion.

Information should be given about timescales concerning the child protection conference, the process of a comprehensive risk assessment, and ways in which the family can participate as well as the complaints procedure. As much detail as possible should be offered in writing.

If an allegation is unsubstantiated we believe that it is equally important to record fully the enquiry and provide a written copy for the family. In these circumstances, however, families often request that such records be destroyed and are unhappy when the agency's policy is that such records remain on file. From the family's point of view there is an understandable fear that the very existence of a record will leave a question mark over them. However, the advantage to the family of retaining an accurate written record is that, should a future allegation be made, reference can be made to it by those making the enquiries, whereas simply knowing that a previous enquiry took place could prejudice a new one. Nevertheless we would suggest that agencies should respect the family's wish to have all copies of such records destroyed (when appropriate) provided that they are made fully aware of the dangers to them of so doing. The exception would be if there are other reasons that the local authority should keep the records for a period of time (and if this is the case the reasons should be explained to all concerned).

Conclusion

This chapter has examined the complexity of the relationship between the ethical, legal and practical considerations involved in conducting initial child abuse enquiries. We have argued that this complexity can only be managed effectively by careful planning. We have identified seven stages in a child protection enquiry and have discussed the need for careful planning throughout. We agree with the need to keep the nature of the child protection system under critical scrutiny. Consequently, our concern has been to emphasise the role of a consciously planned approach in minimising and checking the inherent tendency of the system to inflict damage on families. Planning offers no guarantee of this but a failure to plan is almost certain to increase the risk of a cascade of mistakes. We conclude, therefore, that it is only by means of good planning that the overriding objective will be achieved of keeping families together while minimising the risk to children.

BIBLIOGRAPHY

Amphlett, S. (1992) 'System abuse and gatekeeping', in *Partnership in Child Protection* Office for Public Management/NISW.

Brown. C. (1984) *Child Abuse Parents Speaking: Parents' Impressions of Social Workers and the Social Work Process*, School for Advanced Urban Studies, University of Bristol.

Burns, L. M. (1991) *Partnership with Families: a Study of 65 Case Conferences in Gloucestershire to Which the Family were Invited*, Gloucestershire Social Services Department.

Cleaver, H. and Freeman, P. (1995) *Parental Perspectives in Child Protection*, London: HMSO.

Corby, B. (1987) *Working with Child Abuse*, Milton Keynes: Open University.

Department of Health (1988) *Report of the Inquiry into Child Abuse in Cleveland 1987*, London: HMSO.

Department of Health (1989) *The Care of Children: Principles and Practice in Regulations and Guidance*, London: HMSO.

Department of Health (1991) *Child Abuse: a Study of Inquiry Reports 1980–1989*, London: HMSO.

Department of Health (1991) *Working Together and the Children Act 1989*, London: HMSO.

Department of Health (1992) *Memorandum of Good Practice*, London: HMSO.

Evans, M. and Miller, C. (1992) *Partnership in Child Protection: The Strategic Management Response*, Office for Public Management/NISW.

Farmer, E. and Owen, M. (1995) *Child Protection Practice: Private Risks and Public Remedies*, London: HMSO.

Gibbons, J. (1993) *Operation of Child Protection Registers*, Department of Health.

Glaser, D. and Frosh, S. (1988) *Child Sexual Abuse*, London: MacMillan.

Gormley, C. (ed.) (1994) *Section 47 Investigations: Tensions in Safeguarding and Promoting the Welfare of Children in Need*, Social Information Systems.

Hallet, C. and Birchall, E. (1992) *Co-ordination and Child Protection*, London: HMSO.

Marneffe, C. (1985) 'Can the action of the social worker lead to child abuse?' *Child Abuse and Neglect*, 9, 3, pp. 353–7.

McGloin, P. and Turnbull, A. (1986) *Parent Participation in Child Abuse Review Conferences*, London Borough of Greenwich.

NISW (Leeds) (1990) *Report on the Issues for Front Line Managers in Managing Child Protection Services*.

NSPCC (1990) *Child and Parental Participation in Case Conferences*, Occasional Paper 8.

NSPCC/Family Rights Group (1992) *Child Protection Procedures: What They Mean for Your Family*.

Parents Against INjustice (1991) (reprint 1994) *Working in Partnership: Coping with an Investigation of Alleged Child Abuse or Neglect*.

Ryan, M. (1994) *The Children Act 1989: Putting It Into Practice*, Family Rights Group.

Sedgwick, A. (1994) 'Towards differentiating levels of assessment in child protection cases', in Gormley, C. (ed.) *Section 47 Investigations: Tensions in Safeguarding and Promoting the Welfare of Children in Need*, Social Information Systems.

Shemmings, D. and Thoburn, J. (1990) *Parental Participation in Child Protection Conferences*, report of a pilot project in Hackney Social Services Department, University of East Anglia.

Thorpe, D. (1994) personal communication to the authors.

10

The potential for recorded agreements

Dendy Platt and Terry Burns

Introduction

Under current practice you may well have to sign more documentation to put your car through its M.O.T. than if your child were to become subject to a child protection enquiry which could change the lives of the whole family. The purpose of this chapter is to put recorded agreements for enquiries (section 47, Children Act 1989) into alleged abuse and neglect firmly on the practice agenda.

A recorded agreement (sometimes known as a written agreement) is a document which, within certain limits, is agreed between the child, the parent(s) and the agencies involved in making the enquiry. It covers the main details of how the enquiry is to be conducted. Agreements have been used by social workers in a number of areas of child care practice, but their application to enquiries into child abuse allegations is a controversial development which has not yet been explored adequately. This chapter examines the development of recorded agreements in social work. It reviews the reasons for using agreements in the context of section 47 enquiries, the dilemmas of doing so, and current approaches to good practice. Finally, it will set out some of the issues which should be included in an agreement of this kind.

The developing use of recorded agreements

Recorded agreements have their historical and theoretical origins in a behavioural approach to social work where 'contracts' are commonly used as the basis for some therapeutic interventions (Sheldon, 1980, 1982). The approach gained particular prominence during the late 1970s. It was the

1980s, however, which saw agreements taking on more significance in terms of the service aspects of social work. This led to what Sheldon described as a 'service contract', which is:

> ... *drawn up between social workers and their clients for the purpose of giving greater definition and sense of direction to working relationships. Service contracts are useful as a means of specifying and allocating agreed tasks to the different parties concerned, and act also as a continual reminder of the agreed goals and purposes of intervention* (Sheldon, 1980).

Some of the first areas of application were related to fostering (Thomas, 1989), and the admission of children into local authority accommodation or care. Tunstill (1989) described the potential for written agreements to help address key difficulties identified by research, especially the way in which child care decisions are made, what happens after an admission to care and the relationships between social workers and natural parents. Other applications included child protection plans and comprehensive family assessments (Platt and Edwards, forthcoming).

An important factor behind these developments was the desire of professionals to work in partnership with families and to promote an empowerment model of practice. For families and advocacy workers recorded agreements are a means of enabling families' opinions to be heard, their rights respected, and for defining more clearly the tasks of statutory agencies (Atherton and Dowling, 1989). The use of recorded agreements:

> ... *has evolved from a dual concern about the inequality and powerlessness experienced by service users in relation to professionals, and about the effectiveness of social work intervention* (Braye and Preston-Shoot, 1992).

A requirement to use recorded agreements is now contained in the guidance accompanying the Children Act 1989. Model forms, developed by the Family Rights Group and the National Foster Care Association, have become part of routine practice in many areas. However, the requirement is limited to aspects of residential care; family placement (DoH, 1991b); and the child protection plan (Home Office, 1991). Their use also is encouraged, but not required, in other situations (e.g. DoH, 1991a, para. 2.10). The enquiry into alleged child abuse, however, is an area where the use of recorded agreements is in its infancy.

Why use recorded agreements when child abuse or neglect is alleged?

The recorded agreement is potentially a powerful tool enabling the planning of an enquiry (as described earlier in Chapter 9) to be opened up to a partnership approach. As is proposed throughout this book, better working relationships can be achieved with children and families if they are involved and consulted properly. The still too familiar tendency to inform parents that an enquiry is being carried out, and then leave them in temporary limbo while this is being done, is likely to alienate the whole family and create an uncertainty that cannot be justified. As noted elsewhere in this book, of those cases which go on to a child protection conference, only a very small proportion of parents will be prosecuted, or the children removed. It is clearly in the interests of the local authority to ensure that sound working relationships are established with parents and children from the beginning. The recorded agreement offers an opportunity to do so.

Recent research has confirmed the start of an enquiry as a crisis-point for parents and children (Farmer 1993; Sharland *et al.*, 1995; Farmer and Owen, 1995; Cleaver and Freeman, 1995). In a significant number of cases, this crisis is exacerbated by the way the enquiry is conducted. For example:

> *In cases of sexual abuse mothers quite often discovered that their child had already been interviewed and they had been neither informed nor involved* (Farmer, 1993).

This type of feeling was in no way confined to parents:

> *Both parents and children spoke of feeling swept along by the investigation without being consulted or, in some cases, informed about what would happen next ... One child described how, after she had told her tutor at school about her sexual abuse, no-one explained what would follow. She was taken to the police station and found herself 'going down a corridor and not knowing what was going to happen next'* (Farmer, 1993).

Enquiries are most likely to begin in an atmosphere of understandable hostility or resentment on the part of the parents. The relationship is forced upon them, it is coercive, and its legalistic nature means that things happen which not only are out of their control but also are often outside the control of the worker. Using recorded agreements gives an opportunity for more positive issues to be addressed. Both parent and child are able to test out the honesty and openness of the worker and their willingness to listen, to compromise and to acknowledge the family's perspective. In the view of one of the DoH research teams, a number of improvements to current practice suggest themselves:

(i)   *more information to help smooth the interaction of professional and parent;*

(ii) *more encouragement to social workers to reflect upon the nature of their task;*

(iii) *greater effort to safeguard the rights of individuals caught up in an enquiry* (Cleaver and Freeman, 1995).

Our contention is that the recorded agreement can assist in achieving each of these ends.

In other contexts there is evidence that the structure and clarity afforded by recorded agreements can be of considerable assistance in developing partnership practice. They have been shown to contribute to the prevention of out-of-home placements; to the successful reunification of children with their families; and to the accomplishment of plans for permanent placement (Maluccio, 1989; Etter, 1993; Stein *et al.*, 1978). Generally they are valued by service users (Atherton and Dowling, 1989). They can help workers identify and make more explicit the value base from which they are working (Braye and Preston-Shoot, 1992). This awareness can be particularly important in encouraging appropriate responses to minority groups such as children with disabilities, single parents and Black families. The growing evidence that, for example, Black families are over-represented in child protection interventions emphasises the need for such steps to be considered carefully (Thanki, 1994). The practice underpinning recorded agreements is consistent with the principles of practice with black families outlined by Ahmad (1990). Their use in the area of planning an enquiry into alleged abuse and neglect, however, raises some new issues.

Dilemmas of using recorded agreements when beginning an enquiry

The level of service-user involvement in decision making implied by a recorded agreement is significant. It raises anxieties which strike at core dilemmas of 'child protection' work. The responsibility to address the safety of the child on the one hand appears to conflict with the desire to involve parents in making decisions on the other. As an issue which might prevent the introduction of recorded agreements, however, it is more imaginary than real. Whatever the circumstances, the professional will always retain the power to act to protect a child and should never be expected to reach an agreement which undermines the child's safety. This is a 'bottom-line', non-negotiable position which must be accommodated within discussions about any agreement. The change in practice involved in introducing recorded agreements inevitably awakens such concerns. Similar experience has arisen in other emotive areas. As Ahmad (1990) notes, for example, deep-rooted anxieties have been seen to limit the effectiveness of access to records for Black clients.

Concerns will be greatest when a parent is also a suspected perpetrator of abuse. In joint enquiries between police and social workers, there may well be greater resistance to the use of recorded agreements from the police than from social workers. The reason for this is the police tradition of wanting to preserve evidence, which may lead them to keep those subject to enquiries uninformed for as long as possible. This aspect of practice has been confirmed by research:

> When investigations were undertaken, decisions were made about which family members to approach and in which order. In the case of joint investigations these decisions were dictated by police considerations about gathering evidence which could be used in a prosecution. Little attention was given to keeping parents informed about what was happening (Farmer and Owen, 1995).

As 'working together' has become more established, practice experience suggests that values and attitudes of disparate agencies like social services and the police can adapt. A co-operative relationship can become both possible and productive. In an enquiry both the police and social services have common objectives. They also have individual responsibilities which must be met. If a recorded agreement is developed carefully, then these differences can be identified and noted.

The introduction of recorded agreements, however, will present a fundamental challenge to the type of approach which privileges the collection of evidence above other considerations. This concern, as well as many procedural issues, derives in particular from experience of the most serious cases. Certainly there will be a few extreme circumstances when normal communication with family members may have to be set aside in the interests of the child. However, recorded agreements could otherwise be used in a variety of situations, ranging from a brief visit following up a low-key referral, to a full-blown enquiry. As has been shown in earlier chapters, the majority of cases will not be so serious that the involvement of parents and children in planning and decision making would destroy vital evidence. We would want agencies to reserve the right, however, to delay the establishment of an agreement, or to restrict the parties involved, in those extreme cases where to go ahead could have a detrimental effect on the child.

The more pragmatic objection to the use of recorded agreements when making enquiries into alleged abuse concerns issues of expediency and tokenism. Preparing, agreeing and drafting a recorded agreement takes time.

The 'child protection' process tends to be associated with speed. The 24-hour timescales for an initial enquiry imposed in some areas (if not always adhered to) convey a feeling of urgency and haste. It could therefore be argued that recorded agreements are an inappropriate encumbrance which places the child at greater risk. The Department of Health, in its most recent guidance (1995), is lukewarm about the value of involving families in the planning of an enquiry, although it is clear that they should be fully informed. Again, however, we return to a familiar theme. Where parents and children perceive that they have been involved in the decision making, they are likely to be more committed to the subsequent plans (see Burns and Young, Chapter 9, Farmer, 1993). Ensuring that clients have better access to information, resources and choice are important elements of an anti-racist approach with Black people (Ahmad, 1990), as well as constituting good practice with White families. Since approximately 80 per cent of children placed on child protection registers are likely to remain at home (Gibbons, 1993), commitment to the process is of considerable importance in enabling future plans for the protection of the child to be implemented. Technical difficulties associated with the speedy preparation of an agreement, and with writing it up during the negotiation process, could be overcome by the introduction of a suitable proforma.

In spite of the dilemmas, our view is that use of recorded agreements should become standard policy when making an enquiry into alleged child abuse or neglect. The occasions when it is inappropriate will be the exception rather than the rule and should be defined by the needs of the child, not by the needs of the agencies involved. The problem of recorded agreements becoming a routine expectation, however, is that standards of practice are insufficient to make their application more than a token gesture. The negotiation of the agreement is of considerable importance.

Negotiating an agreement

Recorded agreements for enquiries into alleged child abuse inevitably will have a coercive element. The family will rarely welcome an enquiry and the success or otherwise of the agreement is dependent upon the skill, sensitivity and determination of the worker. The key to establishing an agreement which takes account of the family's views, rather than being a one-sided imposition, lies in the approach to its negotiation. It is vital that full consideration is given to family members' race, language, culture and any special needs. The process offers the opportunity for parents and children to question the purpose of the intended action and if necessary raise objections. Workers' responses should be to accommodate the family's view unless it prevents necessary enquiry being made or affects the protection of the child.

A recorded agreement in the context of an enquiry into alleged abuse essentially is a plan of how the enquiry will be conducted and agreed between the agencies involved, the child and the family. It is not an end in itself. It relies heavily on a context of sound policies and good partnership practice. Families caught up in a 'child protection' enquiry cannot but be anxious. As well as the objective threat posed by the involvement of the police and social services, families are aware also of the negative portrayal of the child protection system by the media. The speedy negotiation needed to establish an agreement should address this anxiety. Whilst it cannot be eliminated it must be acknowledged that the anxiety will be increased greatly if the family feel they have no way of knowing what is to happen, and when, or what they can do to influence the process. Unfortunately, evidence of real negotiation over recorded agreements is somewhat depressing. In the context of child protection plans, Lindley (1994) records that:

> *None (of the families) described the plan as being negotiated with them, and some concern was expressed about the ineffectiveness of a plan which was stipulated rather than negotiated with the family: 'We signed the first agreement before the court case, however they didn't stick to their side of the agreement, only some of it. And yet they still came round twice a day and expected us to be co-operative'* (mother).

Similar findings are described by Marsh (1992). The success of recorded agreements relies heavily on those with the power being willing to share it. The context of an agreement for an enquiry into alleged abuse or neglect is complex. Workers may (and indeed should) have a clear agenda for the tasks they wish to achieve. Yet at the same time they must give up a measure of control of these tasks. Families will experience a confusion of emotions and expectations which may well militate against clear thinking. So what are the right conditions for establishing a genuine agreement in such circumstances?

According to Atherton and Dowling (1989), families do not have unrealistic expectations of 'equality' in their relationships with social workers. They do, however, suggest that recorded agreements can be applicable to a wide range of circumstances. In the context of an enquiry under section 47 of the Children Act 1989 recorded agreements could be used to promote clarity and mutual respect in all types of referrals. Atherton and Dowling identify the conditions which families believe should be met before any recorded agreement would be worthwhile.

Families' conditions for written agreements

1. *The social worker's/agency's motivation must be pro-client.*
2. *Agreements should be negotiated, not imposed.*
3. *All participants must have access to advice.*
4. *The family's view is genuinely respected.*
5. *Local authority tasks must be clearly defined.*
6. *The agreement will be both followed and reviewed.*
7. *The agency is willing to reconsider whether both the terms and implementation of the agreement were fair.*
8. *The final written document is agreed by all.*
9. *It is written in clear, unambiguous language.*
10. *Its contents can be appealed against.*

(Atherton and Dowling, 1989)

This list gives a clear indication of the necessary preconditions to achieving partnership through agreements. If recorded agreements are used with planning enquiries into abuse allegations, some of these conditions will give rise to concerns. For example, the social worker's motivation is likely to include some balancing of competing interests whilst maintaining as paramount the child's interests. There may be aspects of the enquiry process which the worker will have to impose. And an appeal against the agreement, however desirable, will be difficult to achieve when authorities are faced with the pressure of timescales.

Given the constraints of the child protection process it will be necessary to establish an approach to the negotiation of the agreement which addresses some of these difficulties. Social workers who use them may need to refine their skills (Marsh, 1992). Isaacs (1991) describes a model of 'principled negotiation' which emphasises the importance for each partner to set out their needs and wishes so that common ground can be sought together. It is a process that should focus on the issues rather than the personalities. It should avoid 'positional bargaining'. By this we mean a form of haggling which starts with a near stand-off and then the participants move their positions closer and closer until they can 'agree a price'.

Unfortunately for the child protection worker certain aspects of their 'position' may have been defined in advance. For example, there may have been a management decision that a medical examination will be required. The implication of Isaacs' model is that all the issues should be put 'on the table' early in the discussion. Consequently, these must include the concerns to which the worker has become party, as well as any constraints (such as procedures or management decisions) placed upon his or her role. Not until discussion of the issues presented by both sides has taken place would

171

options for action be examined, or actual decisions reached. Such an approach is reasonably consistent with the task-centred method advocated by Oppenheim (1992) for the first interview in an enquiry, but allows greater attention to be paid to the explanation and negotiation of the process at an early stage.

Open negotiation of this kind may be assisted by the use of advocates for the child and family. They can be particularly important in ensuring that participants understand what is happening, and what their options are. Particular skills may be needed when children are old enough to be involved in the process. The principles described in this chapter are entirely consistent with partnership objectives when working with both adults and children. As Hopkins and others (1994) identify:

> *Working agreements with young people should ensure that they retain maximum possible choice/autonomy within the working relationship, while having easy access to advice and support outside of it* (Hopkins *et al.*, 1994).

However, workers are likely to encounter a number of tricky circumstances where time and energy spent in negotiating the needs of the child and the wider family, either separately or together, will pay dividends in the long term.

The maximum possible sharing of power will be achieved when workers are clear about the limits of their authority and make room for all other issues genuinely to be up for discussion. For example, where a child has moderate to severe bruising on several parts of the body, and states that his dad hit him, the worker may have been instructed by a manager that the need for a medical examination is non-negotiable. This might be a case where, if the family did not agree to a medical, an Emergency Protection Order would be sought. However, a great many practical details which will be of concern to the family can still be set out in an agreement. They include: the timing of the medical; who should carry it out; whether a parent should be present; whether other children in the family should be seen; whether childcare may have to be arranged for the other children, etc. Other substantive issues also may be open to negotiation, such as whether neighbours or extended family members should be interviewed, or whether there are any particular forms of support which the family would like to use. The more that workers are aware of and are clear about the limits of their own power and authority, the easier it will be for the family to understand what rights they have in the situation.

The approach also is entirely compatible with the Family Group Conference (see Chapter 1). As use of the family group conference develops in many parts of the country, experience is growing of how families can be enabled to take greater responsibility when child abuse is alleged. The potential for using the family group conference in the early stages of an enquiry has been recognised (Tunnard, 1994). It is not difficult to see how a recorded agreement could lead on to a family group conference later in the process, or in some cases family members could be brought together to establish the recorded agreement and make their own decisions about how the enquiry should proceed (provided the child's safety was not compromised).

What would the recorded agreement look like?

If a police officer arrests someone in connection with an alleged offence, the person is given a clear caution and a statement of his or her rights. The enquiry into alleged child abuse is often intended to be conducted in a spirit of greater helpfulness and co-operation than a police investigation. In practice, however, this is not always the case. A 'more co-operative' approach often has become equated with woolliness, lack of clarity and an inability to tell people where they stand. The recorded agreement at the start of a section 47 enquiry should cover all the information necessary to make good this deficiency. It gives appropriate recognition to the parents' definition of the incident, the child's understanding, and their views of how the enquiry should be conducted, who should be seen and what they should be told.

A clear research and practice base for this particular type of recorded agreement currently is unavailable. However, the following is a suggested format for an agreement which is derived from existing practice in related areas, and from the recommendations of Parents Against INjustice (Amphlett, 1991) who have advocated such agreements for some time.

- A general statement indicating that the agreement concerns an enquiry into alleged child abuse or neglect, and including the names of the key participants, their roles and how they can be contacted.

- The reason for the enquiry including:
  —the type of alleged abuse or neglect, or information about why there is concern for the child;
  —details of any injuries or other physical evidence and how they are said to have been caused.

- A statement of the allegation which should be as full as possible. If the intrusion of an enquiry is to be made into the life of a family it must be well considered; if it is, the areas which need investigation can be identified.

■ Details of differences of opinion, if there are any, including disagreement expressed by the child or the child's carers about aspects of the enquiry which the professionals intend to insist on and are unwilling to negotiate.

■ A statement of what might be the possible outcomes of the enquiry (including: further assessment; whether legal proceedings might be considered if the abuse is founded; what kind of support might be available; the possibility of a case conference/registration, and the parents' wish to attend if applicable; and any action to be taken if the allegation is unfounded).

■ What specific actions will be taken (i.e. medical examination; interviews of people involved; video interview under the *Memorandum of Good Practice* [Home Office with DoH, 1992]; liaison with other agencies), and who is responsible. This will include reaching agreement on:
—which doctors may need to be involved;
—who will be interviewed;
—that a parent, or some other person whom the child trusts, will be present at examinations or interviews with the child;
—the use of interpreters or other resources which may help people whose first language is not English, or people with disabilities, etc.;
—for Black families, ways in which the enquiry will include awareness of their experience of racism, the impact of cultural differences and any preference for a Black or White worker.

■ Regarding initial assessments of the social and home circumstances, how and when they will take place and how the positive features will be identified (as well as the negative ones).

■ Time-limits to the enquiry.

■ Provision for ensuring that the child and family will be kept informed (in writing when appropriate) as the enquiry progresses.

■ An undertaking that, following the enquiry, a written report will be given to the child and family stating the conclusions arrived at and any action proposed.

■ Provision for ensuring that the child and family have been informed of their right of access to an appeals and complaints procedures.

Clearly the foregoing represents a significant amount of information to be covered. Given that family members will be in a state of shock at the initial meeting or visit, it may be possible only to discuss the process in outline. Skill and sensitivity will be required from workers to promote the opportunity of working in partnership with carers who may be experiencing such disbelief and numbness that no agreement may be meaningful. A limited agreement recorded in writing is better than nothing at all. It can be built upon at future sessions. However, as the enquiry unfolds, the situation may develop in unexpected ways:

> A most helpful aspect of a written agreement for families who are being investigated is to know when the investigation will be completed. However, by its very nature, an investigation might identify further issues which require further investigation. Both parties need to be aware of this and be prepared to re-negotiate their agreement (Amphlett, 1991).

Conclusion

Our purpose in writing this chapter has been to advocate on behalf of the recorded agreement for section 47 enquiries. We are acutely aware of the pitfalls of doing so. The recorded agreement is a powerful tool only *within the context of good partnership practice*. Without such a framework, however, it is open to misuse. Workers can use their position to include in recorded agreements expectations which are coercive, which further oppress families, or which set them up to fail (e.g. Braye and Preston-Shoot, 1992; Platt, 1993).

Unfortunately, learning to set up recorded agreements with children and families is not a simple matter of achieving certain technical skills. Workers communicate their attitude and approach to families in subtle, often non-verbal, ways. Unless they actually believe in the philosophy behind the practice, in the right of children and families to have some control over the enquiry, the recorded agreement will remain where it began: as mere ink on a piece of paper.

REFERENCES

Ahmad, B. (1990) *Black Perspectives in Social Work*, Venture Press.

Amphlett, S. (1991) *Working in Partnership: Coping with an Investigation of Alleged Abuse or Neglect*, Parents Against INjustice.

Atherton, C. and Dowling, P. (1989) 'Using written agreements: the family's point of view', in Aldgate, J. (ed.) *Using Written Agreements with Children and Families*, Family Rights Group.

Braye, S. and Preston-Shoot, M. (1992) 'Honourable intentions: partnership and written agreements in welfare legislation', *Journal of Social Welfare and Family Law*, no. 6, pp. 511–528.

Cleaver, H. and Freeman, P. (1995) *Parental Perspectives in Cases of Suspected Child Abuse*, London: HMSO.

Department of Health (1991a) *The Children Act 1989. Guidance and Regulations: Volume 2, Family Support, Day Care and Educational Provision for Young Children*, London: HMSO.

Department of Health (1991b) *The Children Act 1989. Guidance and Regulations: Volume 3, Family Placements*, London: HMSO.

Department of Health (1995) *The Challenge of Partnership in Child Protection: Practice Guide*, London: HMSO.

Etter, J. (1993) 'Levels of co-operation and satisfaction in 56 open adoptions', *Child Welfare*, **72**, no. 3, May–June, pp. 257–267.

Farmer, E. (1993) 'The impact of child protection interventions: the experiences of parents and children', in Waterhouse, L. (ed.) *Child Abuse and Child Abusers: Protection and Prevention*, University of Aberdeen Research Highlights in Social Work.

Farmer, E. and Owen, M. (1995) *Child Protection Practice: Private Risks and Public Remedies*, London: HMSO.

FRG/NFCA, Children Act 1989: Written Agreement Forms for work with Children, Families and Carers.

Gibbons, J. (1993) 'Operation of child protection registers', Summary report of a research project commissioned by the Department of Health, University of East Anglia.

Home Office, Department of Health, Department of Education and Science, Welsh Office (1991) *Working Together Under the Children Act 1989: A Guide to arrangements for Inter-agency Co-operation for the Protection of Children from Abuse*, London: HMSO.

Home Office with Department of Health (1992) *Memorandum of Good Practice on Video Recorded Interviews with Child Witnesses for Criminal Proceedings*, London: HMSO.

Hopkins, N. with Butler, I. and Williamson, H. (1994) '. . . and well?' in Butler, I. and Williamson, H. (eds) *Children Speak: Children, Trauma and Social Work*, Harlow: Longman.

Isaacs, B. (1991) 'Negotiation in partnership work', in *The Children Act 1989: Working in Partnership with Families – Reader*, Family Rights Group, London: HMSO.

Lindley, B. (1994) *On the Receiving End: a Study of Families' Experiences of the Court Process in Care and Supervision Proceedings under the Children Act 1989*, Family Rights Group.

Maluccio, A.N. (1989) 'Writing an agreement: an exploration of the process', in Aldgate, J. (ed.) *Using Written Agreements with Children and Families*, Family Rights Group.

Marsh, P. (1992) 'Agreements in child protection', in Thoburn, J. (ed.) *Participation in Practice: Involving Families in Child Protection*, University of East Anglia.

Oppenheim, L. (1992) 'The first interview in child protection: social work method and process', *Children and Society*, **6**, no. 2, pp. 132–150.

Platt, D. (1993) 'The age of mutual consent', *Community Care*, 22 April 1993.

Platt, D. and Edwards, A. (Forthcoming) 'Planning a comprehensive family assessment', to be published in *Practice*, the Journal of the British Association of Social Workers.

Sharland, E., Jones, D., Aldgate, J. Seal, H. and Croucher, M. (1995) *Professional Intervention in Child Sexual Abuse*, HMSO.

Sheldon, B. (1980) *Use of Contracts in Social Work*, British Association of Social Workers.

Sheldon, B. (1982) *Behaviour Modification*, Tavistock.

Stein, T.J., Gambrill, E.D. and Wiltse, K.T. (1978) *Children in Foster Homes: Achieving Continuity of Care*, New York: Praeger Publishers. Cited in Marsh, P. (1992) 'Agreements in child protection', in Thoburn, J. (ed.) *Participation in Practice: Involving Families in Child Protection*, University of East Anglia.

Thanki, V. (1994) 'Ethnic diversity and child protection', *Children and Society*, **8**, no. 3, pp. 232–244.

Thomas, M. (1989) 'Fostering agreements: taking positive steps', in Aldgate, J. (ed.) *Using Written Agreements with Children and Families*, Family Rights Group.

Tunnard, J. (1994) *Family Group Conferences: A Report Commissioned by the Department of Health*, Family Rights Group.

Tunstill, J. (1989) 'Written agreements: an overview', in Aldgate, J. (ed.) *Using Written Agreements with Children and Families*, Family Rights Group.

11

Interviewing children

Wendy Stainton Rogers

The main purposes of partnership

As well as its more general goals, when it comes to interviewing children partnership has two main purposes. The first is that effective partnership will often be crucial to make the interview successful, in terms of it being able to discover the information sought. This applies whether the interview allays any suspicions or concerns or whether it confirms them. In either case, the child's – and indeed usually the family's – interests will be best served by obtaining as much detailed information relevant to the case as possible.

Where there have been wrongful accusations, or where there is a perfectly innocent explanation of the matters which have raised concern, a well-conducted interview with the child is often the most effective means to resolve the issue. Equally, where a child has been harmed – or may be at risk of harm – the child's account can be the most reliable source of information. Indeed, in many situations, enabling the child to talk openly will often be the *only* way to discover what did or did not happen.

Of course children, like adults, can have problems remembering events and in giving an accurate account of them. Also, like adults, children may not tell the truth – for reasons varying from fear (especially if they have been threatened), through loyalty, to having been 'coached', or wanting to cause trouble. However, research evidence (Spencer and Flin, 1990 provide a good summary) suggests that, if anything, children generally tend to give more accurate accounts than adults, if given the proper opportunity to do so. In part at least, this is because children are more concrete in their thinking. They interpret less and so introduce fewer distortions.

What is at issue, then, is the critical importance of interviewing children in ways which encourage and enable them to give as accurate and as comprehensive an account as possible. This means gaining their trust, so that they feel able to talk freely and honestly, and asking them questions which help them recall, while avoiding putting any pressure on them, or 'coaching' or 'leading' them in any way.

Parental co-operation and support can make all the difference to the success of the interview. For instance, a child, particularly a younger child, will find it much easier to answer questions if they have the explicit permission of their parent(s) to do so, and parental reassurance that it is all right to discuss 'private' or 'rude' things with the interviewers.

The second purpose of partnership is to make the experience of being interviewed as unstressful as possible for the child and for the family. Children are used to their parents accompanying them when they have to cope with unfamiliar, difficult or painful situations – like a dental check, or when they start school. It can make the experience all the more distressing for the child to discover that, unlike usual, they are expected to cope with the interview without parental support. Parents too are likely to find the experience much easier to cope with if they have a genuine sense that they are contributing to it, rather than being left out of the picture. Parents can play a key role in preparing children for the interview, in helping the interviewers to plan, and in supporting the child during and after the interview.

But perhaps most crucially, children and young people of all ages are likely to cope far better, however difficult the interview may be, if they have a real sense that their parents and those involved in the interview are taking them seriously. This applies as much to situations where any allegations that have been made have no substance, as to situations where there are genuine causes for concern. Children need to feel they will be listened to carefully, whether what they have to say is that 'nothing untoward happened', 'something is worrying me – but not what you think' or 'something did happen which upset me'. In other words, what is important is to provide conditions in which children who have been harmed in some way feel able to talk freely about it, but also in which children who are unharmed are not left feeling confused and do not get a sense of having been drawn into a system they do not understand. The more, then, that parents and professionals can work together to make children feel that what they say will be treated with respect (whatever it is that they have to say), the less likely it will be that the children concerned will experience the interview as an interrogation in which it is they who are under scrutiny.

Finally, of course, there are the basic and general reasons why partnership should be pursued: in order to treat parents and children with respect; to keep them informed; to allow parents to nurture and care for their children; and to ensure that children continue to receive parental care. In other words, all the reasons that apply in other parts of the process apply just as much in this context.

The context of partnership

Pursuing partnership can be especially difficult when interviewing children. This is because the outcome of the interview will have far-reaching implications for the child's family. If, in the course of the interview, the child discloses information about mistreatment by one or both parents, or by other members of the child's family or household, then the consequence will be full-scale child protection enquiries. If, on the other hand, the child states un-equivocally that nothing untoward happened, then the process may stop there.

Because so much can hang on the interview, it is not surprising that parents may feel very threatened by it. The trouble is, parental antagonism does not mean that the parent(s) are 'guilty'. They may simply be (as described above) worried about its impact on the child. But this makes it very difficult for social workers to know how to respond. Are they dealing with parents who want to prevent the child 'spilling the beans'? Or are they dealing with parents who are simply shocked by the accusations? It takes a lot of skill and professionalism to keep an open mind when parents are being hostile, and then work towards involving parents in the process.

However, the situation is even more complicated because the child's acount may form the basis of evidence that can be used in court proceedings. These may be civil proceedings under child protection legislation or criminal proceedings against the alleged abuser(s), or both. In cases such as this there will be tensions between two different purposes for which an interview may be conducted.

The provisions of the Children Act 1989

Under the Children Act 1989 the focus of the interview prioritises the child's welfare and safety – it is the child's welfare which must be the paramount consideration. Guidance provided in relation to the Children Act (especially *Working Together Under the Children Act*) puts a lot of stress on the importance of partnership with parents, since this is seen to be the best way to discover what has happened and assess the child's circumstances as broadly as possible, including the possibilities of taking measures to protect the child which maintain the integrity of the family.

This Guidance also argues for conducting interviews in a child-centred manner, and for adopting low-key procedures which facilitate the child's ability to recall and recount what did or did not happen. When conducting an interview under this Guidance there are four prime tasks, which are broadly applicable whatever the context:

- to establish the facts about the circumstances giving rise to the concern;

- to decide if there are grounds for concern;

- to identify sources and levels of risk;

- to decide on and be able to plan protective or other action in relation to the child and any others.

Thus, though it may seem self-evident, it is worth stressing explicitly the basic point that what any investigative interview is *for* is to gather the information necessary to plan any action. It is also worth mentioning here that not all interviews conducted with children have a primarily information-seeking purpose. For example, in situations where any legal proceedings have been completed, interviews may be conducted with children where the primary purpose is therapeutic. The child is encouraged to speak about what happened in order, for example, to enable the child to be reassured that it was not their fault and to overcome any residual guilt they may feel.

The provisions of the Criminal Justice Act 1991

By contrast the provisions of the *Memorandum of Good Practice*, produced in response to the child witness provisions of the Criminal Justice Act 1991, prioritise meeting the legal requirements for evidence and consequently pose difficulties for partnership.

The child witness provisions of the Criminal Justice Act 1991 were intended to improve the conditions under which child witnesses to crimes can give evidence in court. In the 1980s there were a number of events which highlighted the difficulties that children face when caught up in the criminal justice system, both in terms of the law itself and the practice of interviewers. Grave reservations had been expressed about the manner in which professionals conducted interviews with children. These so-called 'disclosure interviews' came in for much criticism from lawyers. Some judges condemned the interviews as being oppressive and those conducting them as having closed their minds to any explanation of events other than that the children were victims of abuse; consequently they saw the child's evidence as tainted irredeemably by the questioning practices used.

At the same time the experience of children before the criminal courts had been grounds for concern for much of the 1980s. The Criminal Justice Act 1988 reformed the law by allowing a court to convict on the uncorroborated evidence of a single unsworn child. However, this did not address the issue of the distressing nature of a court appearance for the child who was giving evidence. This was dealt with in part by allowing the child to give evidence by live video link so that s/he did not have to be in the physical presence of the accused.

It was considered important that the law in its operation should be more child-sensitive; that the practice of those working with children should be geared to enabling children to tell their stories more effectively; that the law should not put up artificial obstacles in the way of such accounts; and that children should be spared the trauma of confrontation in court with their alleged abuser if at all possible.

In 1988 the Home Office Advisory Group on Video Evidence, chaired by His Honour Judge Pigot, was set up to consider the use of video recordings as a means of taking the evidence of children and other vulnerable witnesses at criminal trials. It reported in December 1989 and contained recommendations which were acted upon (but only in part) in the Criminal Justice Act 1991 (see Home Office, 1989). The Criminal Justice Act 1991 seeks to improve the position of the child giving evidence in criminal proceedings. Centrally it allows the child witness to give her/his evidence-in-chief by pre-recorded video *but* the child will still have to be available for cross-examination in order to protect the rights of the accused.

A *Memorandum of Good Practice* has been provided to advise practitioners (notably social workers and police officers) on how to conduct interviews with children in order to enable the child's account to be used, if necessary, in subsequent criminal proceedings. It recommends that where there is any possibility of a criminal prosecution, the interview should be video-taped and conducted in a manner which conforms to the rules of evidence for criminal proceedings. The law over the acceptability of a child's evidence is complex and for its detail the Memorandum should be consulted. Its main features are summarised below.

A child's evidence-in-chief may be accepted in pre-recorded video form only in certain circumstances. These are that child is:

1. a witness, not the accused;

2. capable of being cross-examined;

3. *either* under fourteen (or, if under fourteen when the video was made, is now under fifteen) if the offence involves an assault or cruelty to persons under sixteen (section 1 of the Children and Young Persons Act 1933);

or under seventeen (or, if under seventeen when the video was made, is now under eighteen) if the offence is a sexual offence.

Consent from somebody with parental responsibility for the child is not required, although the Memorandum stresses that it is desirable. Children must have the purpose of the interview explained to them, and while their formal consent is not required, the interview should not go ahead without their agreement. Appropriate equipment must be used and the tapes stored securely.

The interview should follow a sequence of phases, starting with rapport-building then moving on to a 'free narrative' account elicited from the child, through to open and closed questions, to a 'closure' phase. Leading questions will seldom be acceptable and child-facilitative techniques (such as the use of anatomically-correct dolls) are discouraged specifically. Wherever possible only one interview should be conducted and it should not last for longer than about an hour.

Conflicts between these two provisions

From these details it can be seen that the two provisions present a number of areas of conflict over what is good practice in terms of partnership. For example, it is recommended in the Memorandum that the child should not be accompanied by a parent in the interview since this may pose problems for the evidential credibility of the child's account. But having the reassurance of a parent may be very important for the child to feel secure enough to talk freely. The child's parent also may find it easier to accept the interview if they can be present. Thus, what may be 'good practice' with respect to partnership is rendered problematic by the legal considerations over evidence.

Civil and criminal proceedings

A video-taped interview of the child's account may also be used in civil proceedings, such as an application for a care order under the Children Act 1989. However, the use of the video is determined by quite different legal considerations in the two situations. In order to make sense of the implications for the way the interview is conducted it is necessary to understand what these differences are. They fall under six main headings:

1. the burden of proof;

2. standards of proof;

3. grounds for making orders;

4. competence of the child witness;

5. attendance of the child in court;

6. rules of evidence.

The burden of proof

The burden of proof is to do with which 'side' in a court case has to prove certain matters. In a civil case it is the plaintiff (i.e. the person bringing the action, such as the local authority or, say, the parent applying for the order) who usually bears the burden of proof. In a criminal case it is the prosecution (i.e. the Crown) which bears the burden.

Standards of proof

The standard of proof refers to the criterion for making judgements in legal proceedings and concerns the degree of certainty that magistrates, judges or juries should consider when making judgements. In civil proceedings concerning children's welfare (e.g. in care proceedings) the standard of proof is 'on the balance of probabilities', i.e. that it is more likely than not that the events alleged to have occurred did in fact occur. The standard of proof in a criminal trial, however, is much more strict. It is that the case against the accused must be proved 'beyond reasonable doubt'. This means that if there is any doubt in the minds of the jury, they should acquit the accused.

Basically what this difference amounts to is that in civil proceedings the court can decide to intervene (e.g. to make a care order to protect the child) once certain facts have been established as true 'on the balance of probabilities'. In contrast, a criminal court cannot convict a person unless it is established 'beyond reasonable doubt' that the accused committed a specific offence.

Grounds for making orders

In civil proceedings for child protection generally these centre around establishing that the child is suffering or is likely to suffer 'significant harm', which is attributable to a failure of parental care or because the child is deemed as being beyond parental control. The focus of evidence is upon the *risks to the child*. In criminal proceedings, however, what has to be established is that the accused committed a specified offence. The focus of evidence here, therefore, is upon *the actions of the accused*.

In civil proceedings (such as an application for a Care Order) all that is necessary is to convince the court that, on the balance of probabilities: (a) the child has been significantly harmed; (b) that this harm is attributable to inadequacies in parental care; and (c) that without a court order s/he is at risk of further significant harm. However, were this same case to reach a criminal trial of the child's father for sexually assaulting her/him then, for the father to be convicted, it must be established 'beyond all reasonable doubt' that it was he who sexually assaulted the child. Thus it is perfectly possible for a child to be placed in the care of the local authority on the basis of a statement in an interview that *somebody* sexually assaulted the child, even though the child's account is not sufficiently clear about who committed this offence in order to provide unequivocal evidence to secure a conviction.

Competence of the child witness

As far as civil proceedings are concerned a child may be called as a witness and give unsworn evidence if, in the opinion of the court, the child understands that he or she must speak the truth and has sufficient understanding to justify his or her evidence being heard. In criminal proceedings the provisions of the Criminal Justice Act 1991 specify that a child witness is to be treated as competent to testify, unless shown otherwise. Unlike adults, children under 14 need not take the oath but their testimony will be considered as if they had. However, when a child (or indeed any witness) proves to be unable to give a comprehensible account of events, that child's evidence will not be allowed to form part of either the prosecution or defence case.

The child's attendance in court

In civil proceedings the court can order the child to attend a particular stage of the court proceedings . However, courts generally are unwilling to force a child to attend, unless he or she is willing to appear, and that this is considered in her/his best interests. The Guardian ad litem will be expected to consider carefully this question and advise the court on this matter.

In criminal proceedings the child's testimony may be critical to the prosecution and so the case may not go ahead unless the child can appear as a witness. The child may testify in person, or by way of a live video-link (where the child sits in a room next to the court which is set up with technical equipment to allow the court to see and hear the child, and for the child to see and hear whoever is questioning her/him). In some circumstances the child's main evidence (evidence in chief) may be given in the form of a video-taped interview (as described above). The video recording will not, however, be admissible unless the child is available for cross-examination although the accused will not be able to cross-examine the child in person, and the cross-examination may be conducted via live video link.

Rules concerning the child's evidence

In civil proceedings, as the rules over hearsay have been relaxed, oral and written reports of what a child has said and video recordings of interviews with children may be submitted as evidence. In criminal proceedings, hearsay and all other rules about evidence do apply, both to the child's evidence in chief (whether given in court, by live video-link, or by way of a pre-recorded interview) and to cross-examination. Whilst these rules regarding evidence and its admissibility have been and are complicated, the idea of evidence is simple – it refers to those matters which have to be established or proved in order to make a case. There is a very useful breakdown of the legal elements – what has to be proved – of the main sexual and violent offences in Annex D to the *Memorandum of Good Practice*.

Rules of evidence and their implications for interviewing

There are four rules of evidence which the Memorandum identifies as being of particular importance in criminal proceedings – those concerning: statements about the bad character of the accused; opinions; hearsay; and leading questions. Together these rules impose restrictions on the way a child can be interviewed .

Statements about the bad character of the accused

Such statements are seen to undermine the accused's right to a fair trial. Thus in criminal proceedings the prosecution may not place evidence before the court which is designed to show that the accused is of 'bad character'. Evidence of past misdeeds falls into this category. For example, if a child talks about something the accused has done to another child – such as, 'He was doing the same when he lived in Leeds, with a little girl there' – this would pose problems and may compromise the interview in whole or in part. In civil proceedings the rule is less strict but the general principle applies that what may or may not have happened in other incidents, not directly related to the proceedings, is of no relevance, even if it throws light on the character of some person involved.

Obviously this poses problems for children being interviewed since it may be very natural for them to talk about other things the person has done. It will be uncomfortable for the child to be steered away from such conversations; the child may feel that what they are saying is being dismissed, they are not believed or, simply, the child may be puzzled and confused by an interviewer wanting a lot of detail about some aspects of their story but not pursuing other aspects which, to the child, are highly salient.

Opinions

Only 'experts' are allowed to offer opinions as evidence in criminal proceedings. Children in investigative interviewing are not 'experts' in a legal sense and hence their opinions are not matters which the court will consider. Thus, so far as the interviewers are concerned, the best evidence will be produced if the interview is conducted in ways which elicit, as far as possible, clear and factual responses. One of the most difficult areas for the court is to distinguish between fact (admissible) and opinion (inadmissible from a non-expert) when evidence emerges in the form of impression or value judgement. Words such as 'drunk', 'dirty' and 'messy' are less helpful than a direct description of the person, house, room, clothing etc.

This is an area where there can be direct conflict between an interview's investigative function and the need to be sensitive to the child's needs and welfare. How the child feels, say, about a particular person may well be important in deciding how best to help her/him. They may have an urgent need to express their distress or anger about what has been done to them. Such conversations, however, will be of limited evidential importance in establishing what has happened to them. Critically, too much emphasis in an investigative interview on 'talking out' feelings, or on making sense of why things have happened, will tend to compromise its usefulness as evidence.

Interviewers therefore have to tread a very careful line between keeping the interview on course, in terms of factual descriptions of what did or did not happen, and being responsive to the child's immediate needs and concerns. Inevitably the child's agenda will often not be that of making enquiries. But to follow the child's agenda alone could run the risk of totally undermining the investigative purpose.

Hearsay

In criminal proceedings hearsay evidence is not generally allowed. 'Hearsay' is where the testimony of a person who was not a direct observer of an event in question is used to prove that the event took place. If the child suffers abuse and then tells, say, a social worker about what happened to her/him, the social worker's evidence about the abuse will constitute hearsay. There are good reasons for the rule against hearsay evidence. These include:

- when statements are repeated second-hand a degree of distortion can be introduced;

- the account of the statement will be out of context, which may alter its interpretation;

- The demeanour of the person who made the original statement cannot be observed, which could affect the sense in which a statement should be understood;

- The person who made the original statement cannot answer questions to resolve confusion or ambiguity, nor can their evidence be 'tested' directly in cross-examination.

The rules about hearsay mean that statements made in the course of an investigative interview normally will not be admissible in criminal proceedings. In contrast to the situation in criminal proceedings the Children Act 1989 changed the rules so that hearsay evidence is now admissible in civil proceedings. Formerly only the child could tell the court about the abuse.

What this means is that, firstly, it can be very difficult to interview a child in ways that avoid hearsay. Often the most natural way to begin is to tell the child, 'Your Mum told me you said to her that Uncle Jimmy did something to you', and then ask, 'Can you tell me about that?'. But this would be quite wrong in terms of the Memorandum's advice – which suggests asking much vaguer questions such as, 'My job is to talk to children about things that worry them. Is there anything worrying you?' Which is, of course, much more confusing and difficult for the child, who has to guess what the interviewer is getting at. The second problem is, again, that the child will find it difficult to make sense of situations when the interviewer steers them away from something they are saying, without having any clue as to why.

An important exception to the usual inadmissibility of introducing material from an investigative interview is where it can be used to show that the child actually made a certain statement, and that this statement has certain implications. This may be of direct relevance if, for example, it shows a child to have knowledge inappropriate to his or her age. For instance, if a child says in the interview, 'He put his willie in my bottom', this would be regarded as hearsay and would be inadmissible as evidence that such an event took place. But it could be presented to a criminal court as evidence that the child had knowledge of this kind of sexual activity.

The statements made in the course of the interview may also be used in some circumstances to support, or to undermine, the child's credibility as a witness. Where a witness has said something different in the past, this can be used to attack their credibility in both criminal and civil proceedings. Of course, cross-examination is a crucial mechanism in law to protect the accused's rights and to 'test' the truthfulness of witness. So a child witness is likely to be asked in cross-examination about a previous statement made on the video. If he or she denies making a previous statement which was inconsistent with his or her evidence in court, then evidence of the previous statement may be given (i.e. the interview recording would be shown). This means that the video recorded interview can become a 'hostage to fortune' for the child. While it can quite properly be used to expose a child's inconsistency, it can also be used to undermine a child in court. How the video is used, and the tenor of the cross-examination against it, are matters over which the judge or magistrates have control. They have the authority to curtail cross-examination which is improper – if, for example, it appears to be being used to confuse or upset the child. However, there have been times when it was felt that this authority has not been imposed in circumstances where the child was being 'badgered'. Thus those making the interview need to proceed cautiously, in the knowledge that the child may well be expected to defend what s/he has said sometimes under extremely aggressive questioning.

Leading questions

Whenever a person is giving evidence in court, he or she cannot be asked leading questions by the side which has called him or her as a witness. The witness must be allowed to tell his or her own story, without being given all or part of the answer expected by the way the question is asked. Leading questions fall into two main categories:

1. Questions that require a 'Yes' or 'No' answer are usually leading questions. 'Did Daddy hurt you?', 'Daddy hurt you, didn't he?', or 'Did the person who hurt you have curly hair?' are all examples of this type of question.

2. Questions based on an assumption about what happened are also leading. An example is 'When did Daddy first touch you there?', put to a child who has not yet alleged that daddy did anything. Even an invitation like 'Tell me about the man who did this', presupposes the

gender of the individual concerned and usually should not be asked unless the child has already volunteered information about gender.

This concern over leading questions clearly is pertinent in terms of the accused's right to a fair trial. It is also crucial to maintain the integrity of the child's evidence. If the defence can argue that a child was led into making an accusation, then the child's statement will be undermined. But it is plain to see how difficult this makes interviewing children in a manner which is helpful and facilitative. Often a child will be reluctant to talk, or will need a great deal of prompting. Just those techniques for helping the child are those proscribed by legal requirements.

Implications for partnership with children

The requirements of the Memorandum can make it extremely difficult, if not impossible, for the interviewer to conduct the interview in a manner which, on the one hand, is facilitative and supportive to the child, and on the other, is open and honest with the child about what is going on and why. At the same time, if the Memorandum is not followed the child's account may not be acceptable as evidence and the child's civil rights to the protection of the law may be undermined.

Possibly the most critical problem, however, comes in terms of seeking the child's consent. While the Memorandum states that the child should have the purpose of the interview explained, and stresses that interviews should not be conducted unless the child agrees, it slides over the full implications of these provisions. If this were always done conscientiously, a moot question is how many children would be willing to take part in an interview. If interviewers were to explain fully all the possible implications – for example, that a large number of people (including the accused) may see the video, or that the child may be cross-examined minutely in court over its contents and any inconsistencies – a large proportion of children may well withhold their consent and the interview could not go ahead.

Interviewers therefore face the dilemma of judging how far they should go in seeking fully-informed consent. The problem is that many professionals working in this field will have had experiences of working with children who have been, frankly, terrified by the threats to which they have been exposed to prevent them from saying what has happened to them. It is often in such cases that, eventually, the most horrific abuse has been uncovered. Not surprisingly this can harden professionals' judgement. Such experiences can convince them that, on balance, it is more important to uncover evidence about the abuse than to respect fully the child's rights to be told, honestly, all the possible consequences of disclosing the abuse they have suffered. They will argue, 'Isn't it more of a betrayal of the child to fail to be able to take action to stop the abuse?'. The problem is, of course, that this can lead professionals into approaching *all* children in *all* circumstances as though there is horrific abuse to be discovered, and into assuming that they are always justified in riding roughshod over the child's entitlement only to participate in an interview when they are informed sufficiently about its consequences to give their consent freely. Clearly this approach is an abuse of children when deployed indiscriminately.

The problem is, of course, that without the interview professionals do not know whether there is abuse to be discovered or not and, if so, how serious it is. So, how far are they justified in running the risk of compromising children's rights to give fully-informed consent in situations when they have no knowledge about whether *this particular child* has been abused?

Interviewers therefore have to develop strategies which balance carefully the duty they owe to children to be completely honest about what they may be letting themselves in for, with the duty they owe to children to protect them. To pursue either to the exclusion of the other will always pose serious risks. The dilemma cannot be resolved simply by maintaining that one or other consideration is paramount. This, therefore, is inevitably a question of professional judgement. What we can be clear about is that this professional judgement *must* be open-minded (i.e. it must not make presuppositions about what may or may not have happened); and it *must not be* an excuse to wield professional power for the convenience of 'the system'. The child's consent must always be sought and obtained and the child must be informed as fully as possible. Professional judgement is not about this; it is about how far it is useful or necessary to go on spelling out every possible consequence. Under no circumstances should a child be misled or given false reassurances. The child's questions about consequences must always be answered honestly and promises must not be made that cannot be kept.

Similar considerations apply to partnership with parents. Whilst there are always going to be situations when parents have every reason to use their authority to prevent a child being interviewed, this possibility must never be used as an excuse, as a matter of course, to forgo seeking parental consent or for not informing parents that an interview is to take place. Such action can only be justified in situations where there is compelling evidence that consent is being withheld maliciously, and then only when other courses of action (for example, seeking a court order to authorise the interview) are impractical i.e. where there is an immediate and serious risk to the child.

Good practice is rather different with older and younger children. Where children are of sufficient age and maturity to be capable of making a decision for themselves, then it is the child's consent which will be critical. Following the Gillick ruling it is lawful to proceed with an interview where a 'mature minor' has given consent, even when their parents have not (or have not been asked). With a younger child the situation is more difficult. Here the law assumes that in all normal circumstances professionals cannot take action unless there is consent from a person with parental responsibility for the child. The best course of action, then, is to seek the consent of such a person. In such cases either parent, or indeed any other person with parental responsibility, can act independently. Where such consent is not forthcoming (or there are serious concerns about the consequences of seeking it) then, wherever possible, authority should be sought from the court (for example, as a direction under an Emergency Protection Order (EPO), or via a specific issue order). Only where none of these avenues is possible may there be a legal case for proceeding without parental consent.

What makes partnership possible – and what makes it difficult?

When it comes to interviewing children partnership can sometimes be relatively easy to achieve, and sometimes very difficult. There are two main factors influencing which of these is the case – and what kinds of hurdles there may be to partnership: the relationship of the parent(s) to the alleged abuser; and whether or not there is a possibility that there may be court proceedings (see above).

Partnership is likely to be most difficult to pursue when there is very strong evidence already, quite independent of the child's account, that one or both parents have abused the child, especially if this abuse was part of a wider system of organised abuse. Such cases may arise, for example, where several other children have made explicit allegations and have reported that other children were also involved. However, the Orkney case highlights the problems which can arise when such allegations are taken on face value by professionals who have failed to maintain a dispassionate, open-minded stance. It is essential in such cases that professionals do not get drawn into a world-view in which every allegation against every person is taken as 'proof' that all those accused are unquestionably 'guilty'. Each allegation, and each person alleged to be involved, must be treated independently on its merits. At the same time there will be cases where children have been abused by their parents and where, in consequence, parents have every reason to subvert or misuse attempts to work in partnership with them.

By contrast, partnership is likely to be easiest where a person suspected of having abused the child is not a parent, or close family member, but is somebody outside the family such as a neighbour, teacher or childminder. Of course even in cases like this partnership will seldom be entirely straightforward. For instance, the parents' emotional reactions – horror at the alleged abuse itself and anger towards the alleged abuser – may be so overwhelming as to undermine their ability to support the child or to contribute to the interview process. Parents may also want to protect the child from further distress. They may be very worried about the impact on the child of giving evidence in court. If they see the interview as inevitably leading to this, they may be resistant. But generally in situations like this parent(s) are anxious to help with the interview in every way they can.

Most cases will fall between the two extremes. For example, partnership will depend to a great extent on the position adopted by the child's other parent (if only one parent is alleged to have abused the child). If this person refuses to accept the need for the enquiry, or, say, sees it as 'meddling', s/he may refuse to co-operate and actively seek to prevent the interview taking place. Even when such parents accept that the local authority has a duty to conduct the enquiry, they may face considerable conflicts of loyalty and be very worried about whether the interview is in the best interests of the family.

Where a father has been accused, for example, of sexually abusing his child, the child's mother may be willing to accept that the abuse took place and that it needs to stop. But she may nonetheless feel that this is something which can be sorted out in the family in ways that avoid its break-up. Women in this position are often very vulnerable. They may be frightened that they will lose everything – their home, their livelihood, their position in the community and even their children. If they are to contribute to the interview process, they will need a great deal of support.

Often social workers assume that partnership can only be pursued with the 'non-abusing parent' so long as s/he is willing to accept that the allegations made are true. This assumption needs to be challenged. Indeed, the very term 'non-abusing parent' is problematic, since it carries the implication that the other parent is the 'abuser' – not the *alleged* abuser. It must therefore be avoided, and a term such as 'non-accused parent' used instead ('alleged non-abusing parent' will not do as it implies doubt over whether this parent was possibly also involved).

It is perfectly possible, and certainly always desirable, to work in partnership with non-accused parents who are convinced that the accusations against their partner are false, or at least, who want to keep an open mind. This should not be viewed negatively, but as a position that in many cases will be a reasonable and rational appraisal of the situation. Indeed, only by working with such parents will it be possible to conduct enquiries, which turn out to be 'false alarms', in ways which leave the family reasonably intact and functioning in the aftermath. Such loyalty and open-mindedness on the part of the non-accused parent will, in such circumstances, be critical in promoting the parental harmony and solidarity that will be needed if the family is to deal with the distress the enquiry has caused. Moreover, the more that professionals can be seen as committed to supporting loyalty between parents who may be wrongly accused, the more willing families will be to work with them, and the less antagonism they will face from the public at large. It is essential for child protection professionals to develop such a reputation if they are to gain the trust and respect of the communities in which they work.

All that is required for partnership with non-accused parents is that they accept that the local authority has a duty to pursue the enquiry and that interviewing the child is a legitimate step to take in the process. Arriving at this position will always take a great deal of tact and skill and may demand considerable negotiation to achieve it. It is, nonetheless, the optimal situation under which to conduct the interview and every effort must be made to reach it. This will be facilitated by:

- being seen as having an open mind (which means *having* an open mind) and making it clear to parents that the decision to interview is not an accusation but a genuine attempt to discover information – including the information that a child has *not* been abused, if that is the case;

- telling parents exactly what is involved in the interview and explaining honestly and openly to what purposes the interview may be put;

- offering support to the non-accused parent to help him/her address any feelings of conflicting loyalty and/or distress over the accusations that have been made against their partner;

- making it absolutely clear that helping with the interview does not in any way imply accepting the accusations as 'true';

- acknowledging that it is reasonable for non-accused parents to continue to be loyal to their partner and that this will make a positive contribution to dealing with the aftermath of the interview, if the allegations turn out to be unfounded;

- explaining what the parent can do to help, including supporting the alleged abuser.

What parents can do to contribute to the interview

As described above, the ideal situation is where one or both parents can support the child. In such circumstances the supportive parent(s) should be involved in the following.

Planning for the interview

This entails drawing on parents' knowledge of things like the child's cognitive and emotional maturity, likes and dislikes, vocabulary and interests. Since parents are likely to know their child best, they can be the most reliable source of the information interviewers need in order to plan, for instance, how best to approach a conversation about sex. Parents' accounts of the composition of the household will help interviewers know, say, what toys to use or what drawings to make.

Preparing the child for the interview

Parents can play a critical role in preparing children for the interview, not only by giving reassurance but also by helping to explain to the child why the interview is happening, what it entails and what may be its consequences. They will need skilful and careful briefing to enable them to do this as well as support to undertake what often will be a disturbing task.

Parental involvement in conducting the interview

The Memorandum specifies that a parent should not be present during the interview, and so, in cases where the child's account may be used as evidence, this will need to be adhered to. However, where this is not the case, there will need to be consideration given to whether a parent can helpfully accompany the child in the interview. Younger children especially may find it more comfortable to engage in conversation with a stranger if they have their mother or father in the room with them. Older children may, by contrast, find this embarrassing, or may be worried to talk about matters in front of parents if they think this will upset them. If a parent does accompany the child they will need to be prepared and briefed carefully to ensure that they do not undermine the child's ability to give her/his own account.

Particular issues arise with children who have communication difficulties or whose first language is not English. With disabled children this is especially so if the child's parent is their usual interpreter. Whilst engaging the parent in this role offers the child the ease and comfort of their familiar mode of communication, it is preferable to separate out these two roles – for the parent to accompany the child but to bring in another person with the appropriate skills to interpret for and communicate with the child.

Supporting the child after the interview

Even when the child is mature enough to be given this information themselves, interviewers should make sure that they give the child's parents information about what (if anything) will happen next, and names and telephone numbers so that the child or parents can contact the interviewers if they want to communicate about anything else.

Parents should also be given guidance about how the child may react to the interview. If the child has communicated information which has distressed them, or if the outcome of the interview may have serious consequences, parents will need guidance on how to handle this.

Where the suspicions which led to the interview are allayed by what the child has to say, the child is likely, nonetheless, to be distressed. Children may well have found it very hard to answer questions which they see as having accused a much loved parent. They may feel guilty that something they said or did, quite inadvertently, led to their family undergoing such an awful experience. Parents will need advice about how to explain to the child why it took place, and how to allay any concerns it has raised for the child. They should also be informed that the child may well need long-term support (from themselves and from services such as counselling), and be offered advice and help to provide this for the child – in addition to any needs they have of their own for such support.

Good practice in interviewing

A number of sources are available which set out the principles of good practice in interviewing children (see for example *Investigative Interviewing with Children*, Open University, 1992). Here I will summarise just the main points which are salient in terms of partnership.

Clarity of purpose

Before they begin, social workers must always clarify and define the purpose of the interview to be conducted. Not only is this good practice, it is essential if they are to be able to inform parents about what they intend to do. They must ensure that there is a clear and agreed understanding of the kind of interview that is to be undertaken, the techniques that will be used and a well-informed decision made about whether they will follow the Memorandum. They should establish, as far as possible, the likely number and duration of interviews that will be required, and any scheduling needed. Whilst there is a strong preference for only one interview to be conducted, there are occasions when more than one is justified.

Keeping an open mind

Critical to achieving this objective is that investigative interviews must always be conducted with an open mind and never with the notion of 'getting a disclosure'. Not only would this quite possibly cause problems in terms of evidence, it can all too easily lead to a failure to uncover information which is essential to making plans for the child's welfare and safety. At worst, it can simply result in reinforcing the interviewer's preconceived, mistaken assumptions about what has happened and fail to establish the true facts. This may leave all manner of problems in its wake. Whatever the outcome untold damage may be done.

Child-centred interviewing

Much of the skill of interviewing is concerned with providing the conditions which enable children to *give their own account*, in their own words, at their own pace, in a setting in which the child is comfortable and feels safe, valued and respected. This is as much to do with creating the right atmosphere as it is with the particular approach taken. Different people can achieve this in different ways, although there are some basic principles that apply to all approaches.

Interviewers must always bear in mind that the child will have her/his own 'agenda' which may be different from that of the interviewers. For example, many disturbing things may be going on and the child may be preoccupied with questions about what will happen next. Their focus may be about the future, not what happened in the past. This divergence of concern needs to be handled sensitively. This takes tact and skill if other features of the interview are not to be prejudiced.

Some children will have particular needs, for example, if their first language is not English or if they have communication difficulties (e.g. because of hearing impairment or learning disabilities). It will be critical to plan for these before the interview and address them appropriately throughout. Similarly children will often communicate best with those who share their world-view and understandings of things like family life. This means that consideration must be made about the child's racial and cultural background as well as ensuring that interviewers share this with her/him, whenever possible. Consideration must also be made about whether the child will be more comfortable talking to a man or a woman.

In general terms child-centred interviews proceed at a pace with which the child feels comfortable and which allows the child to understand what is going on. They combine achieving the interviewer's objectives of gathering information with encouraging the child and validating her/his experience. Children who have experienced abuse may need considerable reassurance that they are right to tell and that any problems in giving their account are acknowledged. If children become distressed they should be comforted but it is important not to 'invade' the child's space or touch the child. If the distress is severe the interviewer must be prepared to terminate the interview or offer the child a break. Telling when this is demands considerable skill and well-informed and sensitive professional judgement.

When the interviewer has a specific 'agenda' this may dominate their perception of where the interview needs to be taken. It occurs far less often when the interviewer is really listening, and is clued in to the child's account. The Clyde Report strongly criticised interviews which pursued the inter-viewers' agenda, when material offered by the child did not correspond to the interviewer's expectation and then the interviewer ignored or failed to pursue matters raised by the child. Other criticisms were about interviewers intro-ducing details of allegations before allowing children a chance to give their own account, or steering conversations on to personal matters of their own.

In general, what the child is saying – the events described – are what should direct the interview. There are, of course, some exceptions, such as when an interviewer is concerned about the child talking about the bad character of the accused (see above) s/he may decide to steer the child off the topic gently (e.g. discussing a previous conviction). However, as a general principle, what the child has to say should usually take precedence and set the agenda for the interview.

Interviewers must focus on listening rather than talking. This is actually very difficult, because it must be achieved in parallel with keeping in mind what needs to be achieved, working out what to say next, and so on. Nonetheless this, perhaps more than any other feature, is what distinguishes competent and successful interviewing. Listening is about directing attention to what the child has to say; it is about the most important thing happening at that moment irrespective of all the other things going on in the interviewer's mind. It is better to pause to collect thoughts, than to miss something because of inattention.

It also means leaving long enough gaps after a child stops talking, to make sure they have finished. Sometimes quite long pauses must be tolerated, and it is surprising how often simply saying nothing – or giving minimal cues (e.g. Uhuh, Yes, Go on, I see) – will encourage the child to continue talking. Another approach is to repeat what the child has just said, with a voice inflection which suggests encouragement to proceed – as in when the child says something like, 'She didn't understand what I said', then the interviewer might say, 'She didn't understand?'.

Body language is critical. This will mean achieving a balance between creating a sense of attention and concern without 'crowding' the child, or making her/him feel too much in the spotlight. Eye contact should usually be with the child (if s/he finds that comfortable) for much of the time. Facial expression and gesture will also be important; head-nodding in response to a child's statement can be encouraging if done naturally. Great care must be taken, however, to avoid using gesture or expression to 'coach' – to imply that some answers are being looked for or approved of.

Listening also means giving the child cues that you are attending and understand – saying 'I see' or 'I'm still listening' in words or gestures. If you fail to understand what the child is saying, take care how you express this. For example, you should not suggest that the child is being stupid. It is better to say something like 'I think I understand what you are saying but could you help me get it clear in my own mind' rather than 'that does not make any sense'.

Interviewers need to be highly observant and 'clued in', not just to what the child is saying but also to the child's body-language and non-verbal intimations of what they have in their minds when they are talking. For example, eye contact is often a critical indicator. A child may speak for some time looking down and then suddenly look directly at the interviewer. This is usually a cue that the child wants some response. This may be for reassurance or it might be to find out how the interviewer reacts to what has just been said. In some cases it may be an invitation to ask for more information; in others it may be a challenge, an indication that the conversation is moving onto 'dangerous ground'. Responses can be quite explicit sometimes, 'Were you just about to say something there?' for example. Only extensive practice combined with skilful feedback can enable people to learn to respond appropriately to such cues.

Another trap that is all too easy to fall into is to get so focused on the need to ask questions in the second stage that the interview becomes uncomfortably inquisitorial for the child. This obviously needs to be avoided; questions need, therefore, to be interspersed regularly with non-questioning kinds of talk. This can also serve a number of functions: encouragement, reassurance, validation or expressions of empathy. The skill is in 'keeping a low-key' to the questioning but without introducing conversation which side-tracks the child into areas which are not salient.

This problem may be particularly acute when two people are interviewing and is one of the main reasons why, at any one stage in the interview, only one person should act as the 'lead interviewer' with the other person, if present, merely offering support and possibly taking notes. This too is difficult to bring off in practice. To have a second person merely sitting there can feel uncomfortable for both interviewers and child. At the same time, it can be disturbing for children to have two people firing questions at them.

One way of tackling this is to keep the pace relatively slow and to address the important principles described above; so long as listening is the major focus, and the child's cues are responded to, it should be possible to follow a style of questioning which is non-threatening. Another method, increasingly used in localities with appropriate equipment and facilities, is to have only the lead interviewer in the room with the child, with their partner guiding and advising by audio-link.

Dilemmas for partnership

The decision whether or not to pursue a Memorandum-based interview will often be the most difficult to take, given its severe implications for partnership. Considerations will include:

(a) concerns about the impact of a formal, constrained interview on the child with the down-side costs, to the child, of taking this approach;

(b) conflicts between protecting 'this child' and protecting 'children in general';

(c) concerns about pre-empting the possibility of pursuing a criminal prosecution, and of undermining the possibility of a successful conviction;

Often, the main problem is that at the stage at which an interview is being planned, there is simply insufficient information to know what will be the best (or least harmful) approach to take. The interview is, inevitably, a 'catch 22'; until it has been conducted, professionals often do not have much to go on. Its purpose is to supply information; the very information which is needed to know what kind of interview to conduct! The pressure will always be to 'keep the options open', to follow the Memorandum in case the interview turns out to have evidential potential. On the face of it this seems a rational strategy. However, potentially there are severe costs to adopting it, particularly in terms of the constraints it imposes on the ability of professionals to work in partnership. These include:

(a) constraints on the interview itself – where it can be conducted, when, by whom, etc., (parents will seldom be allowed to accompany the child in the interview itself);

(b) pressures to 'keep people in the dark' for fear of risking evidence thus undermining openness and honesty;

(c) the risks of 'escalating' the investigation and antagonising parents;

(d) issues of consent.

This implies three main areas of professional practice which need to be considered:

1. how partnership can be pursued within the decision-making process about whether or not to conduct a Memorandum-based interview;

2. how partnership can be pursued when an 'informal' (i.e. non-Memorandum-based) interview is conducted;

3. how partnership can be pursued when a Memorandum-based interview is conducted.

Crucial areas of practice which need to be approached in terms of partnership are:

(a) gaining consent for the interview to take place whenever this is possible – always accepting that it may be necessary to work hard to make this possible;

(b) similarly, always informing parents whenever possible, even if their consent is not obtained;

(c) involving parents in planning the interview, including finding out about any special needs the child may have;

(d) informing parents and children about its purpose and briefing them about the form it will take;

(e) involving parents in supporting the child before and after the interview;

(f) providing support for parents during the interview and afterwards;

(g) informing parents about the outcome of the interview and what will happen next;

(h) informing parents about the storage of tapes (where they have been recorded) and who has access to them.

Conclusions

The tensions between working with the family and gathering potential evidence are seldom easily resolved in such cases. The best managed, best-principled practice will always entail making difficult judgements about relative risks. But it is crucial to stress that this is not to condone defensive or autocratic practice, whereby parents are treated as 'the enemy' with no efforts made to gain co-operation. Child protection workers have an obligation to conduct interviews in ways which treat children and parents with respect. They must actively seek to avoid underhand, evasive and positively deceitful practices, or simply keeping parents in ignorance to avoid confrontation. Above all they must be wary of 'jumping to conclusions' and they must keep an open mind. They must never allow prejudice or preconceptions to act as excuses for avoiding doing all they can to engage parents in the interview process.

Equally, the pressures imposed by the potential for the interview to be used as evidence in criminal proceedings must not be allowed to dominate the decision about whether or not to follow the Memorandum; nor must they divert social workers away from conducting interviews in child-sensitive and child-facilitative ways. It is still a fact that the majority of cases of child abuse do not result in the conviction of the abuser. If children are to be protected, the paramount goal for social workers must always be to uncover the information they need to assess properly the risks to the child, and then consider the possible avenues that can be followed to make that child safe. This should not be compromised by the desire to produce an evidentially sound, video-taped interview. As far as possible the approach should be one which is both best for the child and the family, and best in terms of legal requirements. But where a conflict arises, then the child's welfare must be the first consideration.

REFERENCES

Home Office (1989) *Report of the Advisory Group on Video Evidence* (the Pigot Report) London: HMSO.

Spencer, J.R. and Flin, R. (1990) *The Evidence of Children: The Law and the Psychology*, London: Blackstone.

12

Medical examinations

Jan Welbury

Introduction

The aims of this chapter are:

- to offer all practitioners in the field of child protection an understanding of the issues involved in the medical contribution to an enquiry;
- to assist non-medical practitioners in assessing the nature of the medical input required for individual cases;
- to illustrate that the medical contribution does not always require a physical examination;
- to accept that examination will not always be possible even when indicated;
- to clarify both the value and the limitations of the physical component of the examination;
- to assist practitioners in preparing and referring children and their carers for a medical assessment;
- to identify good practice in carrying out the medical assessment.

The medical contribution will vary widely depending on:

- the circumstances of, and reasons for the concern for, the child;
- the perceived nature of the abuse, its timing and duration;
- the needs and wishes of the child and his/her carers;
- the doctor carrying out the assessment.

Each district health authority is responsible for the provision of a comprehensive service for children at risk of abuse and to their families. All health provider units concerned with children should have child protection policies and procedures in place. They should also have a designated doctor (usually a consultant community or hospital paediatrician who serves on the local ACPC) experienced in child protection and who is competent to ensure:

- child protection policies are in line with local area child protection committee (ACPC) policy;
- effective communication between the different provider units, including an efficient transfer of records;
- advice is available to all doctors and health professionals;
- doctors know how and when to refer children to the SSD and how to use the Child Protection Register;
- adequate training (including multi-disciplinary and multi-agency) is available and accessible;
- provision and dissemination of information, and advice on child protection;
- that the doctor acts as a reference point for other agencies, e.g. SSD, Education;
- that the doctor works with a designated senior nurse.

Any doctor (a general practitioner or clinical medical officer, i.e. community doctor, paediatrician or psychiatrist) who sees children, or adults who are in contact with children, has a role to play in the protection of children.

Medical examination – determination of need and scope

The need for and timing of a medical assessment

The request for medical input to a child protection investigation should be an early consideration and may happen through a variety of health professionals. Medical input assists the investigation by providing knowledge and information regarding the child and his/her carer. Discussion will indicate the need for a more comprehensive medical assessment which *may* include a medical examination.

The need for urgent examination in child protection (for example, a baby with bruising) is not a common scenario. And there may be valid reasons to delay the actual examination following the request for a medical assessment:

- to allow the child time to build up trust in those working with the child;
- to allow the doctor to collect additional relevant health information;
- to ensure that the examination is carried out in suitable surroundings, by the most appropriate doctor and with an adequate time period allocated to allow a comprehensive assessment.

However, an urgent examination is required:

- to assess and treat possible acute injury;
- to document recent injury;
- to collect forensic evidence.

Assessment and treatment of possible acute injury

- Suspected or overt physical abuse with injury.

  Where there is suspected or overt physical abuse with injury (including burns, scalding, bruising, possible fractures etc.), these injuries need to be assessed with reasonable speed to document evidence, provide appropriate treatment and ensure the protection of the child.

- Suspected cases of abuse associated with certain current symptoms.

  Similarly, urgent examination is needed to handle any suspected case associated with certain current symptoms such as complaints of a sore bottom, bleeding from the anus, urethra or vagina (except in the case of pubertal girl with expected menstrual period), difficulty in passing urine or pain on passing a bowel motion.

Documentation of recent injury

Where there has been alleged sexual abuse within the past 72 hours, prompt action may be necessary to detect the presence of transient genital signs – e.g. redness, swelling and/or bruising – from friction or rubbing (this can occur through intracrural intercourse, i.e. rubbing the penis over the external genitalia between the legs).

The earlier a child with overt injuries is seen the better the chance of observation and documentation of transient signs which may be present. More substantive injuries can then be evaluated for their severity and timing by re-examination at an appropriate interval.

Collection of forensic evidence

Forensic evidence may be acquired during examination of the child, the alleged perpetrator and/or the scene of the alleged abuse. The evidence may be 'robust' in that it can be detected or measured using formal testing techniques at the official Forensic Laboratories. It may be considered less robust when it is based on the clinical findings and opinion of the examiner.

The 'robust' or laboratory evidence comprises :

- swabs of body fluids and secretions, e.g. blood, saliva, semen etc.;
- swabs of infection, e.g. sexually transmitted infection;
- nail clippings, hairs, cuttings, skin scrapings etc.;
- blood samples for alcohol, drugs etc.;
- urine for pregnancy testing, drugs etc.

Less 'robust', or clinical, evidence includes:

- injuries – bruises, bites, fractures etc.;
- changed anatomical appearance that is inappropriate for age/expected life experience (e.g. genital changes).

The strength of this evidence varies greatly from very robust, e.g. certain diagnostic fracture patterns in small children, to relatively weak, e.g. minor changes in the appearance of the anus.

In terms of the forensic evidence the responsibility of doctors is to assess and report whether or not, *in their opinion* and based on their knowledge and experience, the findings are:

- compatible with the disclosure if one has been given;
- compatible with abuse;
- compatible with possible non-abusive causes or 'organic ' disease.

They are also required to state the degree to which compatible evidence is supportive of the possible causes. This again will vary from so strongly supportive that abuse is the only explanation – a conclusion that usually will only be drawn following investigation to exclude possible organic causes – to compatible but not supportive.

Clinical evidence relies on the opinion of the individual examining doctor. It is, however, the clinical evidence that tends to be relied upon in the early stages of the investigation to advise on the direction of the case (i.e. whether there is a possible criminal case to be considered). Normal clinical findings can be compatible with some forms of abuse.

In some cases where sexual abuse is recent, semen or saliva may be detected on swabs taken from the genitalia and elsewhere. This is of extreme importance. Clothing and bedding should also be retained for forensic examination and the child should not be bathed until after the examination has been performed. Semen has been detected in the vagina up to five days after assault but in reality is rarely found after 72 hours. Washing and douching obviously make detection less likely.

These cases are usually presented to the examining doctor by the police and it is important that doctors understand the seemingly 'indecent haste' that can sometimes occur in such cases. The finding of such evidence may be an essential factor in allowing a child or young person successfully to face his/her abuser in court – an action which a substantial number of them strongly desire.

Impact of the nature of the abuse or neglect on the medical examination

Factors determining the need for medical examination

It is unusual for a child to suffer one form of abuse exclusively, though one tends to predominate in the initial stages of disclosure or investigation. The variations in the form of abuse and the perceived severity dictate the need for, type and timing of the examination.

In any examination it is good practice for the doctor to assess the developmental status of the child and to note his/her demeanour and emotional state at the time of examination. Their opinion may inform on the child's:

- understanding of what has occurred;
- communication skills;
- ability to cope with the process of investigation (including possible court proceedings).

Physical abuse The need for medical examination is usually clear in physical abuse as there is visible evidence to document, the likelihood of further detectable injuries and a possible need for treatment.

The aims of the medical are:

(a) to document physical injuries and, where necessary, provide treatment;

(b) to determine the general physical status of the child;

(c) to consider all explanations for the injuries including possible organic disease;

(d) to carry out necessary medical investigations to determine the presence or absence of organic disease (e.g. 'skeletal survey', i.e. X-ray examination of small children which may reveal fractures, or 'clotting studies' i.e. blood tests that can show a pathological tendency to easy bruising);

(e) to consult with senior colleagues or those with particular expertise (e.g. a specialist paediatric radiologist) where findings are unusual or complex;

(f) to offer a considered opinion on the compatibility of the medical evidence with proffered explanations;

(g) to propose an hypothesis where there is no proffered explanation or where the latter is not felt to be compatible with the medical evidence;

(h) to give information, explanation and reassurance to the child and their carer/s regarding the injuries – their extent, severity and prognosis;

(i) to arrange, where necessary, medical follow-up for the child;

(j) to prepare necessary reports and statements.

Sexual abuse There is often a tendency to request a medical examination at an early stage in the investigation. The 'needs' that determine the request are often those of the professionals or carers rather than the 'needs' dictated by the best interests of the child. There is a misconception that the medical examination will produce a rapid answer and justify the 'need' to investigate further.

Many forms of sexual abuse leave no physical signs, or heal rapidly and completely. Hence the medical examination will rarely prove that abuse has occurred. If it does indicate that sexual contact has taken place it is often not possible to state with any absolute accuracy the frequency, timing or exact nature of the abuse. At best the doctor will offer a statement of how consistent are the signs with the disclosure (if one is forthcoming). Not infrequently the signs may be more than expected, indicating that the child may have more to share. The examination can often be the trigger to further disclosure once the child has his/her account confirmed by a doctor.

It is essential to discuss the possibility of *no* physical findings with the child, their carer/s and the professionals involved, before the examination. This is of particular importance in the case where physical findings are unlikely (e.g. digital fondling of the genital area without penetration).

There are situations when examination should occur as soon as possible:

(a) where there may be physical damage which requires treatment or where it may resolve rapidly, leaving no signs;

(b) where there may be forensic evidence;

(c) where the child is worried and requests it;

(d) where the case needs to progress rapidly to provide protection for the child (again it must be noted that the examination may not 'provide' evidence to achieve this).

Where an examination is required the medical examination essentially is the same as those for physical abuse with the additional consideration of:

1. the possibility of sexually transmitted disease and the need to organise appropriate investigation;

2. the possibility of pregnancy in pubertal girls, the opportunity for emergency contraception if the alleged assault was within the previous 5 days and the need for counselling regarding choices;

3. the possibility of inappropriate sexualisation and its detrimental effects on the normal development of sexuality and sexual identity;

4. the issues of continuing vulnerability, particularly of children with learning difficulties, developmental delay and disability.

Emotional abuse and neglect In defining this form of abuse the 'medical examination' needs to provide a picture of the current health status of the child to compare with previously documented examinations as well the expected norm for that child. Hence the requirement is for a paediatric assessment which may include a medical examination. The parameters assessed will include:

1. growth (height, weight, head circumference, where appropriate, and possibly growth velocity);

2. developmental status;

3. physical well-being;

4. emotional status;

5. general level of care and hygiene;

6. consideration of any organic problems (e.g. asthma);

7. consideration of possible concurrent physical and sexual abuse.

The timing of an assessment is important in the management of cases of emotional abuse and neglect. Where children are under surveillance because of concerns for their well-being it is important to encourage regular health contacts to ensure that support and advice is available to their carers and to monitor the stated parameters. This 'preventive' role is essential in encouraging and enabling families with limited resources to provide appropriate care. Such contacts also contribute to the assessment of the family's ability to respond to change and to develop parenting skills.

Where concerns lead to the child being looked after by the local authority an assessment should occur at the earliest opportunity:

- to ensure an accurate evaluation and description of the child's physical and emotional status at the time of admission to the care of the local authority, to contribute to the evidence that should justify that action;

- to enable the doctor to present a comprehensive picture of the changes in the child's well-being up to the time of admission and, by reassessment at intervals following admission, the affects of changed care and environment;

- the child may have unmet health needs which should be addressed.

Emotional abuse occurs in many cases of sexual abuse as well as in cases of physical abuse and neglect. Hence most cases of abuse are best served by a full paediatric assessment rather than a more narrow medical examination.

The occurrence of physical evidence and determination of abuse

Physical evidence frequently is perceived as the most significant and substantive part of the 'jigsaw' of investigation. There is no doubt that there are occasions when this is the case, particularly in pre-verbal children and babies with 'classical' injuries where organic disease has been excluded. However, paediatric assessment of the development, behaviour and emotional status of the child in relation to the alleged or suspected abuse can be equally significant where there is no physical evidence.

Contribution to the welfare and rights of the child

Paramouncy of benefit to child

The welfare of the child must be of primary importance. In terms of the medical examination this means that:

- examination is in the best interest of the child – he/she may require treatment or reassurance;

- the child's needs must come above any self-interest of professionals, e.g. the need to secure a criminal charge;

- a balance must be obtained between avoidance of a compounding impact on the child versus the need for examination.

To achieve this goal it is essential to:

- ensure that the need for examination is defined clearly;

- that the timing of the examination is appropriate as defined by the needs of the child, the requirements of the case and the availability of the most appropriate doctor and venue.

Developmental evidence

A comprehensive developmental assessment will not be required in every case although a comment on the child's general level of development should always be possible. However, a comprehensive assessment should be made and recorded where the child is known or suspected to be delayed or impaired developmentally. Equally important is an assessment of the young child, whose ability to comprehend their situation, to understand the concept of 'truth' and accurately report events, may be in question.

A recorded developmental assessment may also assist the doctor and other professional witnesses interpret the child's account of events which may appear to conflict with an adult concept of reality and possibility.

Right of refusal

Children rarely are aware of their rights. Abused children often have poor self-esteem and are used to adults inflicting their will upon them. In practising the belief of paramouncy of benefit for the child the professionals and carers must enable and allow children their rights (including the refusal to be examined).

It is good practice to explain to the child and their carers:

- the reason for the examination;

- the nature of the examination;

- the benefits/disadvantages and possible outcomes of the examination;

- their right to refuse part or all of the examination.

It is also appropriate to negotiate with the child:

- who they would like to accompany him/her at the examination;

- how they wish the examination to be conducted.

Some children are so disempowered that they cannot refuse verbally but will demonstrate, by their body language, their wish not to comply. Professionals should be able to interpret these messages and positively give children permission to terminate the examination without fear of disapproval.

Their refusal may be the result of coercion by the perpetrator, a situation which produces intense anxiety for the child. It is still appropriate to comply with their expressed wishes and delay attempts to examine until the situation allows them to consent. Children who refuse examination initially often give consent later if they feel more secure.

Conducting the medical examination following such explanation and negotiation infrequently is a more positive, and less intimidating, experience for the child. The overall effect of the experience, whether or not the examination is carried out, can be empowering and therefore therapeutic for the child.

However, the immediate benefit may be less apparent to the child's family and to professionals who may believe that the medical examination will determine whether or not abuse has taken place. They will require a great deal of support, a realistic understanding of the place of the medical examination in the investigative process and the ability to recognise the potential it has for harm if forced upon the child.

Perspective of other involved parties

Substitution of a medical examination for other more relevant actions

When child abuse is suspected or disclosed the medical examination rarely is urgent or essential in instigating and carrying out the investigation. Information collection and collation usually are more appropriate actions and may well modify the need for or type of examination. The findings of the medical should not influence the decision to investigate child protection issues (except where it is the examination that has raised the suspicion). It is not appropriate to either impose on, or allow, the examining doctor the exclusive responsibility for diagnosis.

Need for alternative treatment when a medical examination is not needed

During the process of investigation health issues (physical or emotional) may arise which require attention. When a formal medical examination is not part of the investigative process these issues should be addressed through the usual channels (i.e. the family practitioner) unless there is a specific reason to act differently, e.g. the child is already under the care of a paediatrician , child psychologist or child psychiatrist .

The importance of co-ordinating information

Comprehensive collection and collation of information from all involved agencies are essential in child protection investigation. Health information is available on all children and is collected in a number of places:

- the Health Authority Child Computer System (the information stored varies between districts);
- the Community Child Health Services (i.e. doctors, health visitors and school nurses records);
- the family doctor's records;
- the hospital records (a different set for each hospital and, sometimes, each department attended).

It is essential not only to collect and collate this information but also to ensure that it is interpreted by a competent practitioner (usually a paediatrician).

Limitations of medical examination

It is essential that everyone involved in the investigation of child abuse is aware of the value of the medical contribution but, equally, that they appreciate the limitations of the physical examination. Lack of physical findings does not exclude the diagnosis of abuse, particularly where the suspicion is of sexual abuse. Physical findings can occasionally be diagnostic and are often consistent with and support the diagnosis. However, occasionally they become the main focus of the investigation when they are equivocal or contentious; they can then detract from the overall picture even when the latter would be clear without any physical findings.

Partnership practice

Prior considerations when obtaining consent

Before conducting a medical examination, the doctor should consider all of the following points:

- Who has the right to consent to the examination?
- Is the child subject to a court order?
- What are the directions of the court, if any, in relation to the order?
- Who has parental responsibility and what are their views ?
- Will the assessment be used in court proceedings?
- What are the views of the child?
- Does the child have any difficulty communicating, for which special arrangements need to be made?
- Who will be present at the examination?

The legal requirements and the validity of consent

Depending on their age and ability to understand, and using good practice as a guide, children should be asked for their consent to an examination. Obtaining consent must be carried out in the context of an informed decision. The child must be aware of what he/she is consenting to as well as the possible consequences resulting from the examination. The explanation for the child must include:

- the aim of the examination;
- the process involved;
- his/her freedom to negotiate the way in which the examination is conducted;
- his/her right to withdraw consent.

The child has the right to determine who is present and the right at any stage to withdraw their consent from part or all of the examination. Consent must be given freely without fear, threat, fraud or coercion.

By the age of 16 years, children are regarded in law as capable of giving consent (but there may be exceptions, such as a child with significant learning difficulties). However, young people under 16 years can give their own consent if the doctor feels that they are capable of so doing.

Cases involving court orders, parental authority with local authority etc. should be handled as follows:

Emergency Protection Order (EPO)	Once proceedings have been started, the court's permission for consent should always be sought. The applicant for the EPO has parental responsibility as long as the order lasts and may consent for emergency treatment (although this should be discussed where practicable with the parents).
Child Assessment Order	The court has authority for medical examinations.
Care Order	The local authority (LA) has parental responsibility and may give consent. This authority may be delegated to carers in certain circumstances. The parents also hold parental responsibility but the LA may determine the extent to which this can be exercised.
Child in local authority accommodation	For children accommodated under section 20 of the Children Act, the LA does not have power to consent to medical examination unless delegated by a parent or other person with parental responsibility.
Child placed for adoption	Birth parents retain parental responsibility for children of any age placed under an adoption agency until they have been freed for adoption. The extent with which they are able to exercise this responsibility varies with the legal status of the child, specific arrangements made with the parent and any section 8 order which is in effect.
Wards of court	The High Court has the right to consent to medical examination and direction must be sought on the ward's behalf. Since the Children Act 1989, children rarely are made wards of court.
Local authority parental responsibility	When an LA has parental responsibility it may in appropriate cases delegate the consent to medical examination to others (for example the carers). In

these circumstances it is important that the LA and the parents discuss medical consent, covering various contingencies, before it is needed.

Parental responsibility and involvement

Parents must be involved fully in the procedures for obtaining consent. When children are living at home in the care of their parents, or when the children are too young to decide for themselves, a parent has the power to consent to the medical treatment. Where parents have delegated the care of the child to others they can also delegate their power to consent to medical treatment. Children aged 16 years and over are able in law to give their own consent to medical treatment. In such cases 'parental involvement' does not mean that they may pressurise children or insist on being present during an interview with a doctor, or at an examination.

Good paediatric practice assumes the presence of a parent/carer at any interview or examination. Exceptions to this practice should be rare and occur only when the circumstances have been considered carefully. Such exceptions may be for part or all of the process – more usually the former – and include:

- a clear informed statement by a child or young person that this is his/her choice;
- where the doctor wishes to provide the child and/or the parent/carer with the opportunity to discuss issues that he/she may find difficult, uncomfortable or upsetting.

The opportunity to discuss issues may be offered routinely by some doctors when the child or young person is considered to have an appropriate level of understanding. This can be considered as an example of good practice but should not be seen as:

- an opportunity to invite or induce disclosure;
- an attempt to encourage either party to 'talk behind the other's back'.

It should be seen as an opportunity to discuss:

- sensitive issues, e.g. a young person's possible sexual experience outside of an abusive situation;
- the parent/carer's feelings; particularly important as they may have experienced abuse in their childhood.

It is important to negotiate such discussions and clarify the reasons for offering the opportunity. It is essential that the child and parent/carer understand the limits of the doctor's ability to maintain confidentiality.

Good practice

When medical involvement is requested in a case of possible abuse, the doctor should ask formally for consent from the person with responsibility (usually the parent or child). Reliance on verbal consent is quite normal and rarely is challenged. However, where there exist contentious issues, written and witnessed consent is preferable (wherever possible this should consist of the written consent of the person with parental responsibility, the child and a professional witness). However, consent is equally valid, whether given orally or in writing, as long as it is informed and given freely.

Written consent should always be sought before any treatment is given involving general anaesthetic except where the operation is essential to preserve life and where consent cannot be obtained within the time available.

The child's view

The Children Act 1989 considers the child's welfare to be paramount, but the child may be vulnerable when given the choice to consent to or refuse medical examination in the circumstances of abuse. Abusers recognise this and may pressurise the child to refuse, fearing the consequences of corroboration of the allegations. Although the Act leaves the giving of consent to the child (in the case of older children), parents and professionals must use care in counselling children so that their anxiety does not compound the impact on the child. It is rare for a doctor to proceed without consent and this should be limited to:

- life threatening circumstances;
- deterioration of forensic evidence.

It is important to recognise that examination without consent may be held in law to be an assault.

Preparation

Referrals, records and medical opinion

When a medical opinion is sought it is important that any such referral is made to the most appropriate doctor. No definite guidance can be given as each district will vary widely depending on the local facilities, resources and the ACPC guidelines. It is important for professionals to build up a working knowledge of the systems in their district and the types of cases which different doctors manage. However in general:

- Cases of **alleged sexual abuse** are likely to be managed by a small, well-defined group of paediatricians. In some districts forensic matters may be handled by police surgeons. In such cases it is essential to involve a doctor who can address any medical, developmental or emotional issues arising from the examination or the investigation. In some cases the general practitioner will be the appropriate doctor to address these issues; in others, it will be a paediatrician. A child psychiatrist or psychologist may be needed in cases where they are involved already or where such a need is identified during the investigation.

- Cases of **suspected physical abuse** will depend on the mode of presentation and the severity of the injuries. Scalds, burns, bites, bruises etc. may be presented to the general practitioner, who may feel confident in making a diagnosis but more often he/she will refer such cases on to a paediatrician in the hospital or the community in order to exclude organic disease (which may require X-rays or blood tests).

Similarly cases presenting to accident and emergency departments are likely to be referred on to paediatric staff. Again it is essential that issues of health and illness be addressed actively. Vulnerable children are highly likely to have unresolved health problems and the opportunity to address them should not be missed.

- Cases of possible **emotional abuse or neglect** are assessed most appropriately by a detailed collation of *all* available health information. The information should be given by every health professional providing care to the child. The collation and interpretation of information usually will be carried out by an experienced paediatrician.

Occasionally a second opinion may be required. This does not necessarily require a second examination of the child; in many cases the second opinion can be gained by a re-examination of the medical information on which the first opinion was based. Second examinations should be avoided whenever possible.

Strategy meetings and clarification of scope of the investigation or examination

Potential importance of a strategy meeting

The potential importance of a strategy meeting cannot be overstated as it can:

- offer the opportunity to clarify issues and plan appropriately focused and timely investigation;
- ensure that the investigation is comprehensive and efficient;
- ensure that the issues are understood by all parties involved.

This co-ordinating process should minimise distress to children and their families.

Participation of all interested parties

Participation of all interested parties is essential, although attendance is not always possible, particularly in view of the tight timescales dictated by procedural guidance. Those unable to attend should be given the opportunity to make representation, in writing or verbally to the chair and they should be informed of the plan arising from the meeting. Occasionally the need for urgent investigation will dictate that this planning process takes place over the telephone between the key parties only.

Consideration of the medical input

A strategy meeting offers an opportunity for careful consideration of the medical input including:

- the need for and format of the medical contribution;
- the need for, timing of and appropriate venue for a medical examination;
- the need to address other health issues.

Assessment of the investigation or examination required

Whilst the examination of a child may have been initiated by concerns about maltreatment or neglect, an assessment of the whole child should be included in the examination. This is particularly relevant for vulnerable children as their general health care may have been neglected.

- General
  This includes a full history including the child's past medical history,

family history, immunisations, medications taken and any allergies. The extent of the examination will vary with the age, circumstances, wishes and needs of the individual child. However, particularly in the case of younger children, a 'full medical ' can be a reasonable and useful way of relaxing the child and gaining their confidence, particularly if there is a need for a genital examination.

- Forensic
  The forensic examination includes assessment of:
  —behaviour;
  —injuries;
  —infection;
  —pregnancy;
  —genital examination – where indicated.

Minimisation of examinations and co-operation between the parties

It is essential to limit the number of occasions that a child is examined during a child protection investigation. This can be achieved by ensuring:

- contact with and involvement of an appropriate doctor (guidance should be available in the ACPC guidelines);

- collection, collation and sharing of information before the examination (except in exceptional circumstances, e.g. injury requiring treatment, and when delay could cause the possible loss of forensic evidence);

- an understanding by all parties of the roles and priorities of each professional group and mutual respect of possible differing perspectives;

- detailed discussion between the parties of the information available leading to a clear definition of the need for and scope of a medical examination;

- the 'informed' involvement of the parents or carers and children at all stages of the process (i.e. ensuring that they understand the issues, the language used and their right to be involved in the proceedings);

- a joint examination (because one doctor does not have all of the skills required or there exists a potentially contentious matter).

Good planning should ensure that only one examination is required. However, there are occasions when a second examination is needed:

- where there is recent injury and the signs are not developed fully;

- where a second examination may help to clarify the timing of events (by assessing the healing process);

- where the suspicion of child abuse arises out of an examination for an unrelated matter carried out by a doctor not experienced in child protection;

- where the findings are unusual and/or contentious and the examining doctor feels it essential to share his/her uncertainty with an experienced colleague;

- where solicitors for the parents and/or guardian ad litem, or the child's solicitor, obtain the court's consent to carry out a second independent examination.

Further examination may be required for the management or treatment of injuries or for the investigation of sexually transmitted disease. Where this can be predicted, and where there is a need for a second child protection examination, every attempt should be made to combine the examinations. Ideally all of the examinations should be carried out by the same doctor.

Handling of preparatory interviews and anxieties

When the decision to carry out a medical examination has been made it is essential to plan the time and place to suit most adequately the needs of the case. In reality the timing is often a compromise depending on the availability of the doctor, the existence of appropriate accommodation for the examination and the urgency of the need to examine. There are relatively few doctors qualified to carry out child protection examinations and they all have other commitments which cannot always be postponed. Again good preparation is essential:

- Ideally the venue should be a dedicated suite of rooms that are 'child-friendly' and age-appropriate.

- The unit should be relatively anonymous. Often this is achieved best when it is an integral but discrete part of a paediatric unit.

- The unit should be staffed appropriately with adequate nursing or nursery nurse cover in order to provide support to the child and family and to assist and chaperone the doctor during the examination.

- Where possible the joint interviewing/video unit should be part of the same site to allow optimal co-ordination of the investigation and to minimise distress to children and their families.

- There should be enough rooms to allow the parents/carers privacy during interview or counselling while their children are provided and cared for comfortably.

- The procedure can be time-consuming and so appropriate refreshments should be available.

As stated above initial discussion with all parties is required to ensure that everyone understands the reason for carrying out the examination. This discussion is particularly important with respect to the families and children. It is good practice to offer time individually to both the parent/carer and child in order to allow them to share anxieties that may otherwise be distressing. This can be useful to all parties and should be offered as a positive approach (otherwise it could appear to be devious or divisive). It may become necessary for the doctor to speak to different parties individually if there appears to be a tension between the child and his/her parents/carers but this should be expressed openly and co-operation sought in order to gain a more complete understanding of the situation.

Again the examination should be explained in detail to the child and the revelant family members. Where the child is able to participate in the discussion he/she should be encouraged to decide how they wish the examination to be conducted (i.e. who should be present, where they want to be examined, e.g. on their parent's/carer's knee or on the examination couch etc.). When the child can write, or has an understanding of consent, it is good practice to ask them to sign the consent form; this is also an important consideration for a person with parental responsibility and it is particularly empowering for adolescents.

Involving a child in the preparatory interviews, discussions and consent can transform the examination process from a frightening (and occasionally a humiliating) experience into an empowering one. It may also:

- reassure them that what they say is taken seriously;
- promote further disclosures.

Approach to conducting the examination

When planning the medical assessment it is essential to ensure that all of the appropriate people are available and that they manage to attend. The organisation and co-ordination of the timing and the venue therefore are essential. Transport and support should be organised for those who would otherwise find attendance difficult or distressing.

Persons present at the examination

The people present at the assessment will vary according to the circumstances of the case.

- The **parents/carers** are usually present but there are occasions when they would not be, either at the request of the child, or because they themselves do not wish to be present. Whatever the reason, in such cases it is good practice for the doctor to offer to see the parent/carer at another time unless there are specific reasons for not doing so. When a child is not able to give consent, and if a person with parental responsibility is not going to be present at the assessment, it is essential to obtain consent *before* the time and venue are finalised. As already stated, with few exceptions, a doctor usually cannot proceed without consent. When the child is able to give consent it is still good practice to obtain 'parental' consent whenever possible.

- A **social worker** and/or a **police officer** (usually from the local Child Protection Unit but occasionally from CID) are also likely to be present. Their attendance may be part of a co-ordinated investigation where the interviewing and examination facilities are on the same site. In cases where there is an urgent need for examination that will not allow time for the collection, collation and discussion of existing information, the social worker and/or the police officer will need to provide the doctor with information and offer support to the family.

When considering the actual examination the factors that will be considered include:

1. the age of the child;
2. the functional level of the child;
3. the wishes of the child;
4. the wishes of the parent/person with parental responsibility;
5. the need to take samples for forensic evidence.

When it is necessary to collect forensic evidence it is advisable to have a policewoman in attendance to receive, label, time and package the samples.

When this is not possible the doctor may assume the responsibility, or a nurse who has been trained to do this may be available.

A doctor should not physically examine a child on his/her own, unless this is unavoidable. Sometimes there will be a nurse available to assist the doctor and support the family. Unfortunately, particularly in community settings, a nurse may not be available and the social worker or policewoman may be required to be present to support the child and/or family members.

Timing

The timing of the examination should always be in the interests of the child, not for the convenience of the doctor or other practitioners. However, it is in the interest of the child for the examination to be arranged so as to allow the doctor to give their full time and attention to the case.

Child protection examinations out of working hours should rarely be necessary but may arise when:

- there is a need for acute forensic examination (usually these are initiated by the police);
- a child presents 'out of hours' to a family doctor, or to the accident and emergency department, or when issues regarding the safety of the child exist which cannot be resolved without an examination by another practitioner;
- there is a need for treatment.

Venue

Again the venue will be dictated by the needs of the case and the doctor carrying out the examination. For example:

1. When the examining doctor is the **family's general practitioner** it is likely to take place in the doctor's surgery.

2. When the examining doctor is a **hospital paediatrician** he/she may see the child in his/her hospital out-patient clinic, on the ward, in the accident and emergency department or in a dedicated unit in the hospital (if one exists).

3. Where the examining doctor is a **community-based children's doctor** the child may be seen in the local clinic, the school medical room or in a dedicated unit (if there is one in the district).

4. When the examining doctor is a **police surgeon** the child may be examined jointly with a hospital or community children's doctor (and use the appropriate facilities). Examinations should not be conducted at police stations.

Children should be seen in a setting that is most comfortable for them. If the case requires a full paediatric assessment then ideally it should be held in a dedicated unit. The unit should provide child-friendly resources and ambience, and the facilities to carry out the whole investigation (including a video interview). As stated above the typical setting for such a unit is within a child health facility in the community or hospital. Effectively this anonymises the unit, aims to ensure child-friendly facilities and staff are available, and provides the doctor with a fully equipped base.

Reporting the examination

It will not always be possible to provide a complete assessment immediately after the examination, particularly if it has been carried out as an emergency. However doctors usually will share their findings and initial impressions. The reporting should include :

- an explanation to, reassurance of, and discussion with, the child in a manner appropriate to his/her age and understanding;

- an explanation to the parents/carers followed by a discussion of any queries and anxieties;

- sharing the findings and initial impressions with social services and/or the police;

- proposals for after-care arrangements or (rarely) further examination.

Usually the doctor will provide a written report and, if required, a statement for the police. Doctors, particularly general practitioners, find attendance at child protection conferences difficult because of large, pre-booked clinics and especially as a result of the short (albeit appropriate) timescale dictated by *Working Together* (DoH, 1991). However, it is invaluable to have a doctor present to explain a report especially when there are medical findings which could easily be misinterpreted. Where this is not possible it is good practice for the doctor to telephone the chairperson prior to the conference to clarify any contentious issues.

The doctor conducting the examination

Choice of doctor

The choice of doctor will vary with the situation. The doctors likely to be involved include:

- **The general practitioner** (GP). The family doctor will have access to information regarding the child and all members of the family registered with the practice. The GP may be the appropriate doctor to examine the child in suspected physical abuse and to provide information of emotional abuse and neglect and sexual abuse. It would not, however, be appropriate for a GP to examine a child when sexual abuse has been disclosed or is suspected unless he/she had:

    —the appropriate training and expertise;
    —ongoing involvement and experience in the field.

    Few, if any, GPs would fulfil these criteria. Normally they would refer on to a paediatrician to exclude organic disease and to carry out an examination. Often the GP has a great deal of insight into the family and may be the doctor accepted most readily by the family to deal with health issues and to offer support. However, in some cases the child's family may have avoided medical contact, may have moved areas and changed GPs or may have failed to register with a practice.

- **The Paediatrician**. Most paediatricians work in the field of child protection, in particular in the areas of physical and emotional abuse and neglect. Some specialists will deal only with children where the abuse is recognised in the course of their contact with the child rather than through referral. In any district there are usually a few paediatricians who deal with the assessment of cases of child sexual abuse. Cases of suspected abuse should be dealt with by a senior doctor who has the experience and authority to interpret the child protection issues as well as medical findings. A paediatrician will be available in the paediatric unit of the hospital at all times. However this does not negate the need for appropriate planning and discussion regarding the timing and venue of any examination. Often units are extremely busy and undue haste may lead to the child being seen in a busy out-patient department or on the children's ward (where the doctor may have to be interrupted).

227

- **The Police Surgeon**. He or she sees cases of suspected child abuse when they have been identified by the police. However, in most districts the police would use a local paediatrician. The police surgeon may perform a joint examination with the paediatrician if the latter is not trained to take forensic samples.

Attributes

Doctors who see children in the context of child protection require specialist knowledge of issues regarding the investigative and legal procedures as well as possessing the ability to assess the medical status of the child. They also have to understand the needs and different perspectives of the other members of the investigative team.

Specialist knowledge

They need specialist knowledge of :

- the medical contribution to child protection investigations;
- the normal range of growth, development and behaviour, and the possible affects of child abuse on these parameters;
- the forensic examination, its value and limitations and the procedures for presenting forensic evidence;
- ACPC guidelines, policy and procedures;
- the legal processes involved in child protection;
- ways of communicating with children, and parents/carers regarding child protection issues.

Appreciation of the need to involve other parties

- The doctor should be a member of the team participating actively in the process of decision making rather than being a technical expert delivering the details of an examination.
- The doctor should appreciate the roles, perspectives and statutory obligations of other members of the investigative team. Such an appreciation assists the doctor to understand the imperatives and time constraints felt by some members and will guide the doctor in preparing reports appropriate to the needs of the case, as well as the professionals and the child and family members.
- The doctor should have a good working knowledge of local services

(both statutory and voluntary) in order to enhance the co-ordination of the investigation as well as allow them to advise on the potential therapeutic input for the child and the family.

Approach to medical examination – handling issues of age, gender, culture and disability

In any interaction between individuals each should recognise the other's right to be treated with consideration and respect. This is essential when the interaction is between a child and family members, and professional workers, during a child protection investigation. Care must be taken to ensure that all parties understand the issues, the process of investigation, the decisions regarding the case and the management plan. This is important especially where there is an obvious reason to believe that there may be difficulties for individuals arising from issues of age, gender, culture or disabilty.

Consideration of these issues may alter the way in which the investigation is carried out as well as affect the management of the case. It may assist in understanding the reason for the abuse but should not influence the diagnosis and decisions of the investigating team in a specific case. If an act committed on a child is considered abusive then it must be so regardless of the child's or the perpetrator's age, gender, culture or disability.

- **Age**. A child's understanding relates strongly to their age, their level of development and their experience of life. It is essential to recognise these factors and to ensure that interpretations of any disclosures pay credence to them. The child may have had bad experiences of doctors in the past and require a great deal of preparation and support to be able to consent to examination. Explanations and reassurances should be given in language appropriate to their level of understanding. 'Age' should not be used as an excuse to avoid talking to the child.

- **Gender**. The issue of gender may involve that of the child and the doctor. In general small children are examined by male and female doctors unless the child exhibits particular gender-related fears. Where sexual abuse is alleged and genital examination is required girls from early puberty usually are seen by female doctors (whenever this is feasible). Adolescent boys, when given the choice, may also opt for a female doctor when they are alleging sexual assault by a male.

- **Culture**. Cultural and religious beliefs and different child-rearing practices must be appreciated to avoid misunderstanding. It is not possible for individual workers to have a working knowledge of all cultural groups, and it is inappropriate to generalise about individuals in any identified group. Therefore, in planning the process of investigation, information regarding beliefs and taboos should be collected from an independent source as well as from the family and individuals. Information of significance to the examination should be given to the doctor to allow him/her, where possible, to tailor the process to cater for their needs. Independent interpreters should be available when English is not the first language of the child or family members or when there are anxieties that communication in English will not be effective. After a consideration of different belief systems or child-rearing practices has been made, the examination will need to focus on the precise nature of the allegations in the context of the evidence available and the relevant legal frameworks.

- **Disability**. People with disability are disadvantaged and vulnerable not only by virtue of their disability but also by other people's perception of them. Professionals involved in examinations with children who have a disability should, wherever possible, be experienced in the field. They should be able to see the child beyond the 'disability', recognise signs and symptoms that relate to abuse and communicate effectively with the child. Disability should not be used as an excuse to avoid communication. When alternative forms of communication are required e.g. signing, lip-reading etc. plans must be made to ensure that an independent interpreter is present at all interviews to explain the examination and consent.

Summary

In summary the medical examination must be seen as one piece of the jig-saw of the process of making enquiries and the management of child abuse. Careful consideration and planning should result in the medical examination, when it is required, being carried out in a timely manner by a doctor with the appropriate level of expertise. The aim of the examination must be to reassure and empower the child and family whilst fulfilling the requirements of the investigative process. The capacity of the investigative process to compound abuse by poor practice is a stark reality with a high price being paid by everyone involved; no-one pays more dearly for such mismanagement than children and their families. Good practice requires a coherent, co-ordinated, multi-disciplinary approach. The key underlying principles must include acceptance of the child's needs as paramount and the need to work in partnership with the child and their family.

REFERENCE

Department of Health (1991) *Working Together under the Children Act 1989: A guide to Arrangements for Inter-agency Co-operation for the Protection of Children from Abuse*, London: HMSO.

13

Evaluating the evidence

Corinne Wattam

The work of child protection is concerned centrally with the identification of cases of child harm and injury or significant risk of harm or injury. The reasons for making such an identification are to ensure the immediate safety and health of a child and to work towards preventing the occurrence of future harm. There are two broadly-defined responses to this identification which need to be drawn out. The first is legal and the second therapeutic. Legal remedies are aimed towards ensuring the safety of the child through the civil courts using the various orders available under the Children Act 1989, and ensuring the future safety of the child and other children in the community through the prosecution of offenders. Both of these remedies are used only in the minority of cases, but because all cases initially stand as potential candidates for legal intervention, there is an orientation to evidence for legal proceedings in the majority of cases (Wattam, 1992). Therapeutic remedies technically should run alongside legal remedies and similarly are concerned with prevention and future safety, though they are also aimed towards repairing some of the damage which comes as a consequence of abuse. Most practitioners will be aware that these two themes often conflict, and can be mutually exclusive. However, evidence in child protection work is gathered for both purposes and there are inherent tensions about the type of evidence required, and the extent to which it is required to warrant intervention.

To have evidence of something, there has to be some agreement as to what that something is. This chapter explores the problems associated with child abuse when evidence is required. The first of these is that agreement on child abuse itself is a difficult area, both for legal and therapeutic purposes. Secondly, this problematic nature of the definition of child abuse leads to allegations of error and mistakes in interpretation. Thirdly, it also has consequences for what can be regarded as indicators of abuse, or risk assessment factors. The problem of definition must be recognised as an intrinsic feature of the interpretation of child protection evidence. Each section concludes with some pointers for practice which acknowledge that decisions must be reached and agreement needs to be achieved on a case-by-case basis, but that this has to happen in the context of contested definitions of abuse.

The social construction of child abuse

One central theme of this, and many other papers on child harm and injury, is that child abuse is a social construction (Butler and Williamson, 1994; Stainton Rogers *et al.*, 1989). This not only means that the definition of abuse varies across time (Ariès, 1973) and cultures (Korbin, 1991) but also that a definition for each case has to be reached, or constructed, on every occasion (Wattam, 1989). The issue of inconsistent definition has consequences for child protection work in at least three ways. Firstly, the professional definition is not always consistent. In 1983, for example, Dingwall, Eekelaar and Murray noted the role that 'cultural relativism' played in the child protection response in the UK. What might be considered an indicator of abuse in one family, (for example, lack of emotional warmth) was not always considered abusive, depending on such factors as cultural background, social circumstances and so forth. More recent research suggests that practitioners find that physical harm and injury is less difficult to detect and define than is sexual abuse in the absence of disclosure. Neglect, when not chronic or severe, and emotional abuse, present most problems in relation to detection and definition (DoH/NSPCC, 1995). Professional relationships also are affected. Different professionals pick up on different signs and symptoms, and at different points. Secondly, statistics which aim to show the nature and the extent of the problem of 'child abuse' gloss over and disguise the way in which its definition is problematic. Thirdly, those accused, or alleged to be victims, may not see what they have done or what is happening to them as 'abuse'.

This third implication of the social construction of child abuse has received more attention over recent years. The social organisation and construction of the definition of child abuse has at least four repercussions for children, their families and the people thought to be responsible for their abuse. Actions by alleged perpetrators are open to various interpretations and are available to be justified as non-abusive and benevolent. Examples of such justifications have been detailed in work with sexual offenders (Wyre and Swift, 1990) where men and women will maintain that they were, for example, educating children or showing natural love. Thus, there is often an anticipated disjuncture between the professional view of abuse and the perpetrator's view, which is now accepted as an expectable feature in 'abusive' behaviour, and which means inevitably that the treatment of offenders involves them seeing their actions differently, i.e. as abuse. One of the difficulties of this view is that it does not allow for any positive sexual contact between adults and children. This may be unacceptable to many but essentially it constitutes a moral position which is rarely made either explicit (Howitt, 1992) or uniformly enforced, particularly in relation to sentencing in the criminal courts. A second consequence is that for victims, who themselves may not perceive what has happened to them as abuse, actions are also available for justification and interpretation. This can prevent recognition and reporting, but more significantly, it can invoke further trauma for children when they reconstruct past experiences, previously viewed positively, as negative and damaging. A third consequence of the social organisation of the definition is for families caught up in the process of enquiry, particularly for 'safe parents' who may be penalised for not accepting the professional view (Hooper, 1992). Finally, the presentation of 'child abuse' as a public image means that 'child abuse' can come to be defined by those images. This allows the public to distance itself from child abuse, generally portrayed in the worst case scenarios, and constructs a further definition for public consumption (Wise, 1991).

Whilst it is clear that some children are seriously harmed, injured and even killed by their caretakers, it is not clear just how many victims there are overall. Indicators drawn from the numbers of registered cases are unreliable because criteria for registration varies between authorities and includes a subjective assessment of risk of future significant harm. Up to 75 per cent of allegations will be filtered out prior to case conference (Gibbons *et al.*, 1993; Giller *et al.*, 1992; Thorpe and Denman, 1993). A proportion of these will be unfounded allegations, some will present problems that are not serious enough to warrant intervention, some will be founded but not recognised (false negatives) and some will be founded with a variety of solutions reached. Some of those registered will be false positives. Only a minority of children will end up in substitute care, and only a minority of families will receive some form of social work intervention after the enquiry.

Interpretation of the evidence is central to deciding whether children are designated as abused or not, or at risk of abuse. In order to comprehend this we also have to be able to understand what is meant by evidence. A distinction has been made between 'social' and 'legal' evidence (Dingwall *et al.*, 1983). The difference lies not in the presenting information but in the test to which information is put. For example, a woman may phone social services and report that her son is being abused. The social worker investigating the case is likely to accept that this woman is the child's mother until information comes along to challenge that assumption. In the majority of cases that assumption will be correct. In criminal proceedings, however, it is customary for children who are the alleged victims of an offence to be identified by production of their birth certificate, which also details their parentage. There are many characteristics of child harm and injury which are difficult to prove by stringent legal standards, but which nevertheless indicate concern. Thus, the distinction between social and legal evidence remains. The social construction of child abuse, along with the social nature of most evidence in such cases, means that the evaluation of evidence essentially is a moral judgement. This observation does not undermine the existence or 'correctness' of confirmed cases, but identifies the making of moral judgements as central to child protection work.

Practice implications:

- The issue of consent needs clearer guidance; for example, in relation to the sentencing of offenders where the child is judged as consenting, in cases of teenage pregnancy where the putative father is an adult, and with respect to children's rights.

- Training in cultural difference (beyond race awareness) is necessary for all involved in child care work and judgements.

- It is essential to be clear with parents and children about what is and is not acceptable, and why. Professionals need to state the evidence which forms the basis of concerns and then discuss it.

- It is necessary to be sensitive to different professional concerns. For example, rather than dismissing preliminary reasons for referral (or shelving them for future reference), professionals should set up systems for monitoring, recording and information sharing in schools, or in daycare etc.

The notion of error and the interpretation of evidence

The use of 'social' evidence in every day decision making is one reason why there is so much confusion about whether 'errors' in judgement have been committed. There are cases when practitioners will say they are '100 per cent' certain something has occurred, where a child will make a clear statement to that effect, but where a court will not find sufficient evidence to support a guilty verdict (Wattam, 1991). Those accused can then continue to deny that they committed any crime, or 'abused' a child. There are also a large number of cases where suspicions exist but where no-one can be sure one way or the other. The term 'error' can be used when determining whether the correct procedures were followed and the appropriate decisions and actions taken, such as in case reviews under section eight of *Working Together* (DoH, 1991a) and in Government Inquiries. It has also been suggested that routine day to day decision making in cases is intrinsically prone to errors of reasoning (Howitt, 1992).

The result of Inquiries tends to be advice around changing procedures and practice guidance and improving channels of communication. A summary of the findings of Inquiry reports (DoH, 1991b) states that many deaths are a consequence of unpredictable factors. However, in identifying factors that prevented social workers from assessing what transpired to be a real risk to a child, the review suggested that there may be certain 'blocks'. Some of these are noted as being to do with a lack of knowledge, of signs and symptoms, the law and so forth. This fits within the more conventional notion of 'error', in that it suggests that there is a right, or optimum, level of knowledge available about the signs and symptoms of child abuse. Whilst, of course, there are a number of lists of signs and symptoms (see for example, Glaser and Frosh, 1988; Jones *et al.*, 1987) there is also a general acknowledgement that no sign or symptom, of and in itself, constitutes conclusive evidence of abuse (Royal College of Physicians, 1991; Dingwall *et al.*, 1983). Even the orthodox advice is around taking medical, physical and social indicators (though these rarely are defined) into comprehensive account when making an assessment of whether or not a child has been harmed or injured by a caretaker. However, many of the 'blocks' were related to what might be termed 'information processing', such as not being able to sift out relevant information, or not appearing to separate fact from opinion. Others included a lack of appreciation of the importance of information, particularly if its source was discredited in some way: being decoyed by different problems, having a false sense of security about a particular interpretation, or not putting information together. A further difficulty in information processing was to do with the way in which information could be ignored or played down if it did not fit the current mode of understanding in child protection work. This has also been described as a loss of objectivity, and the importance of supervision is highlighted. The report does not, however, cover the way in which dominant 'modes of understanding' come about or identify what they might be. More importantly in taking these examples it does not explore how they might affect practice in general rather than the isolated and relatively rare tragedy. It may be that in cases where children die it is erroneous to have accepted the mode of understanding, for example, which assumes that families are better together and that clients have a right to self-determination, but in the majority of 'grey area' cases this assumption could be helpful.

236

The study of the Inquiries endorses the Beckford case finding that 'high risk' is difficult to define, and further states that it is not possible, 'confidently to predict who will be an abuser, for the potential for abuse is widespread and often triggered by the particular conjunction of circumstances which is unpredictable (DoH, 1991b, p. 63).

Thus, whilst it may be possible to screen cases on the basis of available evidence, it is not possible to state categorically, on the basis of such evidence, that abuse will occur. The report does identify early warning 'themes'. These include: violence in adult relationships, outside the family and towards children, and in particular the use of corporal punishment in a disciplinary context; child development problems and behaviour change; and warnings from other people.

The report also notes 'critical patterns'. For example, most of the families were known to agencies. This reinforces a finding from the recent report on section 8 reviews which stated that in 26 out of a sample of 30 case reviews the child was already known (James, 1994). It also adds strength to the point that evidence must constantly be re-evaluated in the light of new information. There were also indications of resistance to professional intervention and to attempts by families to cover up signs of harm or injury to their children. This, however, is an anticipated response by parents who may feel threatened when having their child-rearing practices placed under the public gaze. Recent research on parental perspectives reveals that the enquiry in itself constitutes a crisis for many families (Cleaver and Freeman, 1995). Finally, violent behaviour was noted; to self, and particularly towards social workers. The Carlile report notes that 'every effort must be made to make sure that the social worker's assessment, on which might hinge the safety of a child, is not disarmed by the possibility of violence or the fear of its possibility'. Fear of violence, 'burn out' and the effects of stress all constitute factors in the initial interpretation of evidence.

Earlier, the distinction between social and legal evidence was noted. A similar conceptual difference applies to formal and informal rules of decision making. Government Inquiries examine adherence to formal rules, but there are also informal 'rules' or methods for interpreting information which are separate from (though they may contribute to) the way in which procedures are followed, and which are also important in determining whether 'abuse' has occurred. Howitt (1992; 1993) endorses the way in which social work reasoning may lead to 'errors' and identifies three principles which operate in relation to them: 'templating', 'justificatory theorizing' and 'ratcheting'. 'Templating' refers to a process whereby social workers match presenting clients against a 'social template'. 'Justificatory theorizing' describes the way in which theories justify the decisions made. The term 'theory' is used loosely, however. Howitt claims that the 'classic example' of this in his research was something termed 'contrition theory'.

This assumes that in order for a family or a family member to be 'treatable' (i.e. 'they can be worked with' in the professional parlance), evidence has to be shown that the full implications of what has happened are understood and acceptance of responsibility confirmed (Howitt, 1992, p. 355).

Justificatory theorizing means that actions can be seen in terms of the 'cognitive distortions' or justifications that alleged perpetrators may make for their actions, or that parents (particularly mothers) for not acting to protect a child. Finally, Howitt identifies a process called 'ratcheting' which refers to the way in which the child protection system 'moves in a single direction'. Once in the system the reason for entry becomes secondary to the existing circumstances, and 'unwinding' or going back tends not to happen. Thus it becomes quite difficult to get out.

Practice implications:

- All practitioners require an agreed and assessed standard of basic knowledge of signs, symptoms and legal requirements.

- Training is required which includes awareness and negotiation of 'blocks' in information processing, and a clearer understanding of the theoretical frameworks within which everyday practice is conducted.

- There is a need to recognise 'referral information' in long-term cases and for professionals to be able to stand back and re-assess.

- Practitioners should attempt to 'verify *verifiable* facts' during enquiries.

- Attention should be paid to the effects of working with child harm and injury and to the 'knock on' effect this may have on the work, particularly in relation to obtaining and evaluating evidence. There should be minimum requirements about how practitioners are supervised as well as guidance given on the maximum number of workers for each supervising officer.

What constitutes evidence in child abuse cases?

Over the last decade research into the prediction of child harm and injury has burgeoned. There are a large number of studies which seek to identify the features that may predispose children to risk (see for example, Browne *et al.*, 1988). On the whole this research treats child abuse as a 'real', clearly definable and measurable phenomenon. In doing so, it gives a quasi-scientific gloss to the activity of risk assessment. One outcome of the research, and of the desire to predict and prevent child abuse, has been the development of risk assessment systems. However, an overview of the research on which these systems are founded reveals a weak methodological base and cautions against adopting such systems or models as the basis for the interpretation of evidence (Parton *et al.*, forthcoming). The problems begin with the cohorts under study, namely the 'abused children' or 'the abusing families'. Whilst the population studied appears to be plausible – for example, all children registered (e.g. Creighton and Noyes, 1989) all children conferenced in a certain area (e.g. Browne and Saqi, 1988) or all children for whom protective court orders are sought (e.g. Murphy *et al.*, 1991) – they do not hold up under scrutiny. None of these children necessarily are the victims of harm or injury, but rather may be in families who fail to co-operate, or who are judged to be at risk by existing criteria. A recent review suggested that the factors which have the most empirical support are:

> . . . the child's age and developmental characteristics, the character of the abusive incident, actual levels of harm, the repetitive nature of the behaviour, the caregiver's impairment, and the personal history of violent behaviour of the caregiver. In addition, parental history of abuse as a child, parent's recognition of the problem and ability to co-operate, parent's response to child's behaviour, and parental level of stress and social support are also important (English and Pecora, 1994).

However, it should be noted that whilst correlations can be found between each of these factors and the various sample populations, none of these factors sufficiently predicts risk to a child or represents evidence of the potential for abuse.

Risk assessment systems are not used routinely in the UK and questions remain around how practitioners assess whether a child has been harmed or injured, or is at risk of such harm, in practice. Wattam (1992) conducted a study of participant observation, documentary analysis of file text and quantitative analysis of outcomes in all reported allegations of child sexual assault over a two-year period in one district. The data suggested that there were at least four related 'structures' for interpreting information presented to agencies. The first of these, categorisation, is a similar concept to that of 'templating' identified by Howitt above. The term refers to the way in which information is oriented to and categorised on the basis of shared-in-common, cultural expectations. The 'template' represents the category or categories that parents, children and referees are assessed against; it is a kind of social profile of expectable sexual behaviour for children of certain ages or stages of development, different family compositions and behaviours at bathtime, bedtime, and during the course of day-to-day routine living. Work by Thorpe (1994) has extended this notion by revealing the way in which 'good' and 'bad' parents are assessed in practice. Thorpe maintains that these assessments are paramount and take precedence over and above any signs of injury. Actual harms and injuries in children referred are in the minority. Many more referrals contain allegations which are judged on the basis of parental behaviours and characteristics, in the absence of physical or verbal signs from the child. The term 'categorisation' extends the notion of templating in that it is not a hard and fast thing. Information is oriented according to the way people are categorised until other information comes along to change it. A second feature, that of 'motive', was found to operate in the decision-making process, either in terms of motive to report, or in terms of identifying motives for the behaviours reported. If a motive other than 'disinterested' concern for the child could be found, such as in custody and access disputes, then the information would be interpreted in the context of this motive. A third feature was that of 'corroboration'. Dingwall *et al.* (1983) suggested that grounds for suspicion could be grouped into three basic categories of evidence: 'the injury', 'the account offered' and 'the demeanour of parent and child' which all appear to be located in a *structure of mutual corroboration*. Practice appears to be concerned centrally with corroboration. Traditionally, the term tends to be associated with legal practice where its meaning is not that different, but the tests of the strength of evidence used in corroboration are different from those used in everyday life. What is being referred to here is the use of corroboration as a common-sense reasoning device: that is, how information is used to stand for, signify or otherwise validate an allegation of mistreatment, and/or the possibility that a child may be in danger of mistreatment in the future. The sexual abuse study revealed that consistency between accounts and events is crucial to how valid a complaint is perceived. The fourth structure, that of 'specificity', is also operating here. Accounts were perceived as more plausible if specific details could be given.

These four structures operated together to increase or decrease the validity of an allegation. In the case of alleged child sexual assault they may be the only evidence available. However, there are at least two reasons why these structures should be questioned. Firstly, where children are known to have been sexually assaulted, indications are that these structures may not operate in the anticipated way. For example, it may be difficult for a child to give specific details of an assault, particularly if it happened a long time ago, or if it happened repeatedly over a long period. Furthermore, children may well wait until their parents separate or they are forced into some access arrangement before telling others about their previous assaults, particularly where a parent is the alleged perpetrator. Secondly, an increasing legal focus on child sexual assault has encouraged the promotion of more 'scientific' ways of checking true and false allegations. One of these in particular, Statement Validity Analysis or Criteria-Based Content Analysis, adopts many of the same features used in day-to-day life, similar structures to those identified in the research, such as specificity and detail, consistency and spontaneity. For the same reasons, these features may not, in actual cases, be expectable, and therefore cannot be relied upon for evidential purposes (Berliner and Conte, 1993; Wattam, 1992).

The importance of 'the account offered' has gathered strength over recent years, particularly with the introduction of the *Memorandum of Good Practice* for interviewing children (Home Office, 1992) and increased awareness of sexual assault. Sexual assault is even less physically symptomatic than physical abuse and neglect. It therefore often depends entirely for evidence on what children say. There is some controversy surrounding the approach which the Memorandum operates and many social workers across the country are expressing concern. The advocated approach takes little account of the trauma of victims of child sexual assault, the group to whom it is most often applied (Wattam, 1994). The interviewing style is acceptable in criminal proceedings because it is non-leading and allows for the child's spontaneous recall of events as soon as possible after they occur. This does not acknowledge the way in which some children may need help and encouragement to tell others of their experience, nor that the event may have happened some time ago, and over a long period of time so that recall may be affected. It also requires thorough preparation and planning, particularly around the child's circumstances and developmental history, but during the early stages of an enquiry this kind of information may be difficult to obtain. Finally, research indicates that there are patterns to the way in which children tell others about sexual abuse (Sorenson and Snow, 1991). These patterns may undermine their credibility as witnesses in the criminal justice system. Initially, a large number of children may deny an allegation, or make a tentative attempt to tell others which involves minimizing and distancing. Thus some children will say that it has not happened, or that it happened to someone else, or that they dreamed it and so forth. Later they may make an active disclosure which will confirm the allegation. This disclosure process does not fit well with an early one-off interview approach; in the criminal justice system it is the first 'story' which counts, and which will be contained on video.

By the end of the first year of implementation over 14,000 video interviews had been conducted, but only 24 per cent of these had been submitted for criminal proceedings. An even smaller proportion, estimated at between 4–10 per cent, had been submitted for use in civil proceedings. Whilst the burden of proof and standard of evidence in criminal proceedings is higher than that of civil proceedings, a worrying trend were reports in some areas that a similar standard was being expected. In summary, the nature of offences concerning children is particularly difficult to process through the courts, and the introduction of pre-recorded video as evidence does little to counteract the overall problems of evidence which, as has been noted already, rarely is hard and fast.

A key question facing many practitioners concerns when it is appropriate to use pre-recorded video to obtain evidence. Local authorities have been formulating their own criteria as implementation of the Memorandum has progressed. In relation to the general categories of child witnesses, an interview will not be considered where:

- circumstances of the offence would negate the evidential value, e.g. where video had been used as part of the abuse, or where the child was confused as to who the perpetrator might be;

- the investigating team does not understand the child adequately;

- the child's evidence is not required;

- the immediate situation is life threatening and a video interview would exacerbate this, e.g. cases of attempted suicide at the point of disclosure;

- the child does not consent;

- after consultation with line management, it is not considered in the child's best interests, or it may be considered detrimental to the child, to pursue a prosecution.

Additionally, the distinction between a referral and a complaint to the police needs to be maintained. Where there is a clear complaint the Memorandum guidance is appropriate. However, very few cases arrive at the door of social services as formal complaints. Most amount to vague accusations or observations which cause concern. In these cases there should be room for further assessment of the evidence and the need to interview prior to interview (SSI, 1994).

If the signs and symptoms of child harm and injury are ambiguous, and if accounts similarly are open to interpretation the third feature of 'mutual corroboration', that is, 'the demeanour of parent and child' becomes important in the evaluation of evidence. More recent research takes this aspect further and suggests that it is also to do with distinguishing between what is 'normal' and what is 'abnormal' in relation to child-rearing practices (Thorpe, 1994). Following on from this observation is the problem that there are very few studies of 'normal' child-rearing (particularly on a large scale). More recently research has sought to rectify this (DoH, 1995) and the conclusions support findings in the United States that lesser degrees of physical punishment and 'sexual' intimacy are in the normal range (Wolfner and Gelles, 1993). With reference to normal childhood sexual activity previous research reveals that 'sexual play' is not uncommon and that children exhibit a wide variety of sexual behaviours (Kinsey *et al.*, 1948; 1953; Friedrich *et al.*, 1991; Lamb and Coakley, 1993).

A further, significant piece of information, used in the process of 'mutual corroboration', is that of the event which precipitates the report. In the case of child sexual assault this can include a number of factors: for example, watching a TV programme, a health education lesson at school, an argument, or a change in family circumstances (Wattam, 1991; Sorenson and Snow, 1991). It is import-ant to inquire into precipitators because they may act to invalidate reports, rather than validate them. The salience of motive to report was noted above as a structure in determining whether the referral is valid or not. However, the reasoning behind this may be faulty. For example, if a child discloses because of an argument her report may be treated as though it was motivated by the argument (Wattam, 1992). This might be so, but because a report is motivated by anger or conflict it does not necessarily mean that it is false.

In relation to physical harm and injury, and neglect and emotional abuse, less research on precipitators to referral has been done. However, Thorpe and Denman (1993) and Thorpe (1994) do look at the context of referral as a variable in outcome. 26 per cent of the UK sample and 21 per cent of the Australian sample concerned allegations made in a conflictual context (custody and access, family and neighbourhood). Approximately half of these were considered not substantiated in the UK sample; however, the percentage for the Australian cohort was 77 per cent. The relationship between conflicting context for reporting and outcome is not clear, and it may be that such a context provides the rationale for finding a report unfounded. An overview of reports of child sexual assault in custody and access disputes shows that the research supporting more false allegations being made in this context is faulty (Faller, 1993) where children make reports (Jones and Seig, 1988).

Finally, the person making the report may be a significant factor in evaluating the evidence. The referral can come as an observation by a third party or as a self-report from the child, parent or perpetrator. One of the consistent findings in the risk assessment literature is that reports from other professionals, such as doctors, teachers and the police, are substantiated more often than reports from the general public (Cicchinelli, 1991). It may be that these are the cases that warrant the most attention because investigators are more accountable to other professionals than they are to the general public, rather than that these cases constitute more accurate reports.

Whatever the situation, government guidelines and reviews of child deaths emphasise the importance of taking all reports seriously, whoever refers. Such reports and the ensuing assessment may indicate that there is sufficient evidence to warrant therapeutic intervention, even if the legal standards are not achieved, providing the child and the family are willing for this to occur. A worrying trend in implementing the Memorandum is the observation that where interviews fail to obtain sufficient legal evidence the process is halted and children may 'drop out' of the system without further assessment. For all the reasons identified above, it may be that sensitive and longer-term assessment is required particularly in cases of alleged child sexual assault.

Practice implications:

- Be aware of how commonly identified risk factors may operate and discuss these with children and families.

- Clear standards of child care need to be made explicit and publicly available, particularly in relation to 'leaving alone' and parental neglect. These should be drawn up within the context of awareness that it has previously been White, Eurocentric, middle-class, child care standards which have predominated, even in relation to something as apparently value-free as child development assessments (Rex and Wendy Stainton Rogers, 1992). A 'bottom-line' approach is advocated which assesses criteria presenting immediate and serious risk to a child (see for example, Stein and Rzepnicki, 1983).

- Reflect on how the following decision-making processes are operating in individual cases:
  —categorisation and 'templating';
  —expectations of normative behaviour and assessments of difference;
  —structures of 'mutual corroboration', including motive and specificity.

- Greater awareness and sensitivity is required in civil and criminal proceedings of the dynamics of sexual harm and injury and the process of telling others.

244

■ Clear criteria should be set by area child protection committees for obtaining and using pre-recorded video evidence. Children should not be interviewed on video as a matter of routine.

Conclusion

Much of what has been written here suggests that the evaluation of evidence is dependent on informal criteria, rather than on the formal rules of evidence or even procedures. Very few procedures contain advice on how to evaluate evidence and when to take action upon it. This observation should not undermine the quality of the work which is, in the main, conducted with the best intentions. However, it is important to make explicit which criteria are being utilised in the decision-making process in the early stages of enquiries. In particular, increasingly it is becoming important to distinguish between legal and therapeutic evidence in relation to warrants for intervention. Parents and children need to know by what criteria they are being judged. A recent study on parental perspectives reveals very different perceptions, both of the experience of intervention and also of matters which are judged to be important (Cleaver and Freeman, 1995). A failure to appreciate other perspectives can only result in a one-sided evaluation of evidence which could be to the detriment of the children involved.

REFERENCES

Ariès, P. (1973) *Centuries of Childhood*, Harmondsworth: Penguin.

Berliner, L. and Conte, J.R. (1993) 'Sexual abuse evaluations: conceptual and empirical obstacles', *Child Abuse and Neglect*, **17**, pp. 111–125.

Browne, K. (1988) *Early Prediction and Prevention of Child Abuse*, Chichester, Wiley.

Browne, K. and Saqi, S. (1988) 'Approaches to screening for child abuse and neglect', in Browne, K. et al. (eds) *Early Prediction and Prevention of Child Abuse*, Chichester, Wiley.

Butler, I. and Williamson, H. (1994) *Children Speak: Children, Trauma and Social Work*, Harlow: Longman/NSPCC.

Cicchinelli, L.F. (1991) Symposium on Risk Assessment in Child Protective Services, National Centre on Child Abuse and Neglect 9–11 December, Washington DC.

Cleaver, H. and Freeman, P. (1995) *Parental Perspectives in Cases of Suspected Child Abuse*, London: HMSO.

Creighton, S. and Noyes, P. (1989) *Child Abuse Trends in England and Wales 1983–1987*. London: NSPCC.

Department of Health (1991a) *Working Together Under the Children Act 1989*, London: HMSO.

Department of Health (1991b) *Child Abuse: A Study of Inquiry Reports, 1980–1989*, London: HMSO.

Department of Health/NSPCC (1995) forthcoming.

Dingwall, R. Eekelaar, J. and Murray, T. (1983) *The Protection of Children*, Oxford: Blackwell.

English, D. and Pecora, P.J. (1994) 'Risk assessment as a practice method in child protective services', *Child Welfare*, **LXXIII**, No. 5, September–October.

Faller, K.C. (1993) False Allegations in Custody and Access Disputes, Paper presented at Victims and Offenders Conferences, Manchester University, 4–5 November.

Friedrich, W.N., Grambsch, P., Broughton, D., Kuiper, J. and Beilke, R.L. (1991) 'Normative sexual behaviour in children', *Pediatrics*, **88**, pp. 456–464.

Gibbons, J., Conroy, S. and Bell, C. (1993) *Operation of Child Protection Registers*, Report to Department of Health, Social Work Development Unit, University of East Anglia.

Giller, H., Gormley, C. and Williams, P. (1992) *The Effectiveness of Child Protection Procedures: An Evaluation of Child Protection Procedures in Four ACPC Areas*, Manchester: Social Information Systems Ltd.

Glaser, D. and Frosh, S. (1988) *Child Sexual Abuse*, Basingstoke: Macmillan.

Hallett, C. and Birchall, E. (1992) *Coordination and Child Protection: A Review of the Literature*, Scotland: HMSO.

Home Office (1992) *Memorandum of Good Practice*, London: HMSO.

Hooper, C.A. (1992) *Mothers Surviving Child Sexual Abuse*, London: Tavistock/Routledge.

Howitt, D. (1992) 'Injustice to children and families in child abuse cases', in Losel, F., Bender, D. and Bliesener, T. (eds) *Psychology and Law: International Perspectives*, Berlin: de Gruyter.

Howitt, D. (1993) *Child Abuse Errors: When Good Intentions Go Wrong*, London: Harvester Wheatsheaf.

James, G. (1994) *Discussion Report: Study of Working Together 'Part 8' Reports*, Presented at ACPC National Conference, 8 March. Department of Health.

Jones, D., Pickett, J., Oates, M. and Barbor, P. (1987) *Understanding Child Abuse*, Basingstoke: Macmillan.

Jones, D. and Seig, A. (1988) 'Child sexual abuse allegations in custody or visitation disputes', in Nicholson, B. (ed.) *Sexual Abuse Allegations in Custody and Visitation Disputes*, American Bar Association, Washington DC.

Kinsey, A.C., Pomeroy, W.B. and Martin, C.E. (1948) *Sexual Behaviour in the Human Male*, Philadelphia: W.B. Saunders.

Kinsey, A.C., Pomeroy, W.B., Martin, C.E. and Gebhard, P.H. (1953) *Sexual Behaviour in the Human Female*, Philadelphia: W.B. Saunders.

Korbin, J.E. (1991) 'Cross-cultural perspectives and research directions for the 21st century', *Child Abuse and Neglect*, **15**, pp. 67–77.

Lamb, S. and Coakley, M. (1993) '"Normal" childhood sexual play and games: differentiating play from abuse', *Child Abuse and Neglect*, **17**, pp. 515–526.

Murphy, J.M., Jellineck, M., Quinn, D., Smith, G., Poitrast, F.G. and Goshko, M. (1991) 'Substance abuse and serious child mistreatment: prevalence, risk and outcome in a court sample', *Child Abuse and Neglect*, **15**, pp. 197the 211.

Parton, N., Thorpe, D.H. and Wattam, C. (forthcoming) *Deconstructing Child Protection*, Basingstoke: Macmillan.

Royal College of Physicians (1991) *Physical Signs of Sexual Abuse in Children: A Report of the Royal College of Physicians*, Royal College of Physicians, London.

Sorenson, T. and Snow, B. (1991) 'How children tell: the process of disclosure in child sexual abuse', *Child Welfare*, **LXX**, No. 1, Jan–Feb pp. 3–15.

SSI (1994) *The Child, the Court and the Video*, Liverpool: HMSO.

Stainton Rogers, W., Hevey, D. and Ash, E. (eds) (1989), *Child Abuse and Neglect: Facing the Challenge*, London: Open University/Batsford Press.

Stainton Rogers, W. and Stainton Rogers, W. (1992) *Stories of Childhood: Shifting Agendas of Child Concern*, London: Harvester Wheatsheaf.

Stein, T.J. and Rzepnicki, T.L. (1983) *Decision Making at Child Welfare Intake: A Handbook for Practitioners*, Child Welfare League of America, Inc.

Thorpe, D. (1994) *Evaluating Child Protection*, Buckingham: Open University Press.

Thorpe, D. and Denman, G. (1993) *Family Participation and Patterns of Intervention in Child Protection in Gwent. A Research Report for the Area Child Protection Committee, Gwent*, Lancaster University.

Wattam, C. (1989) 'Investigating child sexual abuse: a question of relevance', in Blagg, H., Hughes, J. and Wattam, C. (eds) *Child Sexual Abuse: Listening, Hearing and Validating the Experiences of Children*, London: Longman.

Wattam, C. (1991) Disclosure: The Child's Perspective, unpublished research report, NSPCC.

Wattam, C. (1992) *Making A Case In Child Protection*, Harlow: Longman.

Wattam, C. (1994) Protection through Prosecution: Myth or Reality. Departmental Seminar Paper, Department of Applied Social Science, Lancaster University.

Wise, S. (1991) *Child Abuse: The NSPCC Version*, Feminist Praxis.

Wolfner, G.D. and Gelles, R.J. (1993) 'A profile of violence toward children: national study', *Child Abuse and Neglect*, **17**, 197–212.

Wyre, R. and Swift, A. (1990) *Women, Men and Rape*, Hodder and Stoughton.

Conclusion: Does it ever end?

Dendy Platt

Writing about the end point of an enquiry into alleged child abuse or neglect is rather like describing the colour of a chameleon. No two endings are quite the same, and the reasons for this changeability are to do with the characteristics of the background. For most professionals involved in the process, the enquiry phase comes to an end around about the time of the child protection conference. Unfortunately, things are not always as simple as they may seem; and for some families an enquiry has no ending. This chapter focuses on the *process* of ending the enquiry rather than on a specific point in time.

Recent practice research has tended to consider the *outcomes* of enquiries, and the subsequent decisions (e.g. Farmer, 1993; DoH, 1991b), rather than the *process* of ending them. This chapter is limited by the shortage of available material, and by the fact that professionals have been concerned mainly with outcomes and subsequent decisions. Prosser (1992) identifies a few of the difficulties faced by families at the end of an enquiry. Although his sample was drawn from those who were particularly dissatisfied with their experience, the study highlights, for example, that enquiries and proceedings could last between five months and three years. Parents' concerns were related to the process of the enquiry, in this case the length of time it took. They were also shown to be concerned about the outcomes of an enquiry, such as the removal of a child from home. Little of the research appears to have been sufficiently specific to present the child's view of the ending of an enquiry. The processes are nevertheless important for the subsequent well-being of the child. With published material on children's and families' views being so limited, it is important to note that it has been impossible to identify additional information which may shed light on the viewpoints of Black families or other minority interests.

This chapter begins by exploring in more detail how, and in what ways, the enquiry may come to an end. Following this analysis, some feelings and concerns of children and parents are identified. Relevant procedural requirements are defined, and then the overall picture is used to draw out implications for practice. Finally the question of whether the enquiry ever ends is addressed.

How might the enquiry end?

The obvious answer to this question is that the enquiry ends when all its objectives have been achieved. As was shown in Chapter 1 (see page 8), there are various different ways of understanding the objectives of the enquiry. These were distilled into a single statement:

> *The task of those making enquiries is to obtain as clear an account as possible of whether abuse or neglect has occurred, and then, if appropriate, how and by whom it was caused, and whether the child remains at risk.*

Theoretically at least, it can be suggested that if evidence is provided to meet each of these objectives then the enquiry can be terminated. As families and practitioners know, however, the reality may be somewhat different.

In terms of immediate decisions which we may take to indicate the end point, Cleaver and Freeman (1995) in their study of suspected child abuse, identified four categories:

   (i)   children placed on the child protection register;

  (ii)   those not registered but monitored by an agency;

 (iii)   cases referred for further investigation, and;

 (iv)   no further action.

This categorisation does not take account of the more serious outcomes such as removal of children and criminal prosecutions (which nevertheless did occur in a number of cases initially classified as above). However, none of these short-term steps, especially if viewed together with the likelihood of partial or inadequate evidence, actually include a means of finishing the enquiry process.

An important aspect of the process is the way in which information unfolds. Some (probably most) enquiries will fail to produce sufficient evidence for conclusions to be drawn on all relevant aspects. Decisions will therefore have to be taken with inadequate information. Details will rarely come to light in a tidy manner. New information can lead to a re-thinking of a case, even up to the point of going to court in care proceedings or for a criminal prosecution. Evidence of abuse may emerge gradually over time, at the pace of those involved most closely (Hallett and Birchall, 1992). From the viewpoint of families, an enquiry is only concluded satisfactorily when concerns specific to their situation have been addressed. These may be very different to the professionals' positions. For example,

> ... as soon as I mentioned this mark, she [social worker] was down straight away, you know 'That's a slap mark' ... Tim [boyfriend] had to spend a week at me mam's because we didn't know who'd done it ... From then onwards I was under a social worker for the year... We found out from a third party [what had happened that night]. [The babysitter] had slapped Ian [aged 3] (Howitt, 1992, p. 148).

When did the enquiry end for this mother? After the diagnosis (the baby was admitted to hospital for two days)? When Tim came back home (a week later)? When they found out about the babysitter (a year later)? Or when the children's names were taken off the child protection register (18 months later)?

Recent research has highlighted the point that parents who are part of an enquiry feel they are presumed guilty until proven innocent (Cleaver and Freeman, 1995; Prosser, 1992). This finding will be recognised from personal experience by a great many practitioners. Equally, social workers and allied professionals aim to embark upon an enquiry with few, if any, preconceived assumptions about guilt. Despite this approach, many parents still feel that they are presumed to be guilty. It is not known whether the existence of this phenomenon has any effect on the length of the enquiry or the timing of its conclusion.

The time-delay in getting criminal prosecutions to court continues to be of concern, and procedures for taking account of the needs of children facing such delays often are unavailable (Plotnikoff and Woolfson, 1994). Clearly this point reinforces concern about the length of the enquiry in some cases. Farmer and Owen (1995) show that an enquiry can take from one or two days to several weeks.

The resolution of outstanding issues clearly is important, and, in keeping with our definition of the enquiry, I shall examine some of the key formal opportunities for such a resolution. They are:

- an internal social services or police decision;
- an initial child protection conference, and;
- via legal proceedings.

It is recognised that this categorisation cannot cover every situation, but it is considered sufficient to address the main principles.

An internal social services or police decision

An internal decision to terminate an enquiry will, in normal circumstances, only take place during the stages prior to a child protection conference. Such a decision is likely to be taken on the basis of one or more of the following:

(a) there is sufficient evidence to disprove the allegation;

(b) there is insufficient evidence to provide reasonable grounds for continued enquiries;

(c) the alleged abuse is of such a minor nature as to render further enquiries unnecessary;

(d) the child is not believed to be at risk of future abuse, or the degree of risk to the child is not considered significant.

This discussion clearly overlaps with the issue of gatekeeping, which begins at the initial stages of an enquiry, and is covered by David Thorpe in Chapter 8. From the perspective of ending the enquiry, it is helpful to review the key decision-making points at which an exit from the enquiry process may be achieved. They have been summarised by Cornwell (1989), and can be adapted to encompass more recent procedures as follows:

Exit 1   At initial referral.

Exit 2   Initial information-gathering stage.

Exit 3   Planning meeting.

Exit 4   After any of the interviews but prior to a medical examination.

Exit 5   After the medical examination but prior to any further enquiries or before the child protection conference.

Clearly there is a significant number of cases now where decisions are being made to end the enquiries before the child protection conference stage, and workers should be supported in making them. Nevertheless, there remains evidence that child protection agencies tend to err on the side of caution by not taking these decisions when they could (e.g. Cornwell, 1989; Cleaver and Freeman, 1995; Farmer and Owen, 1995). Material already presented in Chapter 1 supports the need for careful decision making where alternative routes other than more formal enquiries or investigations are appropriate.

When an enquiry ends by internal decision, it is particularly important that workers are aware of the needs of children and families for support in these circumstances. It is too easy to assume that the 'good news' that the enquiry has been called off is sufficient. Given the current state of knowledge about the possible adverse effects of enquiries, the consequences for the family should be examined in the same way as with any more 'complete' enquiries. Similarly, recent research (DoH, 1995) suggests that annually there are approximately 80,000 families who are the subject of concern, but who themselves may know nothing about it. Particular attention needs to be paid to their rights in this situation, especially since there may be subtle changes of attitude towards them on the part of the professionals involved.

At the initial child protection conference

When discussing the child protection conference as the ending of an enquiry, the first difficulty to be faced is the confusion about the proper role of the conference in general, and the problematic nature of its decision-making strategies. Hallett and Birchall (1992) identify a number of studies which describe,

> ... the tendency of conferences to become preoccupied with gathering and evaluating legal evidence, to the detriment of (their) fuller function which is to assess the overall strengths and weaknesses of the child's situation and to formulate a care plan.

Opinions may vary about the extent to which the conference can become involved in the evaluation of information or evidence. Personal experience supports the general direction of the above finding. Often it is impractical for a child protection conference to undertake a thorough and systematic evaluation of all the information available from the enquiries. As Hallett and Birchall go on to indicate, the solution to this problem may lie in the better preparation of individual submissions to the conference. Even so, the dangers of group decision making are also documented by the same authors. There are limits to the amount of complex information that conference members will be able to assimilate and process, particularly within the confines of a one to two hour meeting. Despite carefully prepared reports it is fairly commonplace for the decisions of child protection conferences to be swayed by the climate of the discussion, rather than by the written information with which they are presented.

Nevertheless, the initial child protection conference is the key, formal, decision-making body in the enquiry process. Under our definition of the enquiry, it is an important point at which a resolution of the enquiry can be

253

achieved. Unfortunately, information is scarce to suggest that concluding the enquiry may be a function of the conference. The main formal recognition of this role was in the previous version of *Working Together* (DHSS and Welsh Office, 1988) which asserted that,

> *The investigative stage is concluded when . . . the conference is able to reach a view on whether or not the child's name should be placed on the local child protection register* (para. 5.16).

Whilst this advice has been dropped from the more recent edition of *Working Together*, registration seems to retain a significance in the minds of professionals as the closing point of the enquiry. As Farmer and Owen (1995) comment,

> *At the close of a conference there was sometimes a feeling amongst professional participants that the 'unresolved child protection issues' had been resolved by the act of registration.*

The role of the child protection register is, itself, problematic. Many writers and researchers have given attention to the kinds of factors considered in making decisions related to such issues as the registration of a child. However, attempts to identify predictive criteria for case assessment have so far produced little clear agreement, and there is no objective information about child and family characteristics which is of any real benefit to the practising social worker (see, for example, Hallett and Birchall, 1992; Wells, 1988; Jones, 1993; Pecora, 1991; Gibbons, 1988). Indeed one study (Campbell, 1991) which compared registered with non-registered children, all attending a family centre, suggested that,

> *. . . either there is little real difference between the characteristics of abusing and non-abusing families, or . . . the process of registration is controlled by a series of events which are not solely related to the characteristics of the families under consideration.*

Here again, attention is drawn to the process which takes place at the end of the enquiry. Other studies offer a similar picture. In Cleaver and Freeman's study (1995) two out of three key factors, which explained registration as an outcome, related to characteristics of the system not to characteristics of the family. And Bingley Miller *et al.* (1993) suggest that,

> *. . . the outcome of a referral for child abuse, while admittedly influenced by the characteristics of the case, nevertheless depends heavily on such accidental factors as who refers to the social services, which social services team they refer to and who chairs the case conference.*

254

Clearly there may be some difficulties in resolving an enquiry from the child's and family's points of view if organisational variables are so important compared to the needs of the individual.

One of the earliest criticisms of child protection registers came from Hugh Geach (1983), who drew attention to their ineffectiveness as a reference-point for professionals who may be concerned about a child. In addition, several writers have identified registration as a means of procuring resources (e.g. Corby and Mills, 1986; Jones et al., 1987; Farmer and Owen, 1995). Whilst they describe the stigma experienced by some families, Farmer and Owen (1995) report that the process can be positive in cases which result in greater support from family and friends.

Registration is criticised also in relation to its quasi-legal status (Hallett and Birchall, 1992), particularly from the viewpoint of parents' rights groups. The views of virtually all the parents in Brown's (1986) study were negative. They were concerned particularly about the associated worry and the stigma. In the context of parents' rights, a number of writers (e.g. Milner, 1993; Farmer and Owen, 1995) have identified a greater likelihood of registration if the person responsible was believed to be the mother rather than the father.

As well as the issue of registration Brown (1986) reports on parents' lack of knowledge concerning the outcomes of child protection conferences. Despite increased attention to parental involvement in child protection conferences, there still appears to be a lack of understanding amongst parents about the meaning of registration (Farmer and Owen, 1995).

The small amount of information available about children's views is fairly anecdotal. Farmer and Owen (1995) demonstrate that many children could not distinguish clearly between different parts of the process. Most of the children in Barford's (1993) study were vague about what took place at child protection conferences, and they knew nothing about the child protection register. It would be consistent with the philosophy of the Children Act 1989 to emphasise that information should be provided to children according to their age and level of understanding.

Via legal proceedings

The third set of circumstances under which an enquiry may end concerns the various court proceedings which may take place. There are two key areas. In the first, care proceedings may be initiated when the local authority (or an authorised person) believes that there are grounds for removal of a child from the family home, and that it would be in the child's interests. A common route is for an outline case to be presented to the initial hearing, when an Interim Care Order may be granted if there is reasonable cause to believe that the grounds for a Care Order would be met. The granting of an order then allows the child to be placed in care quickly while the detailed preparation of a case for a full Care Order may be made. The full hearing would take place a number of weeks later. Certain rules, including the use of hearsay evidence and the standard of proof, are more relaxed in care proceedings than in criminal proceedings.

The second type of court proceeding is the criminal prosecution. Here, the responsibility for initiating the case lies with the police. Following a joint investigation (usually by the police and social services), if the police believe they have sufficient evidence to bring a prosecution against the alleged offender then the papers will be presented to the Crown Prosecution Service. Depending upon their decision, a criminal prosecution may be initiated. It is in this part of the process that the need for clear, factual evidence is high.

Families' perspectives

For families, the end point varies according to their experience. Using anecdotal evidence from a consultation exercise, one parent took the view that: 'The investigation finished on my family ... after the case conference ...' (Parent A, 1993). Another took a different perspective. Despite ongoing care proceedings, which he did not see as part of the enquiries, his view was that, '... for me the investigation finished when I was charged'. However, he would in fact have preferred the enquiries to have continued: '(the police) weren't interested in looking for the truth. The fact that they charged me – they ceased to bother to look for the truth' (Parent B, 1993).

Thus, it may well be important for family members in certain circumstances that enquiries or investigations continue for as long possible so that the fullest possible information may be obtained with a view to an ultimate court hearing. Furthermore, there will be situations where social workers and others continue to gather information pertinent to their investigatory role beyond the point at which traditionally they would see the enquiry as concluded. Such information may well be used as evidence in court (Lindley, 1994), and it is part of a fair and open approach to practice for it to be clear to families when investigatory tasks will continue for some time.

Also suspicion may continue after a case has ended. Families may fear that the concerns will start up again. Professionals may harbour doubts, and continue to be on the look-out for evidence of abuse. When enquiries have ended, for some families it is simply the start of a new phase; perhaps of worry about children being taken away. Uncertainty about how things will turn out is commonplace.

When examining a partnership approach to the ending of the enquiry, one of the key issues is that of '. . . how to achieve justice for the accused and protection for the child without "abuse by proceedings" ' (Hallett and Birchall, 1992).

Given the low proportion of successful prosecutions and the general concensus that the stress for children appearing as witnesses is unacceptable (Hallett and Birchall, 1992), the value of criminal prosecution (as opposed to care proceedings) comes into question. Jones asserts:

> It is probable that some children are helped psychologically by this public, authoritative vindication of their original statement. On the other hand, there are other children who are psychologically harmed by the process of testifying . . . We have studied sexually abused children who attended a criminal court to give evidence, comparing them with similar children who did not attend court. The results suggest that attendance at court is accompanied by greater psychological ill effect over and above the impact of sexual abuse itself (Jones, 1992).

Roberts and Taylor (1993), however, underline the importance of prosecution by highlighting the anger of some children when their testimony appears not to have been supported by an appropriate court response. Perhaps one way of mitigating this effect is to use the Criminal Injuries Compensation Scheme. In cases when clearly a crime has been committed, but a prosecution has been unsuccessful, an award may be seen by the child as recognition that abuse has been suffered.

In the relatively small number of cases when children themselves have disclosed abuse, there were feelings of relief and lessening tension (Farmer and Owen, 1995). For others, particularly older children, the decision was regretted. Lack of support may be an issue; in the following example a lack of support from the child's own family was experienced:

> I hoped that everything would stop. I didn't want to know what happened next . . . I felt, instead of everything getting better, it got worse (see Farmer and Owen, 1995).

As noted previously, a positive outcome in cases of actual sexual abuse may be linked to the presence of support from the child's own family (particularly the mother). When children have regretted disclosing the abuse, there is some evidence that their concern arises from the unacceptability of the consequences (e.g. removal from home) rather than from the enquiry process itself (Farmer and Owen, 1995).

The picture is different when we consider the wider family perspective. The distress resulting from an enquiry for families who claim to have been accused falsely is described in detail by Prosser (1992). The importance to such families of closing the enquiries to their own satisfaction is demonstrated by this example:

> Dr. Newton and Dr Thomas had for months accused and damned us, but this disease [which explained the alleged injuries] had never been mentioned. You would think that they would apologise, but no. For another five months Newton and Thomas continued with their accusations. Finally, in February, after going to court on a total of 15 occasions, their claim was thrown out. No apology. No sorrow. The 'caring profession' who had criticised us for so long walked away that day in the court (see Prosser, 1992).

A particular feature of such families is what Prosser calls the 'film loop', where family members go over and over their experiences in considerable detail, as they try to come to terms with them. The issues are well summarised by quoting from an address given by a parent:

> You may experience months or even years of being treated as guilty but when the investigation finally ends you are not debriefed, there is no redress, no offer of reparation, no apology and no help to rebuild the shattered relationships which were once your family unit. If you had been treated with courtesy throughout the investigation, if it had been a partnership, you might avail yourself of the very tenuous offer of further help from social services or allied agencies, but, having been made to feel less than human, there is no way you will accept now, no matter how desperate you are. Even though the investigation has stopped, the children are off the At Risk Register, no longer in foster homes, or whatever, the fact that no-one actually admits to having made a mistake, leaves you in a state of limbo from which it is very hard to move forwards (Parent C, 1993).

Whilst this viewpoint came from a parent who considered herself falsely accused, there will nevertheless be elements of this kind of experience which affect all families to some degree.

Procedural questions

Referring back to the suggestion that the enquiry ends at an appropriate 'point of resolution', it is now possible to achieve some clarification. In some cases, there will be a decision about the outcome of the enquiry (e.g. registration, the granting of a Care Order, a criminal conviction). In some there will be a decision about a planned action (ranging from no action to the placement of a child in care). However, these decisions do not prescribe necessarily the ending of the enquiry itself. Logically, an actual decision should be taken to terminate or close the enquiry, and then to define the resulting conclusions. These conclusions should indicate whether abuse or neglect has occurred, and include (if appropriate) when and by whom it was caused, and a preliminary assessment of whether the child remains at risk.

The formal closure of the enquiry process receives scant acknowledgement in government guidance. *Working Together* states:

> If it is decided at the child protection conference that the investigation is completed and the level of risk does not warrant registration, this should be confirmed with parents and the child, if appropriate, in writing ... (DoH, 1991a, para. 6.22).

Nowhere else in *Working Together* have I found direct reference to the process of ending an enquiry, other than regarding support requirements (para. 5.14.10). However, the Social Services Inspectorate does identify some of the features of the point of resolution:

> Initial child protection conferences share and evaluate information, identify concerns, determine levels of risk to the child or children, and decide on the need for registration (SSI, 1993).

Working Together provides more detailed definitions of what types of outcome may lead to the placing of a child's name on a child protection register (DoH, 1991a, para. 6.36–6.41). There are also several references to the need to confirm the outcome of the investigation in writing. *Working Together* tends to concentrate on written agreements when drawing up child protection plans (paras. 6.8 and 5.17), the need for a written record of the conference (paras. 6.19 and 6.35), and written notification when the allegation appears to be unfounded (paras. 5.14.10 and 6.22). In all these contexts the parent, and child (if appropriate), should receive copies of the written information. The SSI gives the more pithy description of good practice:

> Parents (or anyone with parental responsibility), the child (if of sufficient age and understanding) and referrer, as appropriate, are informed in person and in writing about the outcome of the investigation including those that revealed no substance to the cause for concern (SSI, 1993, p. 24).

Working Together offers a little more detail of the ways in which local authorities may assist in meeting the needs of families arising from an enquiry. They should:

> ... *acknowledge the inevitable distress caused by an investigation ... explain that there is a statutory obligation to investigate ... Supportive counselling may be appropriate* (para. 6.22).

Also suggested is,

> ... *a suitably worded apology* ... (para. 5.14.10).

Unfortunately these latter points about reparation are limited to situations when, one way or another, an allegation has proved unfounded. The principles could and should be applied to other circumstances as well, for example when an enquiry has been unnecessarily lengthy or has been managed poorly. The distress arising from an enquiry applies to the full range of those subjected to it, not simply those who are accused wrongly.

The only other aspect of the guidance which appears to be relevant concerns the decisions of the child protection conference. *Working Together* points out that:

> ... *it is not a forum for a formal decision that a person has abused a child which is a criminal offence* (para. 5.15.2).

Nevertheless, as has been indicated above, clearly there is a need to make decisions which come very close to this one. Whilst the guidance places some restrictions upon conferences drawing final conclusions about the nature of any offence which may have been committed, there is some encouragement given to evaluate the information properly without trespassing on the proper role of the courts.

Implications for practice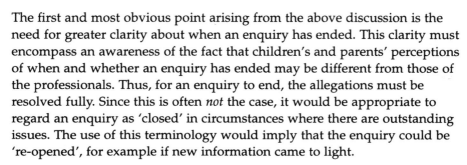

The first and most obvious point arising from the above discussion is the need for greater clarity about when an enquiry has ended. This clarity must encompass an awareness of the fact that children's and parents' perceptions of when and whether an enquiry has ended may be different from those of the professionals. Thus, for an enquiry to end, the allegations must be resolved fully. Since this is often *not* the case, it would be appropriate to regard an enquiry as 'closed' in circumstances where there are outstanding issues. The use of this terminology would imply that the enquiry could be 're-opened', for example if new information came to light.

Furthermore, the decision to close an enquiry should be made jointly where possible. The parents, and if appropriate the child, can be involved in making such a decision. The implication is that family members would have the option to ask for enquiries to continue if there were issues which they wanted to be examined further.

Whatever the circumstances under which the enquiry is closed, a written statement of its result should be given to the parents and, where appropriate, to the child. This should be in addition to any written agreement relating to the child protection plan or to any other arrangement for care of the child. Essentially, the written statement should indicate the conclusions of the enquiry, in the dimensions outlined in the Introduction and adapted from Farmer (1993) as follows:

Commission: whether abuse has occurred or not;

Culpability: who caused the abuse (or neglect);

Risk: the degree of continuing risk to the child.

If the enquiry is closed at a child protection conference, these points should form part of the decision making of the conference. In order to prevent any overlap with the role of the courts it would be necessary to express such decisions as the collective *opinion* of the meeting, not as a finding of guilt. At key points such as at the child protection conference, it will be important particularly to clarify whether the enquiry has been closed or will be continuing, and what the process will be.

For some families, the overlap between the enquiry and an assessment may also be an issue. An assessment, in this context, can be defined as an activity which enables professionals together with the family to assemble information concerning individual and social factors which may contribute either to the risk of future abuse or neglect, or to wider family/social problems. The reason for an assessment would be to inform a decision regarding any future intervention aimed at supporting the family or protecting the child, or both. Any child or family taking part in an assessment will still be under scrutiny, although the focus will have shifted away from the alleged abuse. It is important that children and families understand what is happening at this stage. In circumstances where the removal of a child has taken place, is being considered or other serious action may be taken, it is likely that a comprehensive assessment will be undertaken. Workers are strongly encouraged to use a recorded agreement for such an assessment, in addition to the foregoing documentation (Platt and Edwards, forthcoming).

Additional practice issues arise from the impact of the enquiry itself. Sharland *et al.* (1993) identify a significant lack of follow-through services for both children and parents. A child's needs following proven abuse will certainly include the need for support and possibly for therapy. The wider family, however, will also have needs for support in relation to their particular constellation of experiences at this time. As has been demonstrated, the enquiry may well have a devastating effect, especially on people or families who have been accused wrongly of abuse. Attempts to minimise such effects will begin in the early stages, with the development of appropriate partnership strategies, highlighted by earlier chapters. This approach should be followed up at the closure of the enquiry, by key activities of:

- support (including counselling) for those who need it, irrespective of whether the allegation was substantiated;

- acknowledgement of the distress which may have been caused;

- an apology for any mistakes which may have been made;

- the availability of an appeals process.

For some families there may be quite serious financial needs, particularly if court costs are involved. The legal aid system is recognised as offering very little assistance, especially to those who believe themselves to have been accused wrongly and who are seeking legal redress. Since there is no appeal mechanism in most areas against the decisions of a child protection conference the establishment of accessible processes at this stage might prevent some cases having to go through the courts, thereby reducing the financial impact upon a family. A number of area child protection committees are already establishing such procedures. Beyond that, it is suggested that the question of legal aid be reviewed.

Finally, policies should be developed for handling records after an enquiry has finished. The difficulties of achieving agreement about a common approach to this issue are immense. The following is suggested as a practical way forward. In all cases when abuse is not found, and the child is not assessed as being at risk, consideration should be given to the destruction of records concerning the allegation. Families should be given the option of having records destroyed in all cases of allegations which have been disproved, although for some the retention of such a record may be preferable. Discretion should be given to the child protection conference where proof of the allegations has not been established but where doubt remains. In all cases when records are kept, the family should be informed of the existence of the record and offered the opportunity to view it.

Does it ever end?

Professional agencies working in child protection need to have a set task which is achievable, and which has a beginning, a middle, and an end. They must also understand that children and families cannot simply move on, as professionals themselves do, to the next 'case'; they will live with their own 'case' for the rest of their lives. For some, the end of the enquiry marks a much-needed and welcome resolution of very serious family issues; or at least the beginning of such a resolution. For others, to ask if the enquiry *ever* ends will meet with a resounding 'no'. In spite of the good intentions of enquiry teams, as Cleaver and Freeman (1995) have begun to show, an enquiry can contribute to 'irretrievable damage to family dynamics':

> *The challenge to parents' shortcomings undermines their sense of reality and control. It is as if the door has been opened to a room in which everything said and done assumes sinister significance. At the end of the investigation the door stays ajar; the contents still spill out. Irrespective of the outcome, parents must struggle to integrate what happened into their normal understanding of the world . . .*

In situations where further action has been taken as a result of an enquiry, it may well be irrelevant in practice to consider whether the enquiry has been concluded formally. For the parents of two children taken into care:

> *It's like your child is dead but not dead* (Prosser, 1992, p.43).

BIBLIOGRAPHY

Barford, R. (1993) *Children's Views of Child Protection Social Work*, Social Work Monographs, University of East Anglia.

Bingley Miller, L., Fisher, T. and Sinclair, I. (1993) 'Decisions to register children as at risk of abuse', *Social Work and Social Sciences Review*, **4**(2), pp. 101–118.

Brayne, H. and Martin, G. (1993) *Law for Social Workers*. Blackstone, 3rd edn.

Brown, C. (1986) *Child Abuse Parents Speaking: Parents' Impressions of Social Workers and the Social Work Process*, University of Bristol, School for Advanced Urban Studies.

Campbell, M. (1991) 'Children at risk: how different are children on child abuse registers?' *British Journal of Social Work*, **21**, pp. 259–275.

Cleaver, H. and Freeman, P. (1995) *Parental Perspectives in Cases of Suspected Child Abuse*, London: HMSO

Corby, B. and Mills, C. (1986) 'Child abuse: risks and resources', *British Journal of Social Work*, **16**, 5, pp. 531–42.

Cornwell, N. (1989) 'Decision making and justice: do they register?' *Social Work Today*, **20** (47), 3 September 1989.

Conclusion: Does it ever end?

Department of Health with Home Office, Department of Education and Science and Welsh Office (1991a) *Working Together Under the Children Act 1989: A Guide to Arrangements for Inter-agency Co-operation for the Protection of Children from Abuse*, London: HMSO.

Department of Health (1991b) *Patterns and Outcomes in Child Placement: Messages from Current Research and Their Implications*, London: HMSO.

Department of Health (1995) *Child Protection: Messages from Research*, London: HMSO.

Department of Health and Social Security and Welsh Office (1988) *Working Together: A Guide to Arrangements for Inter-agency Co-operation for the Protection of Children from Abuse*, London: HMSO.

Farmer, E. (1993) 'The impact of child protection interventions: the experiences of parents and children', in Waterhouse, L. (ed.) *Child Abuse and Child Abusers*, Jessica Kingsley.

Farmer, E. and Owen, M. (1995) *Child Protection Practice: Private Risks and Public Remedies*, London: HMSO.

Geach, H. (1983) 'Child abuse registers: a time for change', in Geach, H. and Szwed, E. (1983) *Providing Civil Justice for Children*, Edward Arnold.

Gibbons, J. (1988) 'Prevention: a realistic objective?' *Community Care*, 6 October 1988.

Hallett, C. and Birchall, E. (1992) *Co-ordination and Child Protection: A Review of the Literature*, London: HMSO.

Home Office and Department of Health (1992) *Memorandum of Good Practice on Video Recorded Interviews with Child Witnesses for Criminal Proceedings*, London: HMSO.

Howitt, D. (1992) *Child Abuse Errors: When Good Intentions Go Wrong*, Harvester Wheatsheaf.

Jones, D.N., Pickett, J., Oates, M. and Barbor, P. (1987) *Understanding Child Abuse*, 2nd edn, Macmillan.

Jones, D.P.H. (1992) *Interviewing the Sexually Abused Child: Investigation of Suspected Abuse*, Gaskell.

Jones, L. (1993) 'Decision making in child welfare: a critical review of the literature', *Child and Adolescent Social Work Journal*, **10**, No. 3, June 1993.

Lindley, B. (1994) *On the Receiving End: a Study of Families' Experiences of the Court Process in Care and Supervision Proceedings under the Children Act 1989*, Family Rights Group.

Marshall, K. (1993) 'Reading 3: Investigative interviewing: children's rights', in Stainton Rogers, W. and Worrel, M. (eds) *Investigative Interviewing with Children: Resources Booklet*, Milton Keynes: Open University.

Milner, J. (1993) 'A disappearing act: the differing career paths of fathers and mothers in child protection investigations', *Critical Social Policy*, **38**, Autumn.

Parents A, B and C (1993) Verbal contribution to PAIN 'Thinking Day', 21 June.

Pecora, P.J. (1991) 'Investigating allegations of child maltreatment: the strengths and limitations of current risk assessment systems', in Robin, M. (ed.) *Assessing Child Maltreatment Reports: The Problem of False Allegations*, Child and Youth Services, **15**, No. 2.

Platt, D. and Edwards, A. (forthcoming) 'Planning a comprehensive family assessment', awaiting publication in *Practice, the Journal of the British Association of Social Workers*.

Plotnikoff, J. and Woolfson, R. (1994) 'Victims of time', *Community Care*, 24 March 1994.

Prosser, J. (1992) *Child Abuse Investigations: The Families' Perspective*, Parents Against INjustice.

Reeves, K. (1993) Family Perception of Partnership, address to PAIN 'Thinking Day', 21 June 1993.

Roberts, J. and Taylor, C. (1993) 'Sexually abused children and young people speak out', in Waterhouse, L. (ed.) *Child Abuse and Child Abusers: Protection and Prevention*, Jessica Kingsley.

Sharland, E., Seal, H., Croucher, M., Aldgate, J. and Jones, D.P.H. (1993) *Professional Intervention in Child Sexual Abuse. Summary of Final report to Department of Health*, London.

Social Services Inspectorate (Department of Health) (1993) *Inspecting for Quality. Evaluating Performance in Child Protection: A Framework for the Inspection of Local Authority Social Services Practice and Systems*, London: HMSO.

Wells, S.J. (1988) 'Factors influencing the response of child protective service workers to reports of abuse and neglect', in Hotaling, G. *et al.*, *Coping with Family Violence: Research and Policy Perspectives*, Sage.

Appendix 1

The Steering Committee which supported the preparation of this book included the following:

Chair: Daphne Statham (Director, National Institute for Social Work)

Sue Amphlett, (Director, Parents Against INjustice)
Lyn Burns (Area Manager, Gloucestershire Social Services)
Terry Burns (Area Manager, Gloucestershire Social Services)
David Cooper (Senior Lecturer in social work, University of Plymouth)
Elizabeth Hamilton (Family member)
Keith Hamilton (Family member)
Barbara Hearn (Director, Practice Development Department, National Children's Bureau)
Rachel Hodgkin (representing the Calouste Gulbenkian Foundation; Principal Policy Officer, National Children's Bureau)
Phillip Noyes (Director of Public Policy, NSPCC)
Nigel Parton (Professor in Child Care, University of Huddersfield)
Melanie Phillips (Freelance Trainer and Consultant)
Dendy Platt (Senior Lecturer in social work, New College Durham)
Jane Sadler (Family member)
Trevor Sadler (Family member)
Anne Sampford (Development and Project Officer, PAIN)
David Shemmings (Lecturer in social work, University of East Anglia, Norwich)
Alison Richards (Advice and advocacy worker, Family Rights Group)
Howard Wolfenden (Head of child protection services, Birmingham City Council)

and as an observer

Colin Burness (Department of Health)

Index

abusive enquiries, 152
access to files, 72–5
Access to Health Records Act, 1990, 73, 74, 75
Access to Medical Reports Act, 1989, 73
Access to Personal Files Act, 1987, 73, 74, 75
accountability, 19, 69–70, 71
acute injuries, examination of, 206
adoption, 216
advocates, 172
Afro-Caribbeans, 33, 38–9
  see also Black families
age, 229
agreements, recorded/written, 164–75, 261
  child's participation, 110
  development of principles, 164–5
  dilemmas of using, 167–9
  format, 173–5
  negotiating, 169–73
  reasons for use, 166–7
Ahmad, B., 37, 167, 168, 169
Ahmed, B., 125
Ahmed, S., 31
alcohol problem, 131–2
Alderson, P., 103
Amphlett, S., 152, 173, 175
Anderson, S., 14
answerability, 19, 69–70, 71
Anthony, G., 12, 13–14
apology for mistakes, 260, 262
appeals process, 262
area child protection committees, 147, 262
  children with disabilities, 51, 60
  complaints procedures, 81
Ariès, P., 233
Arnstein, S.R., 79
Asians, 39
assertiveness training, 56–7
assessment, 10, 33
  children with disabilities, 48–51
  overlap with enquiries, 261
  planning enquiries, 161–2

assumptions, xvii
Atherton, C., 165, 167, 170–1
attendance in court, child's, 185–6
attribution theory, 117–18
Audit Commission, 18, 21, 23, 48

bad character of the accused, statements about, 186–7
Bainham, A., 104
Baldry, M., 72
Baldwin, N., 17
Barford, R., 255
Barn, R., 31, 32, 38
Barnardos, 119
Barnes, J., xiii, xxiv
Barnes, M., 33
BBC Childwatch, 21
Bebbington, A., 31
Becerra, R.M., 135
Beckford, Jasmine, 38, 86, 237
  Inquiry, 38–9
'becoming' theory of decision–making, 76
Bell, M., 17
benefits of enquiries, 11–14
Berliner, L., 241
Besharov, D., 13, 133, 134
Biehal, N., 68
Bilson, A., 231
Bingley Miller, L., 254
Birchall, E., 8, 12, 251, 255, 257
  child protection conferences, 253
  impact of enquiry on child, 14
Black families, 28–40, 102
  access to information/records, 168, 169
  child protection, 30–3
  dearth of research, 30
  enquiries, 36–9
  policy and, 16–17
  recorded agreements, 167
  referrals, 125
  treatment or punishment, 33–5
  see also ethnic minorities

267

Index